D1452948

Our American Brethren

Our American Brethren

A History of Letters in the
British Press During the American
Revolution, 1775–1781

by ALFRED GRANT

with a foreword by
H. T. DICKINSON

McFarland & Company, Inc., Publishers
Jefferson, North Carolina, and London

British Library Cataloguing-in-Publication data are available

Library of Congress Cataloguing-in-Publication Data

Grant, Alfred, 1918–
    Our American brethren : a history of letters in the British press
during the American revolution, 1775–1781 / by Alfred Grant.
        p.   cm.
    Includes index.
    ISBN 0-7864-0086-2 (lib. bdg. : 50# alk. paper) ∞
    1. United States—History—Revolution, 1775–1783—Foreign
public opinion, British.   2. Public opinion—Great Britain—
History—18th century.   3. Press and politics—Great Britain—
History—18th century.   I. Title.
E249.3.G74   1995
973.3—dc20   95-1194
                                                                      CIP

Manufactured in the United States of America

McFarland & Company, Inc., Publishers
    Box 611, Jefferson, North Carolina 28640

Acknowledgments

I wish to offer my deepest thanks and gratitude to Margaret Deas and her staff at the Scottish National Library in Edinburgh and to Jeannette Woodward, head librarian at the College of Santa Fe.

Contents

Acknowledgments		v
Abbreviations		ix
Foreword by H. T. Dickinson		1
Introduction		7
ONE	Historical Background	13
TWO	The British Press	25
THREE	Addresses and Petitions to the Crown	42
FOUR	A Ministry Under Seige	59
FIVE	Peace or the Sword	80
SIX	The Sword Unsheathed	102
SEVEN	The Perfidious French	123
EIGHT	Despair	140
NINE	Euphoria	156
TEN	American Brethren and Fellow Subjects	168
Epilogue		183
Appendix A: Henry Woodfall's Account at Newgate		189
Appendix B: Olive Branch Petition		193
Appendix C: British, French, Spanish, and American Relations 1774–1779		197
Notes		201
Index		207

Abbreviations

CM Caledonian Mercury

LC London Chronicle

LC-WC London Courant *and* Westminster Chronicle

MC Morning Chronicle

MP Morning Post

PA Public Advertiser

Foreword

In the Declaration of Independence, the rebellious American colonists naturally claimed to be acting from the highest and purest motives; not surprisingly, they imputed the lowest and worst motives to George III and his British advisers. The American colonists undoubtedly had a legitimate case, and they fought bravely for a noble cause. What really gives the American War of Independence its fascination and, from the British point of view at least, the elements of a Greek tragedy, however, is the fact that it was a war in which both sides could believe that they were defending liberty and fighting for a noble cause.

When we look more closely at the positions taken up on both sides of the Atlantic, we discover that not all the American colonists were fully convinced of the justice and wisdom of their cause and that the British people were also sharply and deeply divided about how best to respond to the American crisis. The colonies had their British Loyalists and the British had their "Friends of America."

No historian now regards George III as an arbitrary ruler seeking to create an absolute monarchy or determined to destroy the liberty of his American or his British subjects. No historian now regards Lord North as a subservient minister ready to assist his monarch in a conspiracy against liberty. While even British historians now readily acknowledge that the American rebels had a good cause and legitimate grounds for protest, and it is also accepted that the British government could not appreciate the American case and could not rise to the occasion created by the American crisis, it is also widely recognized that the British government was defending an honorable position.

The British government was saddled with a huge national debt after the enormously expensive Seven Years' War, and, understandably, British ministers did not see why the American colonists should not contribute a relatively small sum to meet the costs of defending a British Empire which had recently rescued the American colonists from the French threat to their interests. British ministers were mistaken, although the mistake is

I

understandable, when they feared that if Britain did not exercise authority over the commercial activities of her American colonies, then Britain would lose much of her valuable Atlantic trade, probably to her archrival France. British ministers also feared, unnecessarily as it turned out, although the fear was not totally unrealistic at the time, that the American colonists would not be able to create an independent republic, but would divide into smaller units and fall prey to the ambitions of the French and other European powers. What was particularly justifiable in the British position was the belief that no government could allow its subjects to break the law with impunity if civilized government were to prevail and the fear that any acceptance of the legitimacy of the American case would actually destroy Britain's own constitution. When the colonists rejected all attempts by the British parliament to tax them and they resorted on occasion to violence, many in Britain believed that this resistance was the work of a minority of demagogues and subversive spirits who would undermine all law and order in the colonies. No government readily submits to rebellious subjects if it wishes to retain the authority inherent in government.

When the American colonists challenged the whole concept of parliamentary sovereignty, the British government feared that any recognition of this argument would destroy the cherished British constitution which had done so much to bring peace, prosperity, and stability to Britain and her colonies since the Glorious Revolution of 1688. To British ministers (and to many British people), parliamentary sovereignty was not perceived as any kind of a threat to liberty. On the contrary, it was seen as the foundation and the chief bulwark of both liberty and stability. Parliamentary sovereignty was credited with rescuing the country from arbitrary monarchy and with safeguarding it from the social anarchy likely to follow if too much power was conceded to the licentious multitude.

The existing British constitution was seen as a virtuous mean between authoritarianism on the one hand and weak government on the other. It preserved the balance between order and liberty. It was the prime means by which British subjects had enjoyed the benefits of a stable society, the rule of law, rising prosperity, and the most extensive civil liberties in Europe. To see it endangered by a minority of American colonists seemed intolerable, and this threat not unnaturally produced a determination to safeguard what was widely regarded as the best constitution in the world.

British ministers can thus be criticized for not fully understanding the American case, for failing to negotiate a compromise early in the crisis when one might have been reached, and for lacking the vision to rethink the whole relationship between Britain and her American colonies. They should not, however, be condemned as the enemies of stability, the rule of law, or even the civil liberties of ordinary subjects. Although they were men of limited perception, British ministers genuinely thought that their position was a just and honorable one and that it could legitimately be defended by force if necessary.

The fascination, the heroic nature, and the tragedy of the conflict between Britain and her American colonies lie not only in the fact that both proponents believed that they had justice and honor on their side, but also in the fact that both societies were divided within themselves over the legitimacy, the morality, and the wisdom of taking the dispute as far as armed conflict.

In recent years American historians have made some attempt to understand that the Loyalists in the colonies were neither evil nor servile simply because they believed that they still owed allegiance to George III. Historians have also shown in recent years that within Britain too there were men of honor and principle who opposed the policies of their nation's leaders and believed that the American colonists upheld the nobler cause. We now know much more about the ideas and the activities of the British "friends of America," who agreed with the colonists that the British government was indeed engaged in "a conspiracy against liberty."

When war broke out in 1775, the position of the American Loyalists and the British friends of America became extremely difficult. All wars undoubtedly polarize opinions more sharply than ever, and in such a situation, minority views are always endangered. In America the Loyalists were condemned as traitors, and it has taken two centuries to present any proper understanding of their position. This is not surprising since history is invariably written by the victors in any conflict, and time has undoubtedly confirmed the wisdom of those who supported the American Revolution. Within Britain it has taken almost as long for historians to appreciate that public opinion did not rally wholeheartedly and unanimously behind the British government's attempts to restore its authority in the American colonies by force of arms.

As the leaders of the losing side, the British ministers have, of course, long come in for severe criticism, but an understanding of the views and activities of those who opposed them within Britain at the time has had to await changes in how British historians view this period in the nation's history. For too long, British historians were concerned with the history of the governing elite and were not interested in the history of the middling and lower orders of society. They were also distrustful of the role of ideas and principles in politics, and they regarded the printed words as mere propaganda that did little to help the historian understand the real motives of those who acted on the public stage. By concentrating on the royal court and the houses of Parliament and by investigating chiefly government records, the private correspondence of leading politicians and the debates in Parliament, British historians were easily persuaded that the British people rallied strongly behind their government when war broke out with the American colonies. To appreciate the true state of public opinion, however, historians needed to take more seriously the views, arguments, and principles articulated in the British press by ordinary "scribblers" during the War of American Independence.

The British press flourished more vigorously than ever before during the American crisis, and it overcame all attempts by the political elite to restrict the views which could be put before the British people. Alfred Grant has looked very closely indeed at what was printed in the British press during the American War of Independence, and he is able to show how opinions differed and continually fluctuated during this "unnatural conflict." He demonstrates that British opinion was never united in support of the actual conduct of the war and was still less united in support of the wisdom of waging it at all.

The British press informs us of the fluctuating views of the British public, which ranged from euphoria through doubts and fears to despair. It tells us when the British public were well or ill informed about the true state of affairs, it provides evidence of the arguments used by the supporters and critics of the British government, it tells us about the views the journalists and scribblers attempted to put before the British people, and it offers some guide as to how the British people responded to this torrent of news, views, and propaganda. The British press was divided into supporters and critics of the government and into neutrals who hoped to attract readers of all persuasions. It sometimes referred to the Americans as "brethren" and to the war as an "unnatural conflict," and it sometimes berated the colonists as base traitors who would never be able to govern themselves. It printed material that was sometimes grossly biased and material that was patently untrue, but it also produced material that sought to explore, deeply and seriously, the fundamental issues at stake in this conflict. To many commentators in the press, the government was mishandling the war and was placing the liberty of Britons as well as that of the Americans on trial. Most clearly of all, the British press printed material of genuine significance and a wide range of political views that were expressed both in pungent and elegant prose and with great wit and style.

Better than any other source on the war, the British press shows how virulently the ministers were attacked, how the British public rallied more firmly behind the government once the country was at war with its traditional rival France, how the shock of Saratoga was followed by rising optimism as the war in the south progressed well and how that euphoria was superseded by despair following news of the surrender at Yorktown, how journalists discussed different strategies for winning the war, how the British public clutched at straws when defeat stared them in the face, how public opinion sought to reconcile itself to the ultimate and inevitable loss of the American colonies, and how, throughout the conflict, the British public were so much the prey of unfounded rumors and so much the victims of inadequate information that they were prevented from ever fully appreciating the true state of affairs. Most clearly of all, the British press demonstrates that the British public were neither consistent nor unanimous in their views on the justice and the conduct of the War of American Independence.

H. T. DICKINSON
Richard Lodge Professor of British History
University of Edinburgh

Introduction

This narrative is grounded on letters to the printer which appeared in the British press from the outbreak of the American War for Independence at Lexington and Concord to the surrender of the British army at Yorktown.

The choice of newspapers for this work was restricted to those journals which were available for the period from the beginning of the conflict in 1775 to the capitulation of Cornwallis at Yorktown in 1781. It was essential, further, to give due prominence to the London press because that city was the primary terminus for news from America.

For a London daily newspaper, the choice narrowed to the *Public Advertiser*, the *Morning Chronicle*, and the *Morning Post*. The *Public Advertiser* was accessible for the entire period, but the *Morning Post* was no longer extant for 1781, and ninety-three issues of the *Morning Chronicle* for the year 1780 were missing. The *London Courant* was a suitable replacement for the missing issues of the *Morning Post*, and the missing editions of the *Morning Chronicle* were noted, but were not replaced. The *London Chronicle* was the sole London evening newspaper available, and the *Caledonian Mercury*, published in the city of Edinburgh, was chosen as a model of the Scottish press.

The London morning dailies were printed six days a week, every day but Sunday. Each publication consisted of a single sheet, 19" by 26", folded once to make four pages. The first and last pages were primarily composed of advertisements. The evening newspaper, the *London Chronicle*, and the Scottish journal, the *Caledonian Mercury*, were printed on Tuesday, Thursday, and Saturday. The *Morning Post* was distributed in the West End, the residency of the London affluent, while the *London Chronicle* found its readership in the suburbs of London, the dwelling place of the landed gentry.

Each of the morning dailies were faulted at one time or another for being a "ministerial" print, but the *Morning Post* was probably the only one of the three that might deserve that designation. Yet the *Morning Post*, as

7

well as the other journals, maintained an even-handed approach to the news from America.

The *London Chronicle* in general remained apart from much of the controversy that surrounded the American endeavor. Circulated in the evening to its suburban readers, the majority of whom had already read the news in the morning dailies, the newspaper published items that were invariably plagiarized from the morning prints. It was, in a sense, a magazine rather than a newspaper and often printed stories of agricultural interest, travel, and history. The journal reflected the opinions of its readers, the landed gentry.

The *Caledonian Mercury*, printed tri-weekly, was typical of the Scottish press. Newspapers were few, were not influential, and were under government control. When Major Cartwright lectured in Edinburgh circa 1812, no newspaper editor in the city ventured to publish an account of his discourses because he preached the "Radical Doctrine" of universal suffrage and annual parliaments.[1]

The letters to the printer included in this work represent an amalgamation of our present day editorial commentary, op-ed observations, and letters to the editor.[2] The scribblers of this period, whose letters appeared in the press with great regularity, were far different from their modern day counterparts. They were rarely casual correspondents; rather, they were professional journalists whose letters often exhibited some of the finest prose of the eighteenth century. Unfortunately, their identity remains shrouded in mystery, for all wrote under the mask of pseudonyms because the heavy hand of a wrathful ministry and prosecution for libel were constant threats.

The greater part of the London press retained correspondents who espoused either the cause of the ministry or the opposition, or championed the cause of an individual or individuals within those groups. Compensation for these expert journalists was secured from these sources. That they did receive financial benefits for their efforts is well documented in a letter from TIMOTHY SCRIBE which appeared in the *Morning Post* (11/2/78):

> We are perfectly happy to see your labours in the service of your country crowned with success. The seditious leaders of city opposition hang their heads, and sneak into holes and corners, ashamed of their conduct and their cause. Men of probity and character again resume the posts of honour, while the enemies of the state are awed into silence, and offices acquired by faction are resigned with shame. May the stings of conscience gradually reach the whole race of modern patriots! but extend not the progress of your arms too far; remember, Sir, your dependant scribblers must eat. You have established rotation, and hunted licentiousness out of the metropolis; should the senate also feel the influence of your arms, and shrink from your charge, a peace must inevitably ensue; your forces be disbanded and loose, unprovided of their present pay, and good quarters. As you have confessedly acted

the part of a brave, it now becomes you to assume the caution of a prudent General. Excuse our saying, we by no means wish your victory too complete; for scribblers, like soldiers, are never so little regarded, as when they have procured their masters some signal advantages; because their own victories serve to render them useless. Decisive actions terminate quarrels too quickly. Such achievements may rebound to your honour, but not to our interest. You may apprize the enemy's outposts, and force their entrenchments; compel them suddenly to break their encampments; display the same spirit and resolution as compelled them to quit the supposed impregnable one at Coxheath, and remain master of the field; but a signal overthrow must be studiously avoided, prudence forbids it; our finances cannot bear it.

Unlike the letters to the editor and the editorial commentary of our modern press, the letters to the printer, albeit charged with a like function, did not assume the cloak of authority nor attempt to instruct or educate. They were written under the guise of ordinary people communicating with their peers. Never were they admirals or generals, statesmen or diplomats, or authorities of any sort. Lest any reader should think them more, they professed their naïveté openly:

IMPARTIAL (*LC* 10/15/78):
Though I profess myself to be neither a friend nor an enemy to the Ministry, contenting myself with the more humble, though I hope not less honourable, appellation of a friend to my country...

PHILOPOEMEN (*PA* 3/21/78):
To Lord North: I am a plain Man, my Lord, not even Possessing the Privilege of saying Yea or Nay in either House; but the Love of my Country burns as ardent in my Breast as in that of any one who values himself upon such a Distinction.

AN OBSCURE BY-STANDER (*PA* 6/16/78):
I am past the Time of my Life to be of any active use to my Country.... I have never been conversant enough with the World to be a Politician, and therefore don't pretend to judge of the Expediency of whatever has been undertaken, nor of the Propriety or Impropriety with which the Objects have been pursued; but I must feel the consequence in the Events, and be sensible as an Individual concerned.

G.N. (*PA* 8/8/78):
I am not skilled in Maritime Affairs, the Sea is not my element; and therefore am ready to admit when unquestionable Authority shall aver it.... I beg to be indulged in a private Opinion of my own, for though I am not versed in such Matters, I can read, and from reading have gained strange Prepossessions.

SCOTUS (*CM* 1/27/79):
To Lord North: Though I live in obscurity, and am far beneath your Lordship's notice, yet what I beg leave now to suggest may perhaps merit some of your attention.

The means of gathering news used by the printers of the eighteenth-century British newspaper differed greatly from those of their twentieth-century progeny. Foreign correspondents or correspondents of any kind formally attached to a given newspaper were unknown. Official news originated in the *London Gazette*, the approved and sanctioned organ for the ministry. It was so closely tied to the government that the American secretary shared in its profits. Every British newspaper used the *London Gazette* as a major source of news. The extent of the plagiarism depended a great deal on the ministerial or antiministerial bent of the printer.

Plagiarism in the eighteenth-century press was an acceptable practice and an important source of news. Letters to the printer, in addition to all items of news, were considered in the public domain and were reprinted without a hint of credit to the originator of the item. There remained free passage between London, Paris, and Amsterdam throughout the war, so that letters from those cities, as well as letters from America, reached London with great regularity and were printed in toto, abstracted, or ignored.

In spite of the restraints of government, the press prospered in Great Britain. The number of newspapers published in London increased from 4 dailies in 1760 to 13 dailies by 1790.[3] As to the circulation of individual newspapers, of the 18 London newspapers published in 1782, 10 appeared with a daily circulation between 2500 and 3000.[4] During periods of agitation, however, circulation increased vigorously, and it was not unusual for individual newspapers to reach distributions of over 4000. The letters of Junius in the London press so excited the populace that daily circulation rose to an average of 3,400 and in a few instances to 4,100.[5]

The number of readers of British newspapers, however, was far greater than the estimated number of copies in circulation. Newspapers were widely read in taverns, coffee houses, news rooms, clubs, and at public meetings. Members of particular mercantile interests or societies would meet in various coffee houses to conduct their business, and the provision of newspapers was a regular service.[6] The custom of groups of readers purchasing newspapers in order to share the cost was widespread. Although Parliament made the practice illegal in 1789, people of all social classes continued to participate in that custom.[7]

Foreign news came to London first. It was generally some six weeks before this news appeared in the provincial press. For those with more than a casual interest in American affairs, it was essential to subscribe to a London daily.

The colonists who lived in the British provinces in North America, many of whom had never seen Britain, considered themselves Englishmen. Perhaps more importantly, Englishmen considered these colonists Englishmen. Throughout the letters that follow, there are continuing references to our "American Brethren," to our "American fellow subjects," or to Englishmen living in North America. The hiring of German mercenaries by the North ministry raised the cry in Britain that Germans had been retained to kill Englishmen.

The language used by the eighteenth-century scribbler would clearly not be acceptable in the modern press. It was, as a connoisseur of aged cheese might depict it, extremely ripe. Although such language was generally used in censuring the ministry, it was not exclusively the product of antiministerial letter writers. Writing of the martial law proclaimed by General Gage, a Bostonian (*PA* 7/25/75) asserted that "It begins with infatuation, proceeds with falsehood and folly, and ends with a hypocritical affection of prayer." One signing his name as MELA (*MP* 12/16/76) maintained that those ministerial scribblers who wrote of the danger of a French war were using the "language of folly and deceit." Burgoyne's disaster at Saratoga brought this acid comment from J.A. (*PA* 11/10/77):

> As this cruel Devastation and Ravage were begun in Deception, so has every Measure been prosecuted in the same Way, until we have made ourselves hated by America, and scorned by all Europe. To fill up the Measure of our Folly and Wickedness, we invent Falsehoods to deceive the Nation.

The letter writer G.N. (*PA* 3/26/78) cautioned the ministry:

> Let them not try the ultimate Effects of Despair. Corrupt, debased, and degenerate as a Part of us may be, yet the Nation will not tamely submit itself to be ruined by the invincible Ignorance, the deliberate Treachery, or the perverse Obstinacy of any Set of Ministers, and expire without yielding some dreadful Convulsions, at least, in its last Gasp.

The logistical problems faced by the British military were enormous. It was clear from the beginning that virtually all weapons, ammunition, and stores would have to cross the Atlantic. Some rice and flour could be obtained locally at a price, if it could be milled and baked. Fresh meat had to be supplied by raiding the rebel coasts, for in spite of the Treasury's efforts it proved impracticable to ship live cattle from England. Fodder was bulky to ship and hay out of the question, so that extended cantonments for foraging became a dangerous but necessary feature of military operations. Almost everything crossed the Atlantic: oats for the horses, salted beef and pork, butter, oatmeal, pease, and flour for the men. In April 1776, there was an urgent call for horse transports. Every precaution was ordered by the American Department for the horses' health, and some Dutch ships which were too close between decks to give them air were ordered to have their decks scuttled. Nevertheless, of 950 horses which embarked, more than 400 never reached New York.

Westerly passage from Britain to the colonies in North America was long and hazardous. Dispatches from the ministry to the military in the provinces rarely took less than two months from office to office, and many despatches from home took three or four months to reach their destination. A rough check of letters sent by Lord George Germain, secretary of the American Department, to Sir Henry Clinton, commander in chief of the British forces in America, on sixty-three days falling between May 1778 and February 1781 yields the following passage times:

> 1–2 months — 6 letters
> 2 months — 12 letters
> 2–3 months — 28 letters
> 3–4 months — 11 letters
> 4–5 months — 4 letters
> 5–7 months — 2 letters[8]

CHAPTER ONE

Historical Background

The following is a limited account of the relationship between Great Britain and her colonies prior to and during the American War for Independence. It is offered as a primer for those events which influenced the conflict between the mother country and her dominions in North America.[1]

1733
17 May
Molasses Act: This act laid a prohibitive duty on rum, molasses, and sugar imported into the American colonies from the non-British West Indies. Intended to protect the British Indies planters, the act would have ruined American commerce with the West Indies, a trade essential to the well-being of the colonies. The consequence of the act was minimal because the colonists circumvented the law by smuggling.

1761
2 December
Issuance of writs of assistance in Boston: Warrants were to be issued by the courts, on the direction of Parliament, granting British customs authorities the right to search private houses for smuggled goods.

1763
10 February
Conclusion of Seven Years' War by the Treaty of Paris: Britain received Canada and all French claims south of the Great Lakes and east of the Mississippi except for New Orleans. Britain also was left with an enormous national debt. The war had cost Britain more than £82 million. As the burden on the British taxpayer was already great, the Grenville ministry devised a legislative program whereby the colonists would assume some of the financial liability of the war. The Sugar, Colonial Currency, Stamp, and Quartering acts resulted from this program.

(1763 *continued***)**

7 October

Proclamation of 1763: Colonial settlements and land speculation in all territories between the Alleghenies and the Mississippi and from Florida to 50° north latitude were prohibited. The act was viewed by many colonists as an unwarranted restraint on their right to westward expansion.

1764

5 April

Passage of Sugar Act (American Revenue Act) by Parliament: This act was designed to end the smuggling of foreign molasses and to secure revenue for the purpose of protecting the British colonies in North America. The law reduced the tariff on foreign molasses and raised the import tax on foreign refined sugar, wine, coffee, etc. The colonists protested the tax as taxation without representation.

5 April

Passage of Colonial Currency Act by Parliament: This act was primarily directed at Virginia, which had been issuing large amounts of paper money. It prohibited the use of bills of credit as legal tender and was viewed by the colonists as a source of needless travail.

24 May

Colonial protest against Sugar and Currency Acts: The Massachusetts Assembly authorized a committee to maintain contact and correspondence with other provinces in response to Sugar and Currency acts.

1765

22 March

Approval of the Stamp Act by Parliament: All legal papers, commercial papers, newspapers, pamphlets, etc., were now required to bear a stamp. The act was another attempt by Britain to have the colonies share the debt of the late war. The colonists, however, considered the law another attempt to infringe on their rights and impose taxes without representation.

24 March

Quartering Act: Where local barracks and public lodgings were inadequate, troops could be quartered in uninhabited barns and houses. Certain rations and furniture were to be provided at the expense of the local colonial treasury. The law did not include the stipulation that soldiers could be lodged in private homes. Most colonial assemblies refused to pay the cost of quartering the troops.

29 May

Stamp Act Resolves in Virginia: The House of Burgesses adopted Patrick Henry's resolutions asserting the rights of the colonists as Englishmen and denouncing taxation without representation. "Caesar had his Brutus, Charles the First his Cromwell, and George the Third ... may profit by their example.... If this is treason, make the most of it." Other colonies followed Virginia in issuing resolutions denouncing the Stamp Act.

7–25 October

Stamp Act Congress: In response to the appeal of the Massachusetts Assembly, twenty-seven delegates representing nine colonies met in New York and framed a petition to the king and Parliament. The address declared that taxation without representation was a violation of the basic rights of Englishmen and requested the repeal of the Stamp Act. This was the first intercolonial assembly whose acts were endorsed by most of the colonies.

28 October

Colonial protest against Stamp Act: Citizens of New York City adopted a nonimportation agreement, resolving to ban the importation of British goods until the Stamp Act was revoked and other 1764 trade restrictions were modified. Merchants in other port cities later adopted similar nonimportation resolutions.

1766

17 January

London merchants' petition for repeal of Stamp Act: A committee of London merchants presented an appeal to Parliament expressing fear that trade was being drastically upset because of the colonial protest against the Stamp Act and other oppressive laws. The decline in British exports to the American colonies, from £2,249,710 in 1764 to £1,944,108 in 1765, was testimony to the validity of their fears.

18 March

Royal assent to the repeal of the Stamp Act: Repeal was in response to the appeals of the British merchants. Nonimportation was abandoned by the colonies and toasts were drunk to the king.

1766

18 March

Approval of the Declaratory Act by Parliament: Passed on the same day as the Stamp Act was repealed, it was overlooked by the rejoicing colonists. It reaffirmed the supremacy of Parliament.

1767

29 June

Royal assent to the Townshend Acts: These acts included a revenue bill that levied duties on glass, lead, paint, tea, and paper. To enforce the bill, the acts authorized the use of writs of assistance and the trial of smugglers without juries. More outrageous to the colonists was the stipulation that the revenue would be used to pay the salaries of the governors and other royal officials in the colonies, thereby making them independent of all constraints which had been applied by the colonial legislatures.

28 October

Resumption of nonimportation: A Boston town meeting resolved not to purchase British goods. Other nonimportation agreements were later adopted in Providence, Newport, and New York City.

1768

11 February

Massachusetts resolution against Townshend Acts: Drawn up by Samuel Adams, this was an official denunciation of the acts by the Massachusetts Assembly. It declared certain provisions unconstitutional and in violation of the colonists' rights as English citizens. A circular letter carrying the resolution was sent to the other colonies with an appeal for united action against British oppression. This action was regarded as treasonable by the royal authorities, and the Assembly was dissolved by Governor Francis Bernard. Assemblies in other colonies were also threatened with dissolution by Lord Hillsborough, secretary of state for the colonies, if they endorsed the resolutions. Nevertheless, New Jersey, Connecticut, Maryland, Virginia, Rhode Island, Georgia, and South Carolina defied this threat and endorsed the action taken by the Massachusetts Assembly.

23–29 September

Provincial Convention in Massachusetts: Representatives of 96 towns met informally to discuss the refusal of Governor Bernard to call the General Assembly back into session. The meeting was adjourned when British troopships arrived in Boston Harbor.

1 October

Landing of British troops in Boston: Two regiments of British troops with artillery were stationed in Boston.

1769
6 February
Reaffirmation of nonimportation: Philadelphia merchants agreed to stringent nonimportation, prohibiting most British goods after April 1. Baltimore merchants took similar steps, and by the end of 1769 only New Hampshire was not involved in the boycott of British goods.

16 May
Adoption by the House of Burgesses of the Virginia Resolves against the Townshend Acts: Supported by the planter leadership of the colony, these resolutions asserted that it was the sole right of Virginians to levy taxes upon Virginians. They were a response to the Massachusetts circular letter of 11 February 1768. An address to the king expressing these views was adopted. The House of Burgesses was thereupon dissolved by Governor Botetourt.

18 May
Adoption of the Virginia Association: Acting as an extralegal body, the House of Burgesses met in Williamsburg and resolved to prohibit all imports of dutiable British goods, except paper, and many nondutiable imports as well. No slaves brought into the colony after November 1 were to be purchased. Similar actions were taken by other colonies and cities: Maryland (22 June), Savannah, Georgia (19 September), North Carolina (7 November), Providence, Rhode Island (24 October), Newport, Rhode Island (30 October).

1770
19 January
Battle of Golden Hill, New York City: A minor clash between citizens using clubs and 30-40 British soldiers using bayonets. No one was killed, although several on both sides were seriously wounded.

5 March
Repeal of Townshend Acts suggested by Lord North: Lord North proposes to retain only the tax on tea.

5 March
The Boston Massacre: A panicky redcoat guard detail fired on a taunting mob, killing five and injuring six. A general uprising was probably avoided when Governor Thomas Hutchinson withdrew the troops from the city to harbor islands.

7 July
Vote by the New York Assembly to resume importation of British goods except tea: New Yorkers also affirmed their determination to resume nonimportation if other colonies adopted the policy.

(1770 *continued*)
5 December
Acquittal of the Boston Massacre soldiers: A Boston jury acquitted all but two of the redcoats after their defense by John Adams and Josiah Quincy.

17 December
Appointment of Edmund Burke as an agent of New York in England.

1772
9 June
Gaspée Incident: The British revenue cutter *Gaspée*, aground in Narragansett Bay of Providence, Rhode Island, was set afire during the night by patriot raiders.

2 November
Organization of the Committee of Correspondence in Boston: Samuel Adams and Joseph Warren established this committee for the purpose of communication with other towns and colonies to assure united, joint action in resistance to British oppression. More that 80 such committees were established in Massachusetts within three months. Similar committees were later set up throughout the colonies.

1773
27 April
Introduction of the Tea Act into Parliament by Lord North: The purpose was to save the alleged inefficient and corrupt East India Company from bankruptcy by providing a subsidized market in the colonies.

10 May
Passage of the Tea Act by Parliament: The East India Company was allowed to export tea to the colonies without paying regular duty, but with a small tax to be paid by the colonial purchasers. This meant that the East India Company could undersell not only smuggled Dutch tea but also legally imported tea from other sources.

18 October
Protest by Philadelphia citizens against the Tea Act.

27 November
Arrival of first tea ships in colonies.

27 November
Organization by New Yorkers to oppose tea shipments.

16 December
The Boston Tea Party: Boston patriots organized by Samuel Adams and disguised as Mohawk Indians boarded three "Tea Act" ships and dumped 342 chests of tea into the harbor.

1773
17 December
Vote in a New York City public meeting that British tea not be landed.

1774
12 January
Newport, Rhode Island, boycott against all persons buying or selling tea.

14 March
Introduction of the Boston Port Bill in Parliament: Lord North proposed closing Boston Port until the destroyed tea was paid for.

25 March
Passage of the Boston Port Bill by the House of Commons: It was the first of the so-called "Coercive" or "Intolerable" acts. The punitive measure prohibited loading or unloading of ships in Boston harbor, except for food and fuel shipped along the coast, until damages had been paid for tea destroyed in the Boston Tea Party.

12 May
Recommendation by the Boston Committee of Correspondence that all colonies suspend trade with Great Britain.

16 May
Organization of the New York Committee of 51: This was a new committee of correspondence with broad representation, including radicals, moderates, and conservatives.

17 May
Call for a intercolonial convention by the citizens of Providence.

20 May
Approval of two more "Coercive" or "Intolerable" acts by King George: A British official accused of a capital crime committed in pursuit of official duties would not be tried by a provincial court where the official was

(1774 *continued*)

located or where the act was committed, but would be sent to another colony or to England for trial.

The Massachusetts Government Act, also approved by George III, nullified that colony's charter and gave the governor (appointed by the king) control over the town meetings.

23 May
   Calls for a congress of deputies from all colonies by the New York Committee of 51.

26 May
   Dissolution of the Virginia House of Burgesses.

27 May
   Call for an intercolonial congress by the Virginia Burgesses, meeting unofficially.

30 May
   Request from the New York Committee of 51 to all counties to establish committees of correspondence.

2 June
   Reenactment of the Quartering Act by Parliament: This was the fourth of the "Coercive" or "Intolerable" acts.

14 June
   Selection of delegates to Continental Congress by Rhode Island General Assembly.

17 June
   Call by Massachusetts Assembly for delegates from colonies to meet in Philadelphia, 1 September.

17 June
   Recommendation by a Philadelphia public meeting for a congress of delegates from all colonies.

22 June
   Passage of the Quebec Act by Parliament: Considered the fifth "Intolerable" act, it granted religious liberty to French Canadian Roman Catholics and was interpreted as a threat to the generally Protestant

populations of the 13 colonies. The act also extended the frontier of Quebec to the Ohio and Mississippi rivers, reaffirming the Proclamation of 1763 that restricted the other colonies from settlement west of the Appalachians.

29 June
Vote by the New York Committee of 51 to send five deputies to Continental Congress.

10 July
Appeal by the New York Committee of 51 for counties to appoint delegates to the proposed Continental Congress.

22 July
Naming of delegates to the proposed Continental Congress by the Pennsylvania Assembly.

5 August
Naming of delegates to the Continental Congress by the Virginia Convention.

5 September
Convening of the First Continental Congress in Philadelphia: All colonies but Georgia were represented. A committee was established to prepare a declaration of rights and grievances and a nonimportation association.

9 September
Suffolk Resolves: Delegates from towns in Suffolk County, Massachusetts, adopted resolutions protesting the Coercive Acts, urged Massachusetts to form a government responsive to the people and to withhold taxes from the Crown until the acts were repealed, advised the people to arm, and recommended indemnities against Britain. The resolutions stated that the people of Massachusetts would never submit to parliamentary repression but asserted that their authors had "no inclination to commence a war with his majesty's troops."

17 September
Endorsement of the Suffolk Resolves by the Continental Congress.

28 September
Rejection of Loyalist resolution by one vote in Congress: Joseph Galloway, a conservative Pennsylvania delegate, had proposed a "Plan of Proposed Union between Great Britain and the Colonies," including a declaration

(1774 *continued***)**

of abhorrence of the idea of independence. By one vote, Congress deferred consideration, which was tantamount to rejection.

14 October

Adoption of a Declaration of Rights by the First Continental Congress: Eleven resolutions proclaimed that Parliament had deprived the colonists of the rights of English citizens. The resolutions asserted the colonists' rights to "life, liberty, and property," to representation in Parliament and participation in legislation, to trial by peers, and the right to assemble and to petition the king. The practice of keeping a standing army in time of peace without the consent of the legislature was denounced as a violation of rights. Control of legislative power in several colonies by a council appointed by the king was declared to be "unconstitutional, dangerous, and destructive to the freedom of American legislation."

20 October

Adoption of the "Association" by the First Continental Congress: The Continental Association was a nonimportation, nonconsumption, nonexportation agreement. It provided for enforcement by committees of correspondence, discontinuation of the slave trade, and development of American agriculture and industry. Nonimportation was to be effective on 1 December 1774 and nonexportation on 10 September 1775. The Continental Association was operating in 12 colonies by April of the following year, the exception being Georgia, which later adopted a modified version.

26 October

Adjournment of the First Continental Congress: The delegates voted to meet again 20 May 1775 at Philadelphia if by that time Parliament had not acted to reconcile American grievances.

26 October

Recommendation by the Massachusetts Provincial Congress that the towns of Massachusetts prepare for defense: Meeting in Cambridge, the Provincial Congress organized select companies of the militia as "Minute Men" and took measures for the collection of stores and ammunition for public defense.

1775

20 January

Proposal by William Pitt that British troops be withdrawn from Boston: Motion by the elder Pitt (earl of Chatham) defeated by a three-to-one margin in Parliament.

26 January
Refusal by the New York Assembly by a vote of 11 to 0 to consider the proceedings of the Continental Congress: This was a clear demonstration of the Loyalist sympathies of New York.

1 February
Rejection by Parliament of William Pitt's "Plan for Conciliation with the Colonies": The plan would have recognized the Continental Congress, assured the American colonies that no revenue measures would be imposed on them without their consent, and endorsed means by which the Congress would vote revenue to the Crown. It was rejected at the first reading.

9 February
Declaration by Parliament that Massachusetts was in a state of rebellion.

21 February
Opposition to nonimportation by the New York Assembly: By a vote of 15–10, the body rejected a motion to thank the merchants and people of New York City for their nonimportation activities.

23 February
Refusal of the New York Assembly to appoint delegates to a new Continental Congress.

27 February
Passage of the first Conciliatory Resolution by the House of Commons.

30 March
Royal assent to New England Restraint Act: New England colonies were forbidden to trade with any country but Britain and the British West Indies after 1 July and were restricted from the North Atlantic fisheries after 20 July. Later the act was applied also to New Jersey, Pennsylvania, Maryland, Virginia, and South Carolina.

14 April
Arrival of Lord Dartmouth's instructions of 27 January to General Gage: Lord Dartmouth, secretary of state for the colonies, ordered General Gage to take any action necessary to prevent the rebellious faction from perfecting its organization. General Gage was now prepared to take action immediately rather than allow the rebel colonists time to coordinate their organization.

(1775 *continued*)

18 April

Expedition to Concord ordered by General Gage: Lieutenant Colonel Francis Smith was to lead 700 troops there to destroy rebel supplies. Troops began secretly embarking at 10 P.M. to cross the Charles River, thus avoiding the longer overland march via the Boston "neck."

CHAPTER TWO

The British Press

The following announcement appeared in the *Public Advertiser* on 30 May 1775:

A Paper, entitled, *The London Evening Post Extraordinary*, having been printed and published yesterday, containing an account of a skirmish between a part of the King's Troops in the Province of Massachusetts Bay, and a body of the inhabitants of that Province, we are desired by Authority to request that the Public would suspend their judgement upon that event until they can be more authentically informed of the particulars.

An account of the said skirmish was published in the *London Evening Post Extraordinary* and reprinted in the *Public Advertiser*:

From the *Essex Gazette*.
Printed at Salem, in New-England.
Salem, April 25, 1775.

Last Wednesday, the 19th of April, the Troops of his Britannic Majesty commenced hostilities upon the people of this Province, attended with Circumstances of Cruelty not less brutal than what our venerable ancestors received from the vilest Savages of the Wilderness. The particulars relative to this interesting event, by which we are involved in all the horrors of a Civil War, we have endeavoured to collect as well as the present confused State of Affairs will admit.

On Tuesday evening a detachment from the Army, consisting, it is said, of 800 or 900 men, commanded by Lieut. Col. Smith embarked at the bottom of the Common in Boston, on a number of boats, and landed at Phip's Farm, a little way up the Charles River, from whence they proceeded with silence and expedition on the way to Concord....

The savage barbarity exercised upon the bodies of our unfortunate Brethren who fell, is almost incredible. Not content with shooting down the unarmed, aged, and infirm, they disregarded the cries of the wounded, killing them without mercy, and mangling their bodies in the most shocking manner.

We have the pleasure to say, that notwithstanding the highest Provocations given by the enemy, not one instance of cruelty, that we have heard of was committed by our victorious Militia; but listening to the merciful

dictates of the Christian Religion, they "breathed higher Sentiments of
Humanity."

The *Public Advertiser* added the following postscript: "We suppose a
circumstantial account will be prepared and published by authority. The
above is the best we have been able to obtain. We can only add, that the
Town of Boston is now invested by a vast Army of our brave Countrymen,
who have flown to our assistance from all quarters."

And so on this day, 30 May 1775, the people of London and its en-
virons were informed that the American War for Independence had begun,
the unnatural war that would pit Englishman against Englishman and
would forever separate Britons from their American brethren.

The *London Gazette* did not relate the happenings of Lexington and
Concord until 10 June 1775. Needless to say, the official version of the
struggle in Massachusetts Bay differed markedly from that which appeared
in the *Essex Gazette*. The *London Gazette* offered the following account:

> General Gage having received Intelligence of a large quantity of Military
> Stores being collected at Concord, for the avowed purpose of supplying a
> body of troops to act in opposition to His Majesty's Government, detached,
> on the 18th of April, at Night, the Grenadiers of his Army and the Light In-
> fantry with orders to destroy the said stores....
>
> Lieutenant Colonel Smith finding, after he had advanced some Miles on
> his March, that the Country had been alarmed by the Firing of Guns and
> the Ringing of Bells, dispatched Six Companies of Light Infantry, in order
> to secure two Bridges on different roads by Concord, who, upon arrival at
> Lexington, found a body of the Country People drawn up under Arms on
> a Green close to the road; and, upon the King's Troops marching upon
> them, in order to inquire the Reason of their being so assembled, they went
> off in great Confusion, and several Guns were fired upon the King's Troops
> from behind a Stone Wall, and also from the Meeting House and other
> houses, by which one Man was wounded, and Major Pitcairne's Horse was
> shot in two places. In consequence of this Attack by the Rebels, the Troops
> returned the Fire, and killed several of them....
>
> On the Return of the Troops from Concord they were very much an-
> noyed, and had several Men killed and wounded by the Rebels firing from
> behind Walls, Ditches, Trees, and other Ambushes.... As soon as the
> Troops resumed their March, they began again to fire upon them from
> behind Stone Walls and Houses, and kept up in that Manner a scattering
> Fire, during the Whole of their March of Fifteen Miles, by which Means
> several were killed and wounded; and such was the Cruelty and Barbarity
> of the Rebels, that they scalped and cut off the Ears of some of the wounded
> Men who fell into their hands.

The war ended some six bloody years later, not with the Peace of Paris
in 1783, but with the surrender of the British army by Lord Cornwallis at
Yorktown in 1781. The two years that ensued between the capitulation and

the ratification of the treaty were confined mainly to the posturing of the Americans, the French, and the British for the most advantageous peace terms. The capitulation at Yorktown on 20 October 1781 was not reported in England until 26 November 1781, when the London press apprised its readers of the unfortunate news, news so unwelcome that the initial press reaction was that of doubt and disbelief. Both the *Morning Chronicle* and the *Public Advertiser* had difficulty in accepting the unconfirmed reports of the surrender. It was only on the second day that both newspapers confirmed the unhappy event:

> *Morning Chronicle* (11/26/81): It was yesterday evening currently reported, that Lord Cornwallis surrendered (together with the troops under his command) to the enemy on the 20th of October last. We had not an opportunity of enquiring into the truth of this unwelcome report; but shall be extremely happy to find ourselves enabled to assert in tomorrow's paper, that it is wholly groundless.

> *Morning Chronicle* (11/27/81): We are extremely sorry to find, that the report relative to General Cornwallis, and his army, being captured by the enemy, which we stated in yesterday's paper to have been current on Sunday, proves to be a melancholy truth.

> *Public Advertiser* (11/26/81): Last Night it was currently reported that very bad News had arrived relative to Lord Cornwallis, but after the strictest Enquiry it appears to be devoid of Foundation.

> *Public Advertiser* (11/27/81): The disagreeable News relative to Lord Cornwallis, which were circulated about Town on Sunday Evening, were then believed by few except those who wished them to be true. We therefore treated the Matter, in our Yesterday's Paper, as seemingly an idle Tale; but we are sorry to find, in a more particular Investigation throughout the course of the Day, that such Advice have been received that can leave no room for a Doubt of the melancholy Fact.

Some sixty years prior to the conflict between Britain and her colonies in North America there occurred a most important event in the development of the British press. In the reign of Queen Anne (1702-1714), a ministry irked by a recalcitrant press made a special effort to reduce the influence of newspapers. Other endeavors having proved fruitless, the government decided to use the power of taxation to reduce the circulation of the press by forcing publishers to increase the sale price of their newspapers. Her Majesty sent a message to Parliament which among other things stated that great license was taken by the press "in publishing false and scandalous libels, such as are a reproach to any government" and recommended that Parliament "find a remedy equal to the mischief." It was suggested that a more effectual way of suppressing libels would be the imposition of a large duty on all newspapers and pamphlets. To a long parliamentary act which related to soap, paper, parchment, linen and other matters, a few short clauses were added to promulgate the first Stamp Act.[1]

The Stamp Act of 1712 was both an expedient substitute for the lapsed Regulation of Printing Acts for the control and regulation of the press and a means of increasing revenue. It appeared, though, that the principal objective was the control of "licentious, schismatical, and scandalous" publications. By diminishing the possibility of profit, it would render publication more difficult.[2]

The Stamp Act was intended to last for 32 years. It imposed a tax on newspapers and pamphlets, on advertisements, and on paper. As loopholes were found in the act or as the government felt the levy was not sufficient to curb a licentious press, new taxes were imposed. Parliament amended and increased the stamp duties acts in 1725, 1757, 1776, 1789, 1794, 1804, 1815, and 1836. Not until 1853 did Parliament abolish the tax on advertisements; the tax on newspapers continued until 1855, and the tax on paper did not end until 1861.[3]

For a period of some twenty years after the passage of the first Stamp Act, independent newspapers in Britain were, for all practical purposes, forced to suspend publication. Without subsidy from the ministry or the Opposition or some individual of either, a newspaper could not succeed. And no newspaper did so until the first of the "Advertisers" was published on 3 February 1730 as the *Daily Advertiser*. The success of that newspaper was rooted in the belief that readers would regard advertisements as interesting in themselves and that by concentrating on long advertisements the newspaper would be able to pay the "shilling an item" tax and still turn a profit.

The age of the "Advertiser" had begun. Advertisements continued to be essential to the well-being of the British press during the remainder of the eighteenth century. Most newspapers published in London were necessarily "Advertisers" and many bore that logo in their title, namely, the *Morning Chronicle* and *London Advertiser*, the *Morning Post* and *Daily Advertiser*.

It must be allowed that the printers of the eighteenth-century press performed a remarkable task in fully utilizing the four pages of their newspapers. They used the space not only for advertisements, parliamentary debates, and foreign and domestic news, but also for impressing their readers with the excellence and quality of their journal.

It was not unusual for the printer to publish a letter, genuine or invented, as a platform for a commentary to his readers. If members of his public were unaware of the virtue and merit of his journal, he would use such means to ensure their appreciation. The *Public Advertiser*, (10/17/75) published a letter from PROJECTOR in which the author accused the *Public Advertiser* of being a ministerial newspaper. To reassure his readers of the impartiality of the *Public Advertiser* and the patent untruth of such an accusation, the printer responded: "The Printer takes this Opportunity of assuring the Writer of the above letter that he is mistaken with respect to the *Public Advertiser*, as it is not under Ministerial or any other Influence whatever, but open to the free Discussion of all public Subjects, of which PROJECTOR may be convinced whenever he may choose to take up the pen."

Again on 17 February 1779, the printer of the *Public Advertiser* proclaimed his propriety: "In all public Trials, or indeed Disputes of any Kind, different Parties will have their different Partisans; On such occasions, the Printer of the *Public Advertiser* does not ever presume to obtrude his private Opinion on his Readers and the Public, but faithfully publishes whatever is sent to him by both Parties."

If the readers of the *Public Advertiser* wished additional persuasion of the virtue of that newspaper, the printer was happy to reassure them. Not by his own pen, but in this instance by the quill of writer HOMO (11/20/79):

> Mr. Woodfall: I have long corresponded with you, in Preference to every other Publisher, from seeing, by the Impartiality with which you have received the Disquisitions on both Sides of every Question, that you were no determined Tool of Administration, or its professed Opposers; and that your Paper, when it has been at any Time used as a Channel for conveying Poison to the Public, has been, at least equally ready to convey the Antidote.[4]

William Woodfall, the printer of the *Morning Chronicle* and the younger brother of the Henry Sampson Woodfall addressed by HOMO, also felt the need to proclaim the unbiased and objective foundation of his newspaper on 9 September 1775: "Poor old England congratulates Mr. Woodfall on his decision to address the reason rather than the passions of his readers, appealing to the soundness of their judgement rather than the prejudice of their hearts."

A similar message appeared on 24 February 1777: "Several Gentlemen who have written in support of Government, and in favour of Administration, having chosen this Paper for the publication of their Arguments, it is but fair that we should let our readers see what is said by the advocates on the other side of the question."

There was a positive attempt at even-handedness in choosing letters for publication, if for no other reason than to comply with the varied interests of a journal's readers. No British newspaper was secure enough to swim against the tide of public opinion. A newspaper lived by being read. In the great majority of cases, citizens would not buy or read a newspaper, unless they agreed with its opinions. But the opinions of its readers or perhaps subsidies by the ministry or by some member of the Opposition worked to qualify this even-handedness. Yet, in spite of the pressures, the

British press did endure and managed to offer a rostrum for the diverse opinions of its readers.

Not all newspapers, however, were concerned with establishing their absolute objectivity or impartiality. If one was receiving a subsidy from the ministry, it might be well to confirm that relationship. The *Morning Post* at one period was more interested in authenticating such a link than in asserting its impartiality. Neutrality and objectivity were to pay tribute to subsidy: "Detection and Truth (9/11/78): Having long admired your endeavour, as well as power and capacity to repel the force impressed by the present scandalous minority, acting openly with republicans and disgraceful mock patriots of this town...."

Fear of government intervention and prosecution cast a long shadow. Whether to notify the ministry of its purity of intention or to impress its readership with the travail of publishing, the newspaper printer acknowledged self censorship. Prosecution for libel was to be circumvented if at all possible. William Woodfall so apprised his readers:

> An Editors Note (*MC* 8/27/76): The reply to Saturday's Gazette, signed The Scourge of Official Neglect, is doubly unwelcome. To print it would not only be highly unbecoming a Citizen and a Subject, but it would most probably saddle the Printer with a severe prosecution. For God's sake let writers pause for a moment 'ere they take up their pens against the characters of his Majesty's Officers of the army and navy.

The long shadow of a wrathful government was evident in a letter addressed to William Woodfall, printer of the *Morning Chronicle*, from the scribbler PHILALETHES (*MC* 7/8/75) and in Woodfall's reply. Philalethes wrote:

> I am amazed at your partiality for the ministry. .... You have surprised many of your friends and well-wishers, who cannot help thinking that some pecuniary motive must be at the bottom of your apostasy to the cause of liberty and America. We shall find that Three-fourths to the seven-eighth part of the political matter is rank ministerial, and some of it most outrageous.

Woodfall responded:

> The Printer has no cause to step forward as a supporter of the Ministry for last year he was the object of an unjust prosecution and an unmerciful sentence. He wishes not to aggravate a political quarrel and to wound domestic quiet. .... Where essays and articles have been sent with an obvious tendency to inflame the minds of the uninformed, and destroy subordination, he has rejected them with disdain; and he flatters himself his persevering in the same line will rather increase the number of his rational friends than make one man of sense his enemy.[5]

How far and to what limits did the freedom of the British press extend during the American War for Independence? Nowhere did the Revolutionary Settlement of 1688 or the English Bill of Rights mention specifically freedom of speech or press, although several aspects of these freedoms were undoubtedly implicit in the revolutionary principles. Fundamental human freedoms included safeguards for life and property but did not extend to protection for the basic freedoms of expression.

In spite of the restriction and prosecutions, members of the British press felt secure enough to censure Parliament, the ministry, the king, and at times themselves. Indeed, the self-criticism in most cases was well earned. The *Public Advertiser* (9/7/76) offered the following letter from the unlikely correspondent WING, WANG, WONG under the improbable title "Life and Character of China-Stong, Third Emperor of China." The piece discussed the press, its virtues, and its transgressions. No effort was made to single out a "ministerial" or an "independent" newspaper, but the letter sounded a warning to the entire British press:

> The abuse of the Liberty of the Press is, doubtless, the greatest crime that can be committed against society. The best things from corruption become the worst. The press, while preserved in the primitive purity of its institution, is the great instrument of public happiness. The enlightened world, rescued by the press out of a state of darkness and ignorance into light and knowledge, bears witness to the awful truth. It is the watchful Guardian of Wisdom and Liberty, and the scrooge of Tyranny. It keeps Kings and Ministers and Priests in Awe. Despotism and Superstition have fled before it from every Quarter of the Globe where its influence has been felt. The Sense of the many blessings derived from it may well excite the indignation of Society against its Abusers. Now, Sir, is it not notorious that you have, as far as in you lay, perverted the Design of this noble Institution? Have you not employed a Band of mercenary Scribblers to exert their Talents, such as they are, to mislead the Understanding, to disguise the Truth, to maintain falsehood, to puzzle the weak by sophistry, and silence the Modest by dogmatical assertion? Have you not rendered the Press the Champion of Tyranny and Oppression, the Satirist of Freedom, the Channel of illiberal Invective against everything that is wise, and good, and brave, in the Nation.

The letters were unquestionably for "freedom." The problem was to ascertain whose freedom.[6] Was the lack of liberty a product of the ministry or the Opposition? Both, said the press. The *Morning Chronicle* presented PACIFICUS (10/10/76), who was firmly in favor of freedom of the press, save the fact that it was being prostituted:

> I am one of those who have ever considered the Liberty of the Press as the bulwark of English liberty: I therefore lament and every honest Englishman will lament with me that so sacred a blessing should at this alarming crisis, when the immediate interest of the whole empire is at stake, be prostituted to the very worst of purposes . . . men attacked and insulted in the grossest manner, and by whom? By ruffians hired to stab in the dark . . . those for defending the cause of Britain against the very worst of rebels.

The *Morning Post* agreed. "P" (3/27/76): "While, the press once the bulwark of English liberties, is now alas little more than the vehicle of sedition to insult on every occasion not only the Minister, but the three estates of the realm."

The same *Morning Post*, conscious of its circulation and the diverse opinions of its readers, reversed direction and accused "an abandoned administration" of employing prostitute pens "to argue away the liberties of this unfortunate country." This was as obvious attempt to placate those readers who took exception to the "ministerial" attack on the press. SYDNEY (*MP* 6/4/76) denounced the charge:

> Whoever the author of the Plain Questions on the present dispute with our American Colonies may be, it is plain that he is one of the literary Swiss kept in pay by an abandoned administration to argue away the liberties of this unfortunate country.... If our rulers were either distinguished for their understanding or eminent for their honesty, they would not want the assistance of prostitute pens.

The printer of the *Public Advertiser* agreed. While noting the excesses of newspapers, he stressed the importance of maintaining a free and unfettered press. UNSIGNED (*PA* 12/3/76) presented a "political dictionary" defining *real liberty* as "Every freedom consistent with the Laws and Well being of social Government . . . and liberty of the Press," and he described it as "a thing of infinite use, even when it exceeds its bounds, and which when as at present it does exceed its bounds in a shameful degree, and neatly its own destruction, is more imputable to the negligence of government than to the natural insolence of mankind."

In England, Voltaire wrote in 1726, "one can think freely and nobly, without hesitation caused by servile fear. If I followed my inclinations that is where I would settle down, with the sole purpose of learning to think."[7] The publication of books was so open and unfettered that since the beginning of the eighteenth century, the works of Voltaire and other Continental writers were printed in the British Isles. Such freedom was not afforded to the British press, however. Laws of seditious libel became the chief weapon of the government against the advocacy of political reform.[8] It was libelous to condemn the existing government, and it was equally criminal to libel the state as an institution.[9] The term sedition came to be applied to practices which tended to disturb internal public tranquillity by deed, word, or writing, but which did not amount to treason and were not accompanied by or conducive to open violence.[10]

The place for the discussion of public grievances in eighteenth-century Britain was to be Parliament. The Bill of Rights made no mention of the freedom of the press, but insisted "that the freedom of speech and debate or proceedings in Parliament ought not to be impeached or questioned in any court or place outside of Parliament." The right to exclude strangers and the right to prohibit the publication of debates, rights that restricted freedom of speech and press, were expressed in standing orders and defended with the argument that publication would make members accountable outside the doors for what they did within.

The closing of the galleries in the House of Commons did not go without comment from scribblers of both the ministry and Opposition. A REAL PATRIOT (*MP* 11/11/76) educated his readers on the practice of closing the galleries. It was not because of clamor or misconduct, but rather because members of the Commons were loath to expose private greed to public knowledge:

> It was my intention to have got into the gallery of the House of Commons Friday afternoon, as I had been informed the navy supplies were to be voted for, as the current business of the day: upon my asking for admittance, I was answered by a hundred voices; "No admission for strangers!" — Indignant at the refusal, I could not but reflect what was the probable meaning of so flat a denial, in a place, where every constituent has an equal right to attend; for how, Sir, can we otherwise know, whether servants act agreeably to the will of their masters? I have been in that honourable House, when every vacant inch both above and below has been crowded with strangers, and I never could once perceive, that any noise or misbehaviour arising from their admittance, in any sort molested the debate: But other motives have prevailed on our wise Legislators, to exclude us from their Assemblies. Secrecy is the best friend of their designs. To act openly and fairly, is not their aim. And if the love of private advantage, so far supersedes their regard for their country's welfare. England the boasted region of liberty, will soon have occasion to lament the degeneracy of her sons.

Although sympathetic to the ministry and the need for additional supplies to quell the rebellion, TULLY (*MP* 2/13/77) attributed the clearing of the gallery to some devious purpose:

> On shutting the Gallery of the House of Commons: . . . Is this any reason for our giving up our rights, and not exerting every nerve if it was necessary to subdue, and quell the rebellion. This appears to be so clear, that it is amazing any man can think differently, whatever motives he may have to write and to speak so. Why then with so clear and good a cause are Administration afraid of having their sentiments known? To what crooked motive and fear are we to attribute the care with which the gallery of the House of Commons is shut to strangers?

The gallery of the House of Commons could be closed at the request of any member and was automatically closed at times of division. The press might report the debates but never the vote. Any attempt by the press to print or publish intelligence reflecting upon the proceedings of the House of Commons or upon any member thereof for or relating to his service therein was a breach of privilege punishable by the House.[11] Ministers were no more ready than kings to allow their actions to be criticized in the newspapers. Until 1771, Parliament resolutely refused to allow the publication of its proceedings.[12] Politicians who wanted their speeches distributed to the reading public provided copies for the press and often paid for the service. William Woodfall was accused in 1773 of taking £400 per annum from Fox and Sheridan to ensure their speeches were reported at greater length than those of their rivals in Parliament.[13]

The eighteenth-century common law also established the rule that the judge and not the jury should test the criminality of a particular publication. The obligation of the jury was confined to affirming the publication of the article in question. The law was to be the responsibility of the judge; fact was the sole province of the jury. Truth was not considered a defense in the matter of seditious libel.

Convictions on seditious libel charges depended on judges who invariably were appointees of the Crown and natural supporters of the existing political system.[14] During the first thirty years of the reign of George III, there were seventy prosecutions of the press for criticism of the government.[15] The nature of an act that would precipitate the wrath of government was both broad and unpredictable. Standard fines seem to have been £100, with a confinement in Newgate prison until paid.[16]

Parliament demonstrated itself to be most disturbed with any and all critical commentary, all of which resulted in a wide range of prosecutions. Henry Woodfall of the *Public Advertiser*, Baldwin of the *St. James Chronicle*, and Say of the *Gazetteer*, were charged and convicted for reporting the debates of the House. Say of the *Gazetteer* was charged and convicted for printing an article which claimed there was a seat in the House for sale. Meres of the *London Evening Post* and Say of the *Gazetteer* were charged and convicted for publishing a letter of John Wilkes that was said to be a reflection on a member of the House of Lords.

Yet in spite of the many prosecutions of the press for libel during the reign of George III, there was but one prosecution of the press for seditious libel directly connected with the American War for Independence. The strife between Old England and her refractory children on the other side of the Atlantic seems to have involved the British newspapers in little trouble. The tone of the press was zealous, resolute, even violent, but it was a sign of the times that it was allowed to scatter the most explosive material almost unchecked. Government had discovered that the newspapers spoke the voice of the people and to put them down would require an army, not a few crown councils.[17]

It was an advertisement for the Constitutional Society which was the cornerstone for the first and only prosecution of the press for libel in a matter directly concerning the war with the rebellious colonies. The incident began on 7 June 1775 at the King's Arms Tavern, Cornhill:

> At a special meeting, this day, of several members of the Constitutional Society, during an adjournment, a gentleman proposed that a subscription should be immediately entered into (by such of the members present who might approve of the purpose) for raising the sum of one hundred pounds, to be applied to the relief of the widows, orphans, and aged parents, of our beloved American fellow subjects, who, faithful to the character of Englishmen, preferring death to slavery, were, for that reason only, inhumanly murdered by the king's troops at or near Lexington and Concord, in the province of Massachusetts, on the 19th of last April; the sum being immediately collected, it was thereupon resolved, "That Mr. Horne do pay tomorrow, into the hands of Messrs. Brownes and Collinson, on account of Dr. Franklin, the said sum of one hundred pounds; and that Dr. Franklin be requested to apply the same to the above mentioned purpose."
>
> [signed] JOHN HORNE

The above appeared in the form of an advertisement on 9 June 1775 in the following newspapers:

St. James Chronicle—Henry Baldwin, printer
London Chronicle—J. Wilkie, printer
London Evening Post—J. Miller, printer
Public Ledger—H. Randall, printer
Public Advertiser—Henry Woodfall, printer
Morning Chronicle—William Woodfall, printer
London Packet—William Woodfall, printer

On 8 July, John Horne placed the following advertisement in the *Public Advertiser*:

> Sir Stephen Theodore Jansen, having, soon after, transmitted a sum of money, by way of subscription, in as of this object, Mr. Horne published the following note, in the *Public Advertiser*, on the 8th of July: "I think proper to give the unknown contributor this notice, that I did, yesterday, pay to Messrs. Brownes and Collinson, on the account of Dr. Franklin, the sum of fifty pounds, and that I will write to Dr. Franklin, requesting him to apply the same to the relief of the widows, orphans, and aged parents, of our beloved American fellow-subjects, who, faithful to the character of Englishmen, preferring death to slavery, for that reason only, inhumanly murdered, by the king's troops, at or near Lexington and Concord, in the province of Massachusetts, of the 19th of last April."
>
> [signed] JOHN HORNE

The sequence of events which followed this circumstance was significant. The first of the Constitutional Society advertisements was printed only a few days after the London newspapers had reported the skirmish at Lexington and Concord and nearly a fortnight before the official *London*

Gazette had printed the approved version of the clash at Massachusetts Bay. The government, however, chose to ignore the matter and did not begin prosecution proceedings until some thirteen months after the advertisements appeared in the charged newspapers. Finally, on 17 December 1776, John Miller, John Wilkie, Henry Randall, and Henry Baldwin were brought to trial for printing the advertisement of the Constitutional Society. On 1 February 1777, they were sentenced each to pay a fine of £100. Surprisingly, no charges were placed against either William or Henry Woodfall, a circumstance best appreciated in light of the trial of John Horne.

The position of the British government regarding freedom of the press was laid down by Blackstone in the eighteenth century in his *Commentaries on the Law of England* and later restated by Lord Mansfield as lord chief justice of the Court of Common Pleas. It was agreed that liberty of the press was essential to the nature of a free state, but that liberty consisted in laying no previous restraints upon publication and not in the freedom from censure for criminal matters after publication.[18] Subsequent censure instead of previous censorship, punishment instead of prevention, became the rule. Lord Mansfield commented on the liberty of the press accordingly: "To be free is to live under a government of law. The liberty of the press consists in printing without any previous license, subject to the consequences of the law. A man may keep poison in his own closet, but he may not sell them publicly as cordials."[20]

Having completed the prosecution of four printers of the Constitutional Society's advertisement, the ministry turned its attention to John Horne, the prominent liberal who initiated the episode. On 4 July 1778, some two years after the Constitutional Society advertisement was placed in the aforementioned newspapers, the trial of John Horne commenced at Guildhall before Lord Chief Justice Mansfield:

> Our said lord the king giveth the court here to understand and be informed, that John Horne late of London, clerk, being a wicked, malicious, seditious, and ill disposed person, and being greatly disaffected to our said present sovereign lord the king and to his administration of the government of this kingdom and the dominions thereinto belonging, and wickedly, maliciously, and seditiously intending, devising, and contriving to stir up and excite discontents and sedition among his majesty's subjects, and to alienate and withdraw the affection, fidelity, and allegiance of his said majesty's subjects from his said majesty, and to insinuate and cause it to be believed that divers of his majesty's innocent and deserving subjects had been inhumanly murdered by his said majesty's troops in the province, colony, or plantation of the Massachusetts-Bay in New-England, in America, belonging to the crown of Great Britain, and unlawfully and wickedly to seduce and encourage his majesty's subjects in the said province, colony, or plantation, to resist and oppose his majesty's government, on the 8th day of June, in the

15th year of the reign of our present sovereign lord George, the third, by the grace of God of Great Britain, France, and Ireland, king, defender of the faith, and with force and arms at London aforesaid, in the parish of St. Mary-le-Bow, in the ward of Cheap, wickedly, maliciously, and seditiously did write and publish, and cause and procure to be written and published, a certain false, wicked, malicious, scandalous, and seditious libel of and concerning his said majesty's government and the employment of his troops, according to the tenor and effect of the following: [a quote of the article] in contempt of our said lord the king, in open violation of the laws of this kingdom, to the evil and pernicious example of all others in the like case offending, and also against the peace of our said present sovereign lord the king, his crown and dignity; . . . that the said John Horne . . . contriving as aforesaid, afterwards, to wit, on the 9th day of June . . . caused and procured to be printed and published in certain newspapers. . . .

On 19 November 1777, the attorney general moved for judgment. Sentence of the court pronounced that the defendant "do pay a fine of two hundred pounds, and be imprisoned for a space of twelve months, and until the fine is paid, and that he do find securities for his good behaviour for three years, himself in four hundred pounds, and two sureties in two hundred pounds each."

The proceedings were completed two and a half years after the initial grounds for the prosecution appeared. Henry and William Woodfall, who were not prosecuted for libel as were their fellow printers, appeared at the Horne trial as witnesses for the prosecution. Both were called to establish the fundamental case of fact against John Horne, that he, John Horne, had placed the advertisement in question directly with their newspapers.

Although both Henry and William Woodfall were granted immunity from the charges resulting from the printing of the Constitutional Society advertisement, they continued their activities on behalf of a free press. On 16 May 1777 in the *Morning Chronicle*, William Woodfall, printed a letter from PHALARIS. It was an assault on the government's libel position and a defense of the four printers who had been judged guilty of printing the Constitutional Society's advertisement. It was also undoubtedly in defense of John Horne, whose trial was shortly to convene. The letter demanded jury trial in all cases of libel and refuted the government's position of separating fact from law. It is as significant in the twentieth century as it was in the eighteenth.

On Libels, (including the Case of Miller): . . . The law has been said by many able writers to have been abused and violated in the constructions of Lord Mansfield on what constitutes the crime of libel, and, in his doctrine, the law and fact are separable in a criminal mode of prosecutions against the supposed libeller... I propose to examine the sentiments of Judge Blackstone generally, and those particularly which have rung in changes in favour of a free press since the year 1763. And first, after describing the signification of a libel to be immoral and illegal, the worthy Blackstone proceeds to tell us that the direct tendency of these libels is the breach of the public peace by stirring up the objects of them to revenge, and perhaps bloodshed. These are his words: "For the same reason that it is immaterial with respect to the essence of libel whether the matter of it be true or false, since the provocation, and not the falsity, is the thing to be punished criminally, though doubtless the falsehood of which may aggravate its guilt and enhance its punishment. In a civil action a libel must appear to be false as well as scandalous, for if the charge be true, the plaintiff has received no private injury, and has no ground to demand a compensation for himself, whatever the offence it may be against public peace, and therefore, in a civil action the truth of the accusation may be pleaded in bar of the suit. But in criminal prosecution the tendency which all libels have to create animosities and disturb the public peace, is the sole consideration of the law, and therefore in such prosecutions the only points to be considered are, first, the making of the book, or writing; and secondly, whether the matter be criminal; and if both these points are against the defendant, the offence against the public is complete." If we depend upon this as law, which it seems reasonable we should, then it is very plain that the tendency of all libels to create animosities and disturb the public peace, is the sole consideration of the laws, on which ground Lord Mansfield in all his conduct has been substantially right, and Juries are only to find the making or publishing the book, or writing, complained of as a libel. And yet, chaste as this idea may be, and sound as this law may seem, the advantage of a Jury is lost to the defendant, and on the simply finding him guilty of making or publishing the book or writing, he is the at the mercy of the Kings's Judges in regard to the criminality of either, and the punishment in consequence—so that a paper, harmless and inoffensive as it may be to the public, is by this law liable, if offensive to Administration, to be considered as a libel, the author convicted by his Judge of a guilt which his Jury is told they have nought to do with.

Let us now enquire a little into the doctrine contended for on the other side. It is argued, and with much ingenuity that a criminal prosecution can only be had for a crime, and therefore the simple publication of anything not libellous is no crime at all; and to continue the same argument, it is then the publication of what is false, scandalous, malicious, or seditious, that is the crime, and solely gives jurisdiction to the criminal court, and that is what must of necessity be submitted to a jury, for their opinion and determination. Whether the contents of a paper be true or false, or malicious, is a fact to be collected from circumstances, as much as whether a trespass is wilful or not, or killing a man with malice aforethought; whether any act was done, or word spoken, in such a manner, or with such an intent, the jurors are judges. The Court is not judge of these matters, which are evidence to prove or disprove the thing in issue. The strict law (says the same advocate) is pretended to be that the truth of the matter asserted is no defence against the charge of its being a libel, but that he says he shall never receive as law. Now from this latter argument, opposed to what is laid down by Blackstone, we are to understand, that law and fact are inseparable in trials of libels, criminally or civilly before a jury, who ought to determine on both, from plain truth and common sense, unembarrassed by far fetched innuendoes, or artful constructions of a corrupt Judge, otherwise the writer of a ballad lampooning a Prime Minister, may be subject to heavy punishment as a libeller, after being convicted only by his jury of having wrote it. The inconvenience of this doctrine would be very great indeed, were matters to extend far; for instance, suppose any man had wrote a letter, and charged Lord North with dishonour and infamy, all which might be true, why then, according to the prevailing doctrine, he would only have in a criminal prosecution to prove the writing of the letter to entitle him to a verdict, the criminality of it being the sole consideration of the law, and the expounding of the law, if at all complaisant to the Prime Minister, will punish accordingly. From these premises a harmless writer is oppressed without remedy, the law is wrested to iniquitous purposes, and sanctifies the unholy to the injury of the innocent. To review, therefore, the grand question, whether the law and fact are to be inseparably considered by a jury in matters of libel, it clearly appears that if the prosecution be criminal according to Blackstone, and whether the book or writing be true or false, such jury have only to find the making, penning, or publishing it, and that its criminality being the sole consideration of the law, they have nothing to do with that at all.

Suppose then, as in the case of Miller, a defendant has published an advertisement for a subscription in favour of General Lee, or has introduced in his paper, that success to the American cause had been drank in a respectable company of London merchants, or let us even suppose that some bold writer had told us that a late proclamation against law, and that in either of these cases a criminal prosecution was grounded. Why then the jury must only find the fact of publication, and the crime is implied in the indictment on information, and punishment follows; but supposing there to be no crime attending the fact, is it not depriving the defendant of justice to suffer a jury to find the one without the other, and leave his expressed or implied crime to the sole consideration of the laws? Perhaps we may be answered no, because the law, or criminal Court, is counsel for such defendant, who, if he supposes himself aggrieved, may apply to arrest judgement on the verdict against him of the simple fact. But what precedents have we to show that a defendant would succeed in an application of this kind? Would the Judges of the King's Bench, with the Attorney General, when possessed of such a verdict, suffer an arrest of judgement therein to prevail? A Jury of common sense are altogether capable of determining whether the thing proved to be published tends, in the words of Blackstone, to create animosities, and disturb the public peace, or whether it has done so, they then ought to consider laws and fact together, and if they find the latter without a crime, they ought on their oaths as honest men to acquit the defendant, and not by finding the fact only, leave the crime at the mercy of the law's sole consideration, as eventually may be expounded or interpreted. The words tending to disturb or break the public peace are vague and uncertain, and according to the ingenuity or malice of some Judges . . . But it may be here said, that by leaving the crime as well as fact to the jury, a guilty defendant may escape, and he cannot be put on his trial a second time for the same charge. Granted; and much better so, that innocence should be fettered, which ninety-nine times in a hundred it undoubtedly would. Therefore, and to conclude, if impartial justice is to be distributed among us, it is more likely to be experienced by juries exerting an apparent right to determine law and fact, than fact only.

Neither the ministry nor George III were safe from the mockery of the press. In an attack on Lord Sandwich and the poor condition of the British navy, it was the king who endured the ridicule. LOG-BOOK wrote in the *Public Advertiser* (5/4/1778):

> Lord Sandwich, therefore, very wisely seized the Opportunity of the Recess of Parliament to provide himself with another Witness; and this was no less a Personage than the King himself, who, with a Mixture of Condescension and Magnanimity never to be enough loved and admired, has become, out of Affection to the Noble Lord, and Eye Witness of the Strength of his Navy, and the Abundance of his Stores, (particularly Timber) and that through a Series of Labours, Hardship, and Danger, both by Sea and Land, not to be paralleled in the History of any other Prince in the same Space of Time. Of this Royal Military Expedition he has graciously permitted the aforesaid Earl of Sandwich to give a very minute Account in the *London Gazette*; and I may venture to affirm, without being suspected of Flattery, that the Portion of History which will be hereafter supplied by this Gazette, will be one of the most shining Pages in the Annals of George the Third, our present illustrious Sovereign. The Rapidity of his March in a Chaise and Four from St. James's to Greenwich; his instant Embarkation in a Barge at the Hospital Stairs; his quitting the Barge, and ascending the August Yacht; his committing his sacred Person into that Yacht to the Mercy of the Waves of the furious Thames, and, without Convoy, to the Danger of the Enemy, in the Voyage from Greenwich to the Nore; his bold Entrance into the River Medway, and his perilous but successful Push all the Way up to Chatham; the Patience and Constancy with which he endured the Fatigues of the Sea; the Intrepid and daring Spirit with which he passed through the Fire of so many and such great Ships and Batteries; these Exploits ... shall excite as much Respect and Veneration to his Memory in our Posterity, as the faithful, though adorned, narrative given in the Gazette by Lord Sandwich has raised of Wonder and Applause in us to the living Prince.

It clearly was not the ministry's design to prosecute for libel malicious commentaries that were in any way related to the war. By 1778 General Burgoyne had surrendered his army at Saratoga, and the French were openly allied with the rebellious colonies. It was not a joyous time for Lord North and the Tory ministry. Neither was the government a toothless tiger, however. Should the press threaten its powers of restraint, other than in matters of the war in North America, the ministry was ready and able to dispense the severest of punishments.

On 19 January 1781, the *London Courant* printed the following paragraph:

> The several Conferences that have been held between Lord St [Stormont], one of his Majesty's Secretaries of State, and Mons. St, the R__n [Russian]

Ambassador, are thus explained: For some months past, the Ministry have had Reason to suspect his Excellency to be little better than a Spy, and last Week had the good Fortune to get a Packet of his, directed for a Person at P__g, but intended for the French Court. In Consequence of this he was sent for by Lord St, and charged with living here in the Habit of furnishing the Enemies of Great Britain with Intelligence. We do not know what Answer his Excellency gave; but an Express is sent to R__a of the transaction.[20]

The ministry lost little time in announcing to the press that it had not abrogated its rights and intentions of holding the press to a tight rein. Eight printers, seven of whom had reproduced the original article, were prosecuted for libeling the Russian ambassador. The punishments imposed exceeded the norm and were intended to be a warning to the press that the government would continue to use libel as an effective action to restrain the press. The following summation appeared in the *Gentleman's Magazine*[21]:

> The late printers of the *London Courant* and *Noon Gazette*, and the publisher of the *Morning Herald*, with the printer of the *Gazetteer*, received sentence on the Court of the King's Bench, for having published a libel against the Russian Ambassador; viz. the late printer of the *London Courant*, as the original publisher, to be imprisoned for one year, and to stand in the pilary for one hour at the Royal Exchange; the late printer of the *Noon Gazette*, to pay a fine of £100 and to be imprisoned for a year; and, for an aggravating paragraph, to be imprisoned for a additional year, and to pay a fine of £100. The publisher of the *Morning Herald* was fined £100 and imprisoned for a year; and the printer of the *Gazetteer* (being a female) was fined £50 and imprisoned for six months.
>
> The printers of the *Whitehall Evening Post, Middlesex Journal,* and *St. James's Chronicle*, received sentence for the same offence; each was fined £100 and the two former were imprisoned for a year.

The struggle between the government and the press continues to the present day. Progress came slowly. In 1792, Fox's Libel Act established the rule that it was the obligation of the jury and not the judge to determine whether a publication was defamatory or seditious. In 1834 the libel laws were further amended by Lord Campbell's Act, which made truth a defense in criminal as well as civil action.[22] In spite of the resolves of Parliament, many judges continued to pass on the criminality of the writing and to reject truth as a defense. Prosecutions for libel continued with appalling severity throughout the eighteenth century.

Supporters and adversaries of the press have interminably argued the problem of freedom for that bulwark of liberty. Although the debate has remained heated throughout the centuries, resolution remains beyond human understanding. Everyone is in favor of freedom of the press, but few, if any, would tolerate a press without restraint.

CHAPTER THREE

Addresses and
Petitions to the Crown

Astonishing as it may seem, in 1775 the subject of addresses and petitions to the Crown[1] excited the fervor of the letter writers of the British press more than the battles of Lexington and Concord or the carnage at Bunker Hill.[2] The year 1775 might well have been labeled a year of supplications to the throne. The press abounded with addresses to the Crown voicing boundless loyalty and complete approbation for the measures being taken to reduce the rebellious colonies in North America. These fountains of allegiance and fidelity were originally reported in the *London Gazette*, the official organ of the ministry, and then reprinted in the commercial press. Duplication was not universal, but rather dependent on the political and business interests of the printer.

From London, Bristol, and Manchester, from Antigua[3] and Beverly, from the University of Oxford and the Devonshire militia;[4] from the largest and from the smallest communities in Britain came addresses of loyalty and gratitude, expressing the need to reaffirm the authority and supremacy of the British legislature.

From London the *Morning Post* reported (10/16/75):

> *London Gazette*
> St. James's, October 14.
> To the King's Most excellent Majesty.
> Most gracious Sovereign
>
> We, your Majesty's faithful and loyal subjects, Merchants and Traders of the city of London, filled with the deepest concern at the unjustifiable proceedings of some of your Majesty's colonies in America, beg leave to approach your royal throne to testify our entire disapprobation and abhorrence of them; with the most solemn assurances that we will support your Majesty with our lives and fortunes, in maintaining the authority of the legislature of this country, which, we conceive, does and ought to extend over and pervade every part of the British dominions.

With regret and indignation we see colonies, which owe their existence, and every blessing that attended their late prosperous situation, to this their parent country, unnaturally regardless of the fostering hand that raised and supported them, and affecting distinctions in their dependence, not founded in law, or in the constitution of Great Britain.

We are convinced, by the experienced clemency of your Majesty's government, that no endeavour will be wanting to induce our deluded fellow subjects to return to their obedience to that constitution which our ancestors bled to establish, and which has flourished pure and uninterrupted, under the mild government of the House of Hanover.

May that Being who governs the Universe so direct your Majesty's councils and measures, that, from the present confusion, order may arise, and peace again be restored.

That your Majesty may long reign over an happy and united people, is the earnest prayer of

Your Majesty's most faithful and loyal subjects.

From Manchester the *Morning Chronicle* (9/14/75) reported by way of the *London Gazette* the following:

At a General Meeting of the Gentlemen, Clergy, Merchants, etc, of the town of Manchester, held on the 6th instant, the following address to his Majesty was unanimously agreed upon:

To the King's Most Excellent Majesty.

The humble address of the Gentlemen, Clergy, Merchants, and principal inhabitants of the town and neighbourhood of Manchester, in the county palatine of Lancaster.

Most Gracious Sovereign,

Actuated by an affectionate and dutiful regard for your many royal virtues, and firmly attached to that constitution, which secures to British subjects; we presume, in the most loyal and respectful manner, to offer our tribute of gratitude to your Majesty, for the many blessings we have enjoyed under the benign influence of your government.

Since your Majesty's accession to the throne, commerce, the great source of wealth, hath been not only successfully encouraged, but firmly established in this island; and under the auspices of peace hath been carried to an extent unknown to your royal predecessors: manufactures flourish in every part of your Majesty's dominions, particularly in this town and neighbourhood, where they are daily advancing towards perfection, and where the lowest of your subjects are fully employed, and are blessed with the peaceable enjoyment of the fruits of their industry.

Thus happy under your Majesty's government, we look with horror upon every attempt to disturb the tranquillity; and 'tis with inexpressible concern we behold the standard of rebellion erected in some of the American provinces, and our fellow-subjects involved in an unnatural war against their lawful Sovereign. We observe with regret, that the lenity shown by your Majesty towards the insurgents has been of no avail, but, instead of reclaiming, hath seemed rather to irritate and urge them on to more daring acts of violence: and as force is become necessary to bring them to a sense of their allegiance, we think ourselves bound in duty to assist your Majesty in the execution of the legislative authority.

We are not intimidated at the prohibition laid by the Americans on the importation and exportation of goods to and from the British dominions; our extensive trade happily flows in so many different channels, that the obstruction of one can but little distress, much less deter us from our duty to our King and Country. But whatever check our manufacturers may receive by a necessary war, we shall cheerfully submit to a temporary inconvenience, rather than continue subject to lawless depredations from a deluded and unhappy people; as we are fully persuaded, that trade with America can never be established on its true basis, until the Colonies are reduced to a proper submission to the government and laws of Great Britain.

As Englishmen we are led by inclination, as well as impelled by interest, to preserve the authority of the British legislature, and to protect the dignity and prerogative of the crown, (as founded on the principles of the constitution) sacred and inviolate. And we beg to assure your Majesty, that we are ready to support, with our lives and fortunes, such measures as your Majesty shall think necessary, for the punishment of rebellion in any part of your dominions, being convinced, that the sword of justice will be directed by the hand of mercy, towards such of your subjects as have been deluded by the artful designs of a discontented faction.

On 9 October 1775, the *London Chronicle* printed the following Bristol address to the Crown. It reported unqualified endorsement for the manner in which the ministry and the king were conducting the matter of the rebellious colonies:

The London Gazette—St. James's, October 7.

The following address of the Mayor, Burgesses, Clergy, Freeholders and Inhabitants of the City of Bristol, at the Guildhall assembled, has been presented to his Majesty by Charles Hotchkin....

With gratitude we acknowledge the many and great blessings we enjoy under your majesty's mild and auspicious government; during which the trade and commerce of this ancient and loyal city have increased to a degree unknown to former times, to be attributed only to the wisdom of your Majesty's Councils....

We cannot but with astonishment behold the conduct of a few disappointed men, whose sophistical arguments, and seditious correspondence, have, in a great measure, been the occasion of deluding your American subjects into open rebellion.

As British subjects, we testify our abhorrence at this unnatural rebellion ... [and] express our warmest wishes [for the] success of those measures your Majesty hath adopted in support of the legislative authority of Great Britain over all your dominions.

Such was the essence of the addresses inspired and directed by the ministry. Pleased with its exertions and eager for a broad audience, government proposed to send duplicates of these supplications to America. The

Public Advertiser (9/21/75) reported the following: "A great number of Copies of the Addresses already presented, are ordered to be printed, to be sent to America, by the first Transport that goes, and there to be distributed, if possible, in order to set those misled People right, who imagine that nine out of ten in England espouse their Cause."

The position of the ministry was not to remain unchallenged, however. A petition from "the Gentlemen, Merchants, and Traders of London" appeared in the commercial press, but, not surprisingly, failed to be reported in the *London Gazette*. It originated in London, but from a gathering much different from the assembly aforementioned. And the message to the king expressed not approval but marked disapproval of the actions of the government regarding America. The *London Chronicle* reported the petition on 14 October 1775:

> The following Address, Memorial, and Petition of the Gentlemen, Merchants, and Traders of London, unanimously agreed to at a general meeting at the King's Arms Tavern, Cornhill, was presented to his Majesty last by Wm. Baker, Esq; Chairman . . . and it not having appeared in the *London Gazette*, it is thought proper to adopt this method of communicating it to the Public:
>
> To the King's Most excellent Majesty.
>
> The humble Address, Memorial, and Petition, of the Gentlemen, Merchants, and Traders of LONDON.
>
> May it please your Majesty,
>
> We, your Majesty's most dutiful and loyal Subjects, the Gentlemen, Merchants, and Traders of London, beg leave to approach your Majesty with unfeigned assurances of affection and attachment, to your Majesty's person and government, and to represent, with great humility, our sentiments on the present alarming state of public affairs.
>
> By the operation of divers acts of the British Parliament, we behold, with deep affliction, that happy communion of interests and good offices which have so long subsisted between this country and America suspended, and an intercourse (which augmenting as it grew the strength and dignity of your Majesty's dominions, hath enabled your Majesty to defeat the natural rivals of our greatness in every quarter of the world) threatened with irretrievable ruin.
>
> We should humbly represent to your Majesty, if they had not been already represented, the deadly wounds which commerce of this country must feel from these unfortunate measures; that it has not yet more deeply felt them, is owing to temporary and accidental causes, which cannot long continue. But we beg your Majesty to cast an eye on the general property of this land, and to reflect what must be its fate when deprived of our American commerce.
>
> It fills our minds with additional grief to see the blood and treasure of your Majesty's Subjects wasted in effecting a fatal separation between the different parts of your Majesty's empire by a war, uncertain in the event,

destructive in its consequences, and the object contended for lost in the contest.

As was true in the dissenting petition from London, the people of Bristol were not united in appreciation of the manner in which the ministry and the king were dealing with the rebellious colonies in North America. Their dissenting statement did not appear in the *London Gazette* and received only scattered press coverage.

The *Morning Chronicle* (10/2/75) reported a meeting of "Merchants, Traders, and others" on 27 September to petition his Majesty "praying his interposition to put a stop to a ruinous civil war, that our trade may thereby be restored to its former flourishing state":

> At a numerous and respectable meeting of the Merchants, Traders, and others, interested in, and well wishers to American commerce, held at the Guildhall, at eleven o'clock this morning, Mr Hayes, an eminent American merchant in the chair, the following resolutions were agreed to.
>
> Resolved:
>
> 1. That the trade with North America is of very great advantage to Great Britain in general, and to this city in particular.
>
> 2. That any measures which contribute to the destruction of that trade, are an essential injury to the internal commerce and manufacturers of this kingdom.
>
> 3. That the unhappy contest between Great Britain and her colonies had a manifest tendency to destroy the commercial connection, and political union, which have for many years subsisted between the two countries.
>
> 4. That the loss of our trade with America will deprive many thousand industrious poor of the means of procuring a daily subsistence (a melancholy fact!) of which we have already ample experience in this city.
>
> 5. That the late importation of American grain into this city hath greatly contributed to lower the price of all the necessaries of life, and has been the means of preserving multitudes from the calamitous consequences of famine.
>
> 6. That an approbation of measures calculated to destroy the commercial intercourse between the two colonies, and spread the horrors of a civil war over a very considerable part of the British dominions, would be highly disgraceful to the inhabitants of a city that depends solely upon trade for its support; and to every friend to humanity and the general happiness of society.
>
> A motion was then made, that a petition be presented to his Majesty, praying his interposition to put a stop to a ruinous civil war, that our trade may thereby be restored to its former flourishing state. . . . A Petition was then produced, read paragraph by paragraph, and passed without a dissenting voice. A Petition was then signed by the gentlemen present, and afterwards left at the Bush tavern in Corn-street; and when the signatures are fully completed, it is to be presented to the King by our Representative in Parliament.

The *London Chronicle* (10/12/75) reported that the aforementioned petition was presented to his Majesty by Edmund Burke[5] as a representative of that Bristol:

On Wednesday the following petition was presented to his Majesty from the City of Bristol, by Mr. Burke, one of the Representatives of that City . . . It was signed by 979 persons; among whom were most of the principal merchants and manufacturers of that great commercial place; men perfectly acquainted with the advantages derived from American commerce, and sensible of the mischiefs that must be consequent to an American war.

Perhaps the debate became deepened and broadened because Edmund Burke represented Bristol in Parliament and was himself a controversial figure. Burke and the group of merchants whom he supported received little favor in the press. Rather, the ministerial scribblers, most notably those of the *London Chronicle* and *Morning Chronicle*, used the occasion to attack Burke personally and relentlessly.

In the *London Chronicle* (11/21/75), writer A.B. sought the support of the Almighty to bolster his disapproval of the representative from Bristol:

> But Mr.B---ke and his petitioners should have remembered, that though it is not very difficult for an artful man to impose upon the generality of his fellow men, yet there is no imposing upon God who discerneth the thoughts and intents of the heart, and from whom there is no disguise, no darkness or shadow of death, by which the workers of iniquity can hide themselves.

In the *London Chronicle* of December 1775, A WILTSHIRE FREEHOLDER wrote directly to Burke:

> To E---- B---ke, Esq: . . . You were kind enough to manufacture the said petition yourself . . . the petition was actually fabricated in London. . . . I cannot conclude without calling on Mr. B--- to produce to the public the names, the places or residence, and the real occupations of the 138 (I presume signers) "principal clothiers, independent freeholders, and opulent tradesmen" subscribers to his famous petition, which was begot by Ignorance, and dismissed with contempt.

The *Morning Chronicle* offered the following from DIVER (12/8/75), who suggested a censure of both Burke and the petition from the "American advocates." Burke was portrayed as "the present political and anti ministerial orator, Member of Parliament for the City of Bristol, and Agent for the City of New York." As for the petition and the subscribers to that petition, DIVER offered nothing less than utter contempt:

> It is true they have procured a petition to the Throne, in opposition to the Addressers, but so far from being of equal weight with the Addressers, or signed by men of equal property and unbiased sentiments, I am assured by a gentleman of the first character in Bristol . . . that the number of Petitioners amounting to 933, there were but 105 on a nice examination of whom he has the least cognizance . . . the large remainder . . . [are] obscure persons . . . [who] sign or make their marks under fictitious or borrowed names in order to swell the petition.

In the *Morning Chronicle* (12/12/75) AN ADDRESSER expressed not only his revulsion for Burke's political activities but again accused the Bristol petitioners and the "American Advocates" of fomenting the rebellion:

> To Edmund Burke, Esq: Member of Parliament for Bristol: It is almost universally acknowledged that the Americans would never have carried their opposition to these desperate lengths had they not been urged on by letters of incitement and encouragement from this side of the water.

Edmund Burke and the Bristol petition, the one most displeasing to the ministry, remained major targets for the attacks of ministerial scribblers. An unsigned letter in the *London Chronicle* (11/18/75) questioned the veracity of the petitioners and claimed they had "fomented a revolution unprovoked and unnatural."

There was little respite for Edmund Burke. From a constituent of the town of Warminster came this unsigned letter (*LC* 12/12/75) discrediting and rejecting the entire petition:

> As a petition has been presented by Mr. Burke under the denomination of a petition from Warminster and other towns, we whose names are hereunto subscribed, the Gentlemen, Clergy, Freeholders, Manufacturers, and Inhabitants of the said town of Warminster, think ourselves obliged to inform the public that we totally disclaim the said petition; and that it is so far from being the sense of the town that it was procured unknown to the far greater part of it.

In addition to those ministerial scribblers who denigrated Burke and the antiadministration petition from the city of Bristol, the ministry had a plethora of journalists who wrote favorably of the policies of government. Expressions of approval and support were in profusion in the press. A call for the people of Britain to voice demonstrations of loyalty, devotion, and the authority of the British legislature was issued by ROYAL SUBJECT in the *London Chronicle* and the *Morning Chronicle* on 28 September 1775:

> Come forth then, undaunted by the hungry howl of pseudo-patriots here, or savage war-whoops of rebellion yonder. Ye cities, towns, societies, and every class of virtuous men, come quickly forth, in emulous throngs, and show, in public declarations to the throne, your steady purpose to defend, at every hazard, and against all invaders and insurgents, whosoever; the rights of your King, as Sovereign of all the British dominions, and the perfidial authority of the British legislature over the whole empire.

The long hand of the ministry reached into Scotland for blessings. A CITIZEN contributing to the *Caledonian Mercury* (9/20/75) found it unsettling that the city of Edinburgh had not openly pledged allegiance to the Crown: "At a time when one part of his Majesty's dominions are in open rebellion . . . it has been a matter of astonishment to many sober thinking people in this place that no expressions of loyalty have been offered by the Magistrates of Edinburgh."

Again in the *Caledonian Mercury* (10/2/75) SIMPLEX presented an entreaty for the support of the endeavors of the ministry: "It must undoubtedly give every friend to Government great pleasure to hear that the addresses are to be presented to his Majesty from the principal cities and towns in this island, praying him to use the most vigorous measures in order to bring those obstinate rogues, the Americans, to reason; that is to say, to due submission to Parliament."

Approval of the measures of the ministry and of the authority of the British legislature was urged throughout Britain. Such was the declaration from A LOYAL SUBJECT printed in the *Morning Chronicle* (9/28/75): "Every class of virtuous men come quickly forth in emulous throngs and show in public declarations to the Throne your steady purpose to defend at all hazards, and against all invaders and insurgents whatsoever, the Rights of your King as Sovereign of all British dominions, and the prefidial authority of the British Legislature over the whole empire."

Nor could the supporters of the ministry be expected to resist criticizing the petition of the London traders who refused to support the king. An unsigned letter published in the *Morning Post* (10/6/75) stated: "The Electors and Freeholders of Great Britain, In Answer to the Address of the City of London: . . . We hold your address and the transactions of the inhabitants of America in the same light, with utter contempt; declaring this our firm resolution to sacrifice our lives and fortunes in his Majesty's service."

To MANUFACTURER in the *London Chronicle* (11/9/75), the London address critical of the conduct of the king and his ministers might very well have been fabricated by the Americans:

> On reading the address, memorial, petition, of the gentlemen, merchants, and traders of London, I concluded it to be a counterpart to the American instructions: for if penned by Hancock himself, it could not have been better adopted to the most sanguine wishes of the colonists; for as the sum of it is to desire his Majesty to divide his crown and empire with the rebels, as the only measure for a reconciliation. . . . The country they possess, and all they enjoy is derived from the munificence of Old England.

In reply to the city of London address, JUNIUS (*MC* 10/9/75) reminded his readers that the meetings of the citizens of London were as "illegal as they are unnecessary and absurd":

> On City Petitions to the Throne: Whatever may be said of the privileges of a free people to assemble as often as reason or caprice direct to censure Ministers, and uniformly to oppose and condemn the measures of every

Administration, right or wrong, and to petition the King, nothing can equal the absurdity with which the Citizens of London, in their corporate capacity, have for some years past, carried their Addresses, Petitions, and Remonstrances to the Throne. The once honest Citizens forget, that when they have delegated their whole power in the community to their Representatives, this constituent body have nothing to do with matters of state, more than to wish, to pray, and to hope. Hence it happens that they assemble about public affairs that do not immediately concern them; and which, having left to the conduct of others, they cannot sufficiently comprehend, for want of information; and hence it is evident; to men of sense and candour that their meetings on public business are as illegal as they are unnecessary and absurd.

The antiministerial letter writers, however, were not to be bested by their rival governmental scribes. VINDEX (*LC* 12/9/75) voiced his dismay at those who encouraged the conflict with America:

Whether England or America was originally the aggressor, every good man wishes that peace, on honourable terms was restored to both countries.... When, therefore, I hear men, considerable in number, bring up their voices to the Throne for a continuation of the horrors of civil dissension, I am lost in the confusion at the strange infatuation which possesses their minds.

A torrent of protest followed the proministerial Manchester address appearing at the beginning of this chapter and its declarations of the well-being of the economy. An unsigned (*LC* 9/14/75) letter in the *London Chronicle* claimed the opposite:

Manchester, Sept. 8. Of the address and petition to the King whereby the signers were in accord with the policy of the government regarding America, this writer suggests this is not the truth; that trade is in a very languishing condition and that the ensuing winter presents a very dismal prospect ... weavers out of work and thousands connected with them unemployed.

The writer CRITO (*MP* 9/22/75) also questioned the validity of the comments of the "Gentlemen, Clergy and Inhabitants" of Manchester on the American trade. He asserted that the economy was simply not booming and that although the hat and fabric trade might be enjoying a period of prosperity, overall trade and manufacture was not. CRITO declared: "Granting these facts to be true,—what then? Because their town goes on without American trade, from their serving principally the home consumption, are they to address for measures that may be infinitely mischievous to many other places?"

Perhaps more disquieting to the ministry and His Majesty was the judgment of the correspondent INDEPENDENT which appeared in the *London Chronicle* (9/28/75). The expressions of loyalty, duty, and affection for His Majesty, he wrote, did not represent the people:

Upon reading the late addresses from Manchester, Lancaster, and Liverpool, filled with so many expressions of loyalty, duty, and affection for his Majesty, and to the hearty abhorrence of the rebellion, as it is there called, now carrying on in America ... addresses to throne are often times filled with the grossest flattery, and are so far from conveying to the Prince the real sentiments of his people at large, that they contain nothing more than the unmeaning protestations of an abandoned and prostituted few.

The *London Chronicle* (10/24/75) continued on the same course with a letter from VERITAS asserting that these affectionate addresses might well have been procured by trickery:

So far as I understand that political virtue hypocrisy, I profess to hold it in the greatest abhorrence in what shape or form soever it appears, and whether it be practised at St. James's, at Manchester, Liverpool, Lancaster, Coventry, Leicester, etc. What led me at first onto this train of thinking was the many loyal, dutiful, affectionate addresses which have been of late obtained by a certain manoeuvre, or legerdemain.

The writers of the *London Chronicle* were not alone in suspecting subterfuge on the part of the ministry. The writer VERO wrote in the *Morning Post* (10/2/75):

I see by the papers that more places besides Manchester and Lancaster have addressed the King to execute with all spirit the edicts of the Parliament of Great Britain over the Colonies.... As to addresses gained by ministerial arts, they are so well known and understood in this age, that they will never be treated with anything but contempt.... [They are] measures whose only tendency is the dismemberment of the empire.

The ministry, however, was not without champions. For TRUE BLUE (*MC* 10/9/75), the measure of an acceptable address was the respectability of the petitioners: "It must give every man infinite pleasure that is a friend to his King and country to peruse the very loyal address of the towns of Manchester and Lancaster ... from such respectable people."

Of special consideration were the addresses from small towns with little or no manufacturing. Towns, the scribblers claimed, which were often under the authority of a despotic master. Such were the concerns of A FREEHOLDER in the *Public Advertiser* (10/20/75): "Addresses from Boroughs, Market-towns, or little Cities, neither respectable in themselves, nor carrying on any Manufacture of national Consequence, are of little Account. They neither act, nor think freely, being solely directed and governed by the imperious dictates of their Master, and generally consisting of Dependants or Expectants."

The following address from the town of Beverly which was reported in the *Morning Post* (10/4/75) was undoubtedly the circumstance FREEHOLDER had in mind.

From the *London Gazette*
St. James's, October 3.

The following address of the Mayor, Alderman, and Burgesses, of the town of Beverly in the county of York, in Common Council assembled, having been transmitted to the Earl of Dartmouth, one of his Majesty's Principal Secretaries of State, has been presented to his Majesty: Which address his Majesty was pleased to receive most graciously,

To the King's Most Excellent Majesty,the humble address of the Mayor, Alderman, and Burgesses, of the town of Beverly, in the county of York, in Common Council assembled.

We, your Majesty's most loyal and faithful subjects, the Mayor, Alderman, and Burgesses, of Beverly in the county of York, should think ourselves wanting both in duty and gratitude to your Majesty, did we not take this occasion of joining with the rest of your Majesty's loyal subjects, in giving this public testimony of our utmost abhorrence of the present unnatural rebellion, in some of your Majesty's colonies in North America, as well as of those factions and evil minded men, both at home and abroad, by whose means the same hath been, and still is, principally promoted and abetted.

When we consider the many blessings we have enjoyed since your Majesty's accession to the throne of these realms, by the great extension of trade, and the consequent increase of wealth; by the many good and salutary laws which have been enacted; and, above all, by your Majesty's just and lenient government over us; we cannot sufficiently express our detestation of all those societies, or sets of men, who (contrary to the allegiance they owe and have sworn to your Majesty) are now, by their inflammatory letters and publications, in a most daring manner, sowing the seeds of sedition among us, and thereby endeavouring, as much as in them lies, to involve us at home as well as abroad in all the calamities of a civil war.

We beg leave, therefore, in the most respectful and dutiful manner, to assure your Majesty, that we will at all times, to the utmost of our power, be ready to support your Majesty, and the honour and dignity of your crown, as well as the legislative authority of these realms, in the defense of our most valuable constitution, against all such attempts of your Majesty's seditious or deluded subjects either at home or abroad.

Given under our Common Seal, this 27th day of September, in the year of our Lord 1775.

JO. MIDGLEY, Mayor

The Beverly address was destined to bear the brunt of the correspondent's ridicule. Without manufacture and with little or no commerce, Beverly presented a perfect target to the writer of the following unsigned letter in the *Morning Post* of 12 October 1775. The ministry and the "Beverly Gentlemen" were to be held up to ridicule and scorn:

> On the Beverly address: If administration were not sunk lower than even their enemies have thought proper to class them, they would not call to their aid the approbation of the town of Beverly upon measures of a merely commercial nature. Can the Beverly Gentlemen imagine that the world, when

they see them interfering in the commercial question of American measures, will not enquire, What is the commerce of this town of Beverly? In what does it trade: What are its American correspondences? What Mr.Editor, must your readers think when I tell them that this town of Beverly is a mere inland place, without the least pretensions to commerce, and possessing not a single manufacture.

There were other petitions and petitioners which excited the fervor of the British public and the British newspapers. A series of petitions from the lord mayor and the livery of the city of London to George III stirred the scribblers to renewed heights. To be precise, it was not the actual petitions but rather the manner in which the petitions should be received by His Majesty which was the source of the disagreement.

The ill feeling that existed between George III and John Wilkes, now lord mayor of London, dated back to the early 1760s. The first edition of Wilkes's new journal, *The North Briton*, published on 5 June 1762, initiated a continuous attack on the earl of Bute, prime minister and longtime favorite of the king. The dispute reached a climax on 23 April 1763 with the publication of issue 45 of *The North Briton*. For many months George III had brooded in silence while Wilkes and his *North Briton* were reviling his dearest friend and, in addition, hurling shameful insults against George's mother. And now, at last, this scurrilous pamphleteer had made a most outrageous attack on his own person, not only accusing him of a direct falsehood, but what was an even greater offence in the eyes of "a Patriot King," insinuating that the responsibility for his acts and his declarations rested entirely with his ministers. The article which aroused the anger of the king dealt with a speech from the throne and characterized a passage in which the peace of Hubertusburg (which ended the Seven Years' War) was discussed as "the most abandoned instance of ministerial effrontery ever attempted to be imposed on mankind." The pamphleteer even insinuated that the king had been induced to countenance a deliberate lie. The resentment of the king and his court knew no bounds.

A general warrant was drawn up authorizing the king's messengers to arrest "the authors, printers, and publishers of a seditious and treasonable paper entitled *The North Briton*, No. 45." When Parliament convened, the Commons consigned *The North Briton* issue no. 45, to the hands of the common hangman to be burned as a seditious libel.

For the next decade the Parliament, the king, and Wilkes were consumed in controversy. Wilkes was elected to Parliament in 1768 as a representative of Middlesex and was later reelected. Parliament was no less consistent in refusing to seat him. By 1774 the disagreement had eased somewhat, and Wilkes was seated in Parliament and elected lord mayor of London. But there remained a notable lack of harmony between George III and John Wilkes.

In mid–July 1775, the controversy between Wilkes and George III centered on the proper method for the petition of the livery of London to be received by the Crown. More to the point, the support Wilkes and his followers were giving to the rebellious colonies lay at the center of the dispute. An address had been prepared by the livery of London protesting the war in North America:

> The humble Address, Remonstrance, and Petition of the Lord Mayor, Alderman, and Livery of the City of London, in Common Hall assembled.
>
> We, Your Majesty's dutiful and loyal subjects, the Lord Mayor, Alderman, and the Livery of the city of London, beg leave to approach the throne, and to declare our abhorrence of the measures that have been pursued, and are now pursuing, to the oppression of our fellow subjects in America. These measures are big with all the consequences which can alarm a free and commercial people: a deep and perhaps a fatal wound to commerce; the ruin of manufactures; the diminution of the revenue, and consequent increase of taxes; the alienation of the colonies; and the blood of your Majesty's subjects....
>
> Your petitioners do, therefore, most earnestly beseech your Majesty to dismiss immediately, and for ever, from your councils, these ministers and advisers, as the first step towards a full redress of those grievances which alarm and afflict your whole people. So shall peace and commerce and affection of all your Majesty's subjects be the solid supporters of your throne.

The king's answer, delivered to the lord mayor by the earl of Hertford, Lord Chamberlain, rejected the petition:

> It is with the utmost astonishment that I find any of my subjects capable of encouraging the rebellious disposition which unhappily exists in some of my colonies in North America.
>
> Having entire confidence in the wisdom of my Parliament, the great council of the nation, I will steadily pursue those measures which they have recommended for the support of the constitutional rights of Great Britain, and the protection of the commercial interests of my kingdoms.

Was the petition to be received "sitting on the throne," as the livery of London requested, or at a levee? George refused to heed the behest of the livery and declared that he alone must decide the place to receive the petition, an answer which the London livery condemned as "evasive, nugatory, and insulting." Wilkes's response to the king's refusal to accept the petition sitting on the throne sets forth what he considered the responsibility of the crown to hold a public reading of the petition "in the presence of the petitioners" and to receive an answer to that petition. Wilkes also took the opportunity to remind George that the people of London, the commercial people, were opposed to the war with America.

> The privilege, my Lord, for which I contend, is of very great moment, and peculiarly striking. When his Majesty receives on the throne any address, it

is read by the proper officer to the King, in the presence of the petitioners. They have the satisfaction of knowing that their sovereign has heard their complaints. They receive an answer. If the same address is presented at a levee, or in any other mode, no answer is given. A suspicion may arise, that the address is never heard or read, because it is only received, and immediately delivered to the Lord in waiting. If he is tolerably versed in the supple, insinuating arts practised in the magic circle of a court, he will take care never to remind his prince of any disagreeable and disgusting, however important and wholesome, truths. He will strangle in its birth the fair offspring of liberty, because its cries might awaken and alarm the parent; and thus the common father of all his people may remain equally ignorant and unhappy in his most weighty concerns.

Important truths, My Lord, were the foundation of the last humble address, remonstrance, and petition to the King, respecting our brave fellow-subjects in America. The greatness as well as goodness of the cause, and the horrors of an approaching civil war, justified our application to the throne. It comprehended every thing interesting to us as a free and commercial people, the first principles of our common liberty, and the immense advantage of the only trade we enjoy unrivalled by other nations.

As a writer of the twentieth century might comment, Wilkes and the livery of London received a terrible press. Support for the king and disapproval of the behavior of Wilkes and the London livery was commanding.

OPIFEX (*LC* 10/7/75):

The public may see by the instructions given to the Representatives of Middlesex that their Constituents have quite laid aside common decency and respect towards Parliament and that they are not willing to be outdone by their American brethren in phrases of contempt; our inveterate enemies in the present Parliament.

CLERICUS (*MC* 8/7/75):

To the Right Honourable the L--- M---- : For what pray are all the Common Halls, Remonstrances, and Petitions? Why to inflame the minds of his Majesty's peaceable and quiet subjects, and to raise them in open rebellion against him, with you at their head. If you still persist in the unworthy cause you have undertook, ruin and destruction must inevitably attend you, to an ignominious death.

POLITICAL LOOKING GLASS (*MP* 7/8/75):

To the Lord Mayor—On the "disgraceful and factious petitions of the Lord Mayor" . . . shall the lenity of such a King become the sport of a little junto of town clerks, unpractised doctors, or a few interested American merchants? I feel as an Englishmen ought; he who insults my King, insults me; he who disobeys the laws of the legislature, is a rebel; and he who daringly supports that rebel by petitions, or even public sanction whilst in hostility, is equally a rebel to peace, order and society.

MESSALA (*PA* 7/1/75):

The right of petitioning . . . is confined to certain Modes prescribed by the

Constitution. The Livery . . . are no better than a tumultuous Assembly; and nobody is ignorant that tumultuous Petitioning is contrary to an express Law.

Petitioning was not confined to Great Britain. The American Congress, following British tradition, busily petitioned the king about what the colonists considered the injustices of Parliament. The most noteworthy of these petitions became known as the Olive Branch Petition (see Appendix B). Enacted by Congress on 8 July 1775, it was signed by John Hancock and almost everyone who subsequently signed the Declaration of Independence.[6] The petition reaffirmed allegiance and affection to the king: "Attached to your Majesty's person, family and government with all the devotion that principle and affection can inspire, connected with Great Britain by the strongest ties that can unite societies, and deploring every event that tends in any degree to weaken them. . . ." The petition maintained that Parliament and the king's ministers were the source of friction between the colonies and the mother country:

> We shall decline the ungrateful task of describing the irksome variety of artifices practised by many of your Majesty's ministers, the delusive pretences, fruitless terrors, and unavailing severities, that have from time to time been dealt out by them in their attempts to execute this impolitic plan [a new system of statutes and regulations adopted for the administration of the colonies] or of tracing thro' a series of years past the progress of the unhappy differences between Great Britain and these colonies, that have flowed from this fatal source.

The petition was taken from Philadelphia to London by Richard Penn, grandson of William Penn, and a copy of the petition was sent to Lord Dartmouth, American secretary, on 21 August 1775. The reply stated that "as his Majesty did not receive it on the throne, no answer would be given." Lord Suffolk further declared: "The King and his Cabinet are determined to listen to nothing from the illegal congress, to treat with the colonies only one by one, and in no event to recognize them in any form of association." Released to the press, the petition received enough publicity to ensure its being brought before Parliament when it reconvened on 26 October. The king, in an indirect reply, asserted the rebels sought "only to amuse by vague Expressions of Attachment to the Parent State and the strongest Protestations of Loyalty to Me, whilst they were preparing for a General Revolt." It was necessary, he said, to put "a speedy End to these Disorders by the most decisive Exertions."

The *Public Advertiser* of 11 November 1775 described the questioning of Richard Penn in the House of Lords as follows:

> Yesterday about Three O'Clock, the Order of the Day having been read for that Purpose, Mr. Penn was called to the Bar of the House of Lords and

examined. . . . We do not presume to give the Questions and Answers verbatim, but hope, without Offence, we may so far gratify the public Curiosity, as to give the substance of the Enquiry. It appeared that the Congress at Philadelphia spoke the Sentiments of all North America; that they considered their last Position to the King as their Ultimatum, and the treating of it with Neglect, or no Answer, as an effectual Bar to all Possibility of a Reconciliation that it was most probably if it did not succeed, they would fix upon some Form of Government independent of Great Britain, though they did not hitherto intend to throw off their Dependence on the Mother Country, but on the contrary, acknowledged the supreme Authority of the Crown, and of the Parliament and finally, that it was very likely if a Reconciliation did not take place, they might apply to some foreign Power for Assistance.

Although records of the questioning of Penn do not exist, there remains little doubt that the *Public Advertiser* failed to report the occurrence accurately. If the colonists acknowledged the "supreme Authority of the Crown," and there remains some question whether they did, they most certainly did not recognize the supreme authority of Parliament.

Spurned by the king, the Olive Branch petition had a mixed reception in the press. CINCINNATUS (*PA* 11/16/75) found little reason to accept the appeal:

This political Dove [Richard Penn] who came over with the Olive Branch, instead of showing any reasonable ground for negotiating a Peace with the Colonies, has produced the most unanswerable argument for the continuance of the war; and proved that no more dependence is to be placed on the representation of their friends in this kingdom than upon the professions of their pious delegates at Philadelphia.

The *Morning Chronicle* in an unsigned letter (10/28/75) agreed with the government's position:

On the Petition of the Congress to the Throne: . . . For subjects in arms, carrying on a regular plan of military operations against their Sovereign, appointing a commander in chief, taking forts . . . destroying by the most treacherous means the King's troops . . . to petition the Prince for peace, and to expect that their petition will be attended to, is such an insult to the understandings of the King and the people of England, as must justly excite the greatest indignation.

But America was not to be without a champion. The writer MONTEZUMA (*PA* 6/28/75) informed his readers that the appeals of the colonists had been ignored:

No history can show, nor will human nature admit of an instance of a general discontent, but from a general sense of oppression. As there is now no legal provision against such oppression left untried, every Province having in vain, first separately, and then unitedly, petitioned and remonstrated, they are

compelled into a contest the most shocking and unnatural, with a Parent
state which has been the object of their veneration and their love.

For W.J. (*PA* 8/24/1775), the ministerial scribblers appearing in the
Public Advertiser precluded the success of the Olive Branch Petition: "When
three such Ministerial Bloodhounds, as Messala, Numa, and Coriolanus,
are, at this juncture, unmuzzled and let loose upon the Public in your paper
in one day, surely it cannot be difficult to predict what will be the fate of
the new Petition from the American (not Rebel) Congress."

In the end, the petitions were of little avail. The war continued and the
loss of men and treasure persisted. The addresses to the crown professing
allegiance and fidelity were inconsequential and the efforts of the ministry
to stimulate a wave of approbation for the Crown or the administration
were unsuccessful. Wilkes and George III affected a tenuous reconciliation
which was probably less than either desired. And the victory of the
Americans was not the result of petitions—received or rejected.

CHAPTER FOUR

A Ministry Under Siege

Lord North was prime minister throughout the War for Independence. His strength and weakness, his virtue and mediocrity were aptly portrayed by the nineteenth-century historian William Lecky.[1]

> In the new Chancellor of the Exchequer, Lord North, the King had found a parliamentary leader who was prepared to accept office under the conditions he required, and who was in almost every respect pre-eminently fitted to represent his views.
>
> The son of the Earl of Guildford, Lord North had entered Parliament in 1774, had accepted a lordship of the Treasury under Pitt in 1759, had been removed from office by Rockingham in 1765, and had again come into office with Pitt as Joint Paymaster of the Forces. He belonged, however, to none of the Whig parties, and he possessed in the highest degree that natural leaning toward authority which was most pleasing to the King. Since the beginning of the reign there had been no arbitrary or unpopular measure which he did not defend. He moved for the expulsion of Wilkes. He was one of the foremost advocates of general warrants in every stage of the controversy. He defended the Stamp Act. He bitterly resisted its repeal. He defeated for a time the attempt to secure the property of the subject from the dormant claims of the Crown. Most of the measures which he advocated in the long course of his ministry were proved by the event to be disastrous and foolish, but he possessed an admirable good sense in the management of details, and he had many of the qualities that lead to eminence both in the closet and in Parliament. His ungainly form, his harsh tones, his slow and laboured utterance, his undisguised indolence, furnished a ready theme for ridicule, but his private character was wholly unblemished. No statesman ever encountered the storms of political life with a temper which it was more difficult to ruffle or more impossible to embitter. His almost unfailing tact, his singular quick and happy wit, and his great knowledge of business, and especially of finance, made him most formidable as a debater, while his sweet and amiable disposition gave him some personal popularity even in the most disastrous moments of his career. Partly through political principle and partly through weakness of character he continually subordinated his own judgement to that of the King, and carried out a policy not very different from his predecessor.

In 1775 the letter writers of the British press found little in the conduct of the ministry toward the rebellious colonies to warrant their support.[2] Rather than offering approbation, letters to the printer condemned the actions of the ministry as being directed with folly, ignorance, falsehood, and wicked intent.

HERA LITUS (*MC* 12/4/75):

The melancholy appearance of our affairs have from the folly which is seen in the ministerial plans and their execution, ought to alarm every well-wisher to this country; and none but either venal tools, or deluded ignorant can say anything in favour of Administration, who have from some concealed design deceived both King and People.

J. BRUTUS (*PA* 6/26/75):

A series of inconsistent measures has brought this Country to an alarming crisis. The destruction of a wicked and a bad Minister may perhaps, for the sake of example, be a recompense for the danger into which he had led us. Every kind of plan in regard to America has during this Administration been hastily adopted, pursued with Eagerness, defended with Ignorance, and at last dropped through indecision.

A BOSTONIAN (*PA* 7/25/75):

I observe the Ministry are too much ashamed of the Proclamation to admit it into the Gazette.[3] It is the only proof of their wisdom that I have seen. Such a performance would disgrace them over all Europe. It begins with infatuation, proceeds with falsehood and folly, and ends with a hypocritical affectation of prayer. My earnest prayer is that God and the people may in their justice soon bring this foolish General and the abandoned Ministers who sent him to condign punishment.

ONE OF THE PUBLIC (*PA* 7/6/75):

Everything done relative to America has been wicked in the projecting, and foolish in its execution; and, by driving a rising, flourishing people to arms, we shall cut off our resources, the sinews of our strength, and become an easy prey to the next invader.

The ministry's expectation that the Restraining Bills[4] would circumvent the designs of the colonies had the opposite effect, according to CRITO (*MP* 5/30/75):

By the latest advices which have been received from America, and which came to Bristol, we learn that the people of Virginia, Maryland, and Pennsylvania, were enraged to the greatest degree at the news of the restraining bills. Those acts passed under the ministry's expectation, that they would have the instant effect of confounding all the designs of the colonies ... those acts have incensed them almost to madness.

The writer CRITO returned to the attack a few days later (*MP* 6/6/75):

> If conquest gives us command of America, we cannot keep it by force; the only possible plan is to burn and destroy it.... Such a plan would be perfectly consistent with several of the acts we have seen passed this and last session—acts to the full as inhuman and barbarous, though not so immediately bloody, for whether you burn a fisherman's house or tell him he shall never fish, appears to me much the same matter.

The writer A.Z. (*MP* 5/30/75) remained convinced that the ministry was responsible for the unfortunate state of affairs: "There is no true friend of this country who can consider the present situation of it without regret for its danger, and indignation against the Ministers who have brought her into so alarming a state of uncertainty."

Earlier TITUS (*MP* 9/1/75) had informed his readers that the ministers were now terrified at the unexpected resistance of the rebellious colonies: "The fact is, that they have met with a resistance they did not expect, and are now terrified at the storm they have raised. With the true dastardly spirit of every Tory Minister that ever disgraced this kingdom, they dread a war as a signal for the loss of their places, and therefore will recede without peace as they have advanced without war."

CRITO (*MP* 8/4/75) censured the ministry for the manner in which it precipitated the American conflict: "They drove America into resistance by a series of such tyrannical acts as would have disgraced Algiers."

For CLEONITUS (*MC* 8/17/75), the continuance of "this unnatural war with America is a plan of raising butchers to attempt the murder of the injured innocent."

In 1775, Americans considered themselves Englishmen, and Englishmen living in the mother country also considered their brethren living in the North American colonies to be Englishmen.

In *PA* 5/31/75, BRUTUS addressed Lord North: "You have now begun the bloody business. You now find all America united, and that they have Spirit equal to Englishmen, because they are Englishmen."

Another writer, CHARANDES (*MP* 8/28/75), rebuked Lord North for the unconstitutional exertion of prerogative operating in America. He further urged everyone to support the American cause:

> So violent and unconstitutional an exertion of prerogative as that now operating in America hath no precedent either in the annals of this or any other country, and the manner in which these measures have been presented obliges every man, however indifferent about the interest of this kingdom from a matter of prudence and self preservation to exert his power in this cause with our brethren in America.

Using the phrase "best friends" TITUS (*MP* 5/31/75), referred to the colonists. In an unsigned letter the *Public Advertiser* (8/24/75) apprised its readers of the "endearing Ties of Interest, Blood, and Affection" that united America and the British Crown.

VESPUCIUS (*PA* 12/5/75) put a question to his readers. Why should the Americans treat with the present administration? Britain proved powerless to subdue the rebellious colonists; the Americans, although desiring to reunite with Britain, would not deal with an administration they scorned:

> As no advantage has been gained over the Americans, as the inability of this Country to subdue the Americans is evident, and as the Ministers, from Menacers of Vengeance, are turned supplicants for Peace, no man can wonder if the Americans, who treat sword in hand, and backed by powerful armies, are determined to maintain their Liberty as obstinately in Negotiation as they have done in Arms. They cannot Fear, Love, or Esteem the present Administration, who have asserted the highest claims in the most contemptible manner: and though the Americans desire re-union with England, they will treat like one great Nation with another; and as they have not been frightened or beaten out of their Rights, they will take care not to be duped out of them by Ministers, whose capacity and integrity they scorn alike.

Britain was a trading country whose commercial interests greatly benefited from their exclusive trade with America. It not was surprising, therefore, that at this early date recriminations were heard about the loss of that trade.[5] The difficulty was laid at the feet of the ministry. BECKFORD'S GHOST (*PA* 7/7/75) held the ministry responsible for the misfortune which had befallen British commerce: "They feel no compunction for the ruin of many hundreds of capital merchants whose failure must bring on a bankruptcy of half the tradesmen and manufacturers in this kingdom—they feel no compassion for the misery of millions which is at hand."

CAMMILLUS (*PA* 7/29/75) agreed with this opinion: "Nothing less than a miracle can crown the measures of the present administration with success.... They care not to how great a degree they irritate the people of England. Our manufacturers are on the point of starving, and our merchants on the verge of bankruptcy."

Support for the ministry by the scribblers of the press in 1775 was probably less than the administration expected. But government did have its champions. Demonstrating to his readers that the judgment of the ministry was sound and the behavior of the press scandalous, FACTION (*MC* 8/14/75) wrote:

> Gratitude and allegiance weighed nothing with the Americans when the prevailing pleas of interest and ambition made it necessary to advance new creeds and to support them with sophistry and deception.... Every judging mind will justify the conduct of the administration ... and treat the scandalous imposition which the press constantly offers to the credulity of the public with sovereign and judicious contempt.

A REVOLUTIONARY WHIG (*LC* 12/7/75) found it difficult to understand why the Americans could reject British liberty:

> Whether there ever was, or ever can be a people more happy in the enjoyment of the most perfect liberty than the subjects of Great Britain are at present in every part of the empire; and whether, therefore, those men (Americans, Patriots, Clergy who support American rebels) are not the greatest enemies of the state and to mankind in general, who, by false reasoning and gross misinterpretation attempt to overturn that government by which we are secured in the possession of such distinguished privileges.

Another writer, ANTI FACTION (*MC* 11/10/75), assured his readers that the administration did not have "hostile designs" against America: "The people of England can never be made to believe that administration have any hostile designs against the constitutional liberties of America; on the other hand, they are firmly persuaded that the coercive measures now pursuing, so far from being inimical to freedom, are indispensably necessary to support the freest constitution the world ever produced."

The letter writer R. FIGG (*MC* 8/2/75) also defended the ministry and advised his readers that it was nonsense to surmise anything but that "America is fighting for the annihilation of the authority of Parliament." In vindication of the ministry and a scrupulous Parliament, CURIOUS DENTATUS (*PA* 6/6/75) wrote: "The present firm and vigilant Minister is only enforcing those Acts, which the Legislature after ample investigation, and in thorough conviction, have passed an order to secure a necessary dependence on the Crown of Britain."

Not all letters criticizing the ministry did so in the cause of America. The writer CRITO (*MP* 9/29/75), OLD TRUEPENNY (*PA* 9/29/75), and RESPONSE (*PA* 8/25/75) held the ministry responsible for the lack of military supplies, for instructions impossible to execute, and for shameful and wicked insinuations.

By 1776 the attacks on the administration increased in both number and severity. The ministry was censured for the precipitation and the conduct of the war. For MELA (*MP* 9/20/76), the manner in which the ministry conducted the war was ineffectual and inept and large sums were being squandered:

> The circle of History cannot present a view of such management as that of administration in the conduct of the present war with the Americans. If Congress had bribed our Ministers to go into a system of attack calculated only to discipline the troops of the Americans, it certainly would have been just such a scene of operations as the two last years have exhibited; the nation at the next meeting of Parliament will have stood the expense of twenty millions sterling; expended for no other purpose whatever, but to render the Colonies able to prolong the war.

The letter writer A MODERATE MAN (*PA* 1/9/76) added to the report of ineptitude and ignorance on the part of the ministry: "It is therefore the duty of every good citizen to join in an unanimous remonstrance to the King requesting him to put an end to the horrors of a civil war which was begun through the folly and ignorance, not to say worse motives, of his ministers."

A BRITON (*PA* 1/11/76) appreciated the accusations of ineptitude and folly:

> Is it possible for any worthy mind to see without a painful sensibility the present chaos of anarchy and perdition; to see power in the hands unequal to the smallest objects, and grasping at the management of the greatest, affecting to govern two immense Empires in the East and West, without appearing to have any the least knowledge of either, or so much as of their own country.

The ministry was not only accused of bungling the war, but of being responsible for acts of cruelty that were perpetrated by British troops and their mercenary allies. Referring to the battle of Long Island, AN OLD CORRESPONDENT (*MP* 10/23/76), accused the ministry of being party to brutality:

> It is an old and a trite observation that cruelty and cowardice are inseparable; and surely the wretch who is capable of justifying so inhuman a massacre, as that committed on the Provincials on Long Island. . . . Surely all good Christians, all lovers of peace, and their country, will sincerely join with me in praying for a speedy end to a war which cannot it seems be supported by G[overnmen]t, but by acts of cruelty which a virtuous Heathen would blush at the recital of.

Confirming the acts of cruelty but placing the blame on auxiliary troops, AN OBSERVER (*PA* 6/29/76) wrote:

> A large mixed army of chosen Britons and mercenary Foreigners are judged necessary to subdue the once despised Colonists; lest this should fail, every art has been practised to arm Savages on their Frontiers, and negroes in their Settlements, two unprincipled foes, who slaughter women and children. . . . With this motley crew, conjured up against the rights of Freemen, the Ministry hope at length to succeed.

MARCELLUS (*PA* 11/26/76) also condemned the excesses committed against the Americans:

> Whilst we execrate and echo from the Gazette [*London Gazette*] to one another invectives against the Wretches who set fire to New York, denying their right to dispose of their own property in any manner, we cannot, without a blush, and perhaps if we have any principle left, without remorse, recollect the burning of Charles-Town, Portsmouth, and Gosport [Gulfport] by the people who are in the King's pay. Is everything lawful to us, tho' unjustifiable to others? May we call Folly Wisdom, and Cruelty Clemency? Does similar Acts of Villainy, as we call it, of the Americans, cease to be so, when committed by the British People?

CATO (*PA* 1/30/76) singled out and condemned Lord North: "Boast, my Lord, of having imbrued your hands with the blood of brethren and fellow-citizens, of having severed every sacred tie of natural affection, once subsisting amongst Englishmen, and of bringing your country to that abyss of ruin, from which the abilities, prodigious as the follies of the present Junto, who dictate to your Lordship, would vainly attempt to extricate her."

With the news of Lexington and Concord barely a year old, there began to emerge a sense of despair and frustration. Again, it was the ministry that was held blameworthy. ARMINIUS (*MC* 11/30/76) argued the hopelessness of facing "more burthensome" taxes and the loss of beneficial commerce, only to perpetrate unconstitutional actions against the Americans:

> Can it appear in the least advantageous to you to have daily more and more burthensome taxes heaped upon you, together with the loss of a beneficial commerce, to no other purpose than that of pleasing the whims of Administration, who any one of common sense must perceive are pursuing the most unconstitutional and arbitrary purposes, which you suffer with unaccountable insensibility and are made the instruments of displeasure against your brethren the Americans.

Concurring with ARMINIUS, JUNENIS (*MC* 8/23/76) blamed a profligate ministry for ruinous debts, declining trade, and a despotic administration:

> A civil war is now the consequence of preferring falsehood to truth—tyranny to moderation—slavery to liberty: for it is certain where a disposition to rebellion appears among any people, the chief cause is tyranny in the rulers. The function of the Nation is truly melancholy: She is overwhelmed with debts, her revenues are wasted, her trade declined, and the affections of her Colonies alienated.

The writer HOSPICE (*MP* 5/22/76) apprised his readers that even victory over America would not be worth the cost in lives and treasure:

> No wise government ever plunged into an enormous expense to support a war without having some great end in view, the accomplishment of which promised in some way or other to recompense the loss of blood or treasure. Few wars are to be read of where the end proposed, supposing it attained, should be utterly worthless—yet of this sort appears to be the present one with America.

Defenders of the ministry were not as abundant in 1776 as they had been in the preceding year. To those writers who appreciated the ministry, it was a compassionate and considerate British administration that restrained the North American colonies with understanding, sympathy, and justice:

PROBUS (*PA* 11/29/76):

England never erected a single battery in all her American Empire, but against native Indians or Foreigners; and if she laid any restrictions of their manufactures where they interfered with her own, she took care to balance the inconvenience by encouraging other branches of their commerce, on which they might employ their industry with equal advantage.

"z" (*MP* 9/19/76):

The ministry could have done nothing but what they have done; as long as there was a chance for conciliation, they held forth peace; when they saw the clear tendency of their actions, they used the sword, and whatever may be the event of the quarrel, they are completely justifiable for their conduct, which from the beginning has been founded in justice.

To "E" (*CM* 4/1/76), it was the wicked Americans who were at fault:

Let it be marked in the annals of this age; let posterity know that the Americans were wicked enough to rebel against the best of kings and the mildest government; and that the contagion spread so far at home as to affect ... some few more men of education; but that all good men despised their folly and wickedness; and that the majority of the nation were unanimous in supporting Government, and chastising the rebels.

A VETERAN OF SEEN SERVICE (*MC* 11/19/76) suggested to his readers that too much forbearance had been shown towards the American rebels: "In the appointment of this Nobleman [Germaine] to conduct American affairs at home, and of the two noble brothers [Howe], to execute his well-concerted plans abroad, his Majesty has shown the most solid judgement and fatherly tenderness for his people, too long the dupes of their tender feelings and pacific forbearance towards a set of puritannick ingrates."

Writing for the *Morning Post* (8/8/76 and 12/20/76), ANTI-MELA decried all the talk of the ruin of trade and commerce:

After such a loss [American trade], to find ourselves never more prosperous, our manufactures fully employed, our commerce increasing, and our revenue rising, altogether form a picture which ought to fill every breast with satisfaction and ought to be esteemed as the clearest defence of the wisdom and propriety of those measures which we have heard so repeatedly and so unjustly condemned.

Where does agriculture flourish more? Where does commerce make greater strides? In what country more flourishing manufacture? Where is public wealth greater or more used? Let any man but open his eyes and he cannot fail being convinced that this country is the happiest and freest society in the world.

By mid-1776 the loss of America was considered by some in the ministry as within the bounds of possibility. ANTI-MELA, chief ministerial writer of the *Morning Post*, sought to diffuse the responsibility of the ministry

(6/10/76): "I am persuaded that whoever might have been in power and whether war or conciliation had been the plan, America would have been equally lost."

The harsh realities of the war in North America became more evident in the letters in 1777. The cost of the war in blood and treasure; the recognition of the difficulties, if not the impossibility of conquering and holding America, the ministerial invention of military victories, all of these, and general despair, became the subject of scribblers' attacks on the ministry.

Disclosing to his readers the realities of the conquest of the North American colonies, AN ENGLISHMAN (LC 3/18/77) suggested that to subdue and to hold them would be very difficult:

> Even those who are most strenuous for the prosecution of this war, acknowledge that should we be able to conquer the towns on the sea-coast of America, we shall be obliged to maintain them by a military force; and that too at an expense which all the advantages we derive from them will not be sufficient to compensate. . . . As to the interior parts of the country, these I take to be entirely out of the question. Into these we never can penetrate, at least we never can secure them.

While the ministry spoke of victories, MELA (MP 1/23/77) counseled his readers that "those enormous burthens, which are heaped upon the shoulders of this devoted nation, have all the effects of the most cruel defeats." ANTI-FORESTIERO (MP 9/1/77) denounced "Our Ministers [who] in their turn take the field and in order to spend our few remaining millions compel the reluctant nation to a deed of desperation, to imbrue its hands in the blood of its own children." GEORGE LANE (PA 1/3/77) compared the ministry to the "like of Don Quixote and Sancho Pancha . . . as nothing will convince them of their mistaken American War, they to all appearance will go on not only rising up the people, but spending millions in pursuit of it."

By 1777, the British people, or at least the readers of the press, were more than ever resentful of the liberties that the ministry was taking in reporting military victories in North America. Growing increasingly weary and disenchanted with the war, the populace, via their scribblers, became ever more critical of the ministry.

JUNIUS JUNIOR (MC 9/12/77) wrote:

> To Lord N____: To your obstinacy, more than your honour, do we owe your continuance in an office which leaves you obnoxious to the censure of your dearest friends. Your hopes of success, as it is falsely termed, accumulate with your wishes to please your royal master by novelty. The subjugation, however, of America at this period, will be no conquest; the military operations there have brought you no nearer the object of your heart, but they have afforded you ample proof that a skirmish or two has not terrified her people

into your purpose. The nation yet groans under the increased weight of taxes, and you have levied among us immense treasure to aid you in your pursuit of human slaughter, rather than territory wealth.... Where is the money you have taken from us to widen the breach between her (America) and Britain? Some new fangled story raised on a stolen march by part of our troops, on the Provincial army, may fill our Gazette with a courtly language, and promise success in a third campaign.

Another letter writer, ARMINIUS (*MC* 1/16/77), was infuriated by the bias of the *London Gazette*:

Though Administration may have had some successes on the other side of the Atlantic (which they only let us have their own account of) that appear so totally contradictory and inconclusive, for when their Gazette Extraordinary is published, which always takes care to be sufficiently partial, yet even in the next day's papers will their scribbling vermin give an account in forged letters from pretended officers, etc., quite different to it, making the loss of the Rebels (as they are pleased to term them) treble the number of those contained therein, and their own the same, if not less so; that by the partiality of the Gazette, and the damned falsehoods fabricated by their hired rascals, the ministerial success is often magnified at least six fold more than it really is.

Widespread apprehension over the conduct of the war found the scribblers increasingly critical of government. The writer J.A. (*PA* 11/19/77) found the ministry impervious to public resentment:

Although the Lives of Men is a Matter of small Account with those in Power, yet, when wantonly sacrificed and profusely lavished, it becomes the general Concern. Administration has acted in this unhappy War, as if it feared no Retrospect of their Conduct; indeed, being supported by Parliament in the Violence, they esteem themselves safe from any popular Resentment. The commercial Interest also, although so greatly injured by the Captures of their Ships, have been debauched from the public Good by personal Emoluments; thus a Contract, well divided among several, gains twice the Number of Proselytes as those not being so fortunate, accommodate their Attachments to their sordid and venal Expectations. This unhappy War was begun from a wicked Intention, has been prosecuted in Folly, supported by Artifice, and, lately, by the Fabrication of Lies - has been endeavoured to sustain drooping Hopes. Thus with the Colonies we shall lose our Respectability and Credit abroad, and every Degree of Confidence at home, as every man must distrust his Neighbour, and disbelieve his Testimony.

Venting his anger and frustration on Lord North, JUNIUS JUNIOR (*MC* 10/21/77) asserted it was absurd to speak of honor when Britain was at war with America:

But with regard to the honour, simply, of our nation, it is remarkable, that this word has never been so much used as lately, in respect to the subduing of America. Before the war something else was talked of, such as national commerce, the Newfoundland fishery, the seamen bred in that part of the world for our service, and pitch, tar, and lumber; all these things were spoken of as highly necessary for us to preserve; and when sounded through such conduit pipes as your friends in both Houses of Parliament, we were to expect that a handful of men would have frightened the cowardly Americans into an obedience to a latent tax on tea, after a bolder attempt had been made to take away their property. But you have not yet frightened them, and it is now more than three years since it was intended. You have, with your hopeful partisans, carried us out of the road of our interest and happiness to answer your ends. You have occasioned many lives to be lost, much waste, and a greater dissipation of our money at home and abroad; and at last, finding the Americans yet unfrightened, but more resolute to resist, you have diffused among us that little paltry word, of no meaning, called honour, which makes us sick when uttered by noodles, and those who neither know of its true meaning, or the real purpose of using it on the present occasion. Where virtue and heroism are wanting, and where profit is sacrificed to power, there can be no honour. The idea is an insult to common sense, and fit only for the minds of wicked despots and their subservient tools.

To BRUTUS (*PA* 6/26/77), Lord North was the initiator of the predicament of Great Britain and the cause of the disillusionment with government:

These are the Services, these are the blessings you have conferred upon your Country; these are the Obligations that it owes you and may yet reward. A disjointed, mutilated Empire. America deluged with the Blood of its brave and free Inhabitants; the East-Indies lost, the West in no little Danger; Ireland oppressed.... Constitution daringly infringed; Trade and Industry declining, and new accessions of Wealth and Power to the Crown, already too formidable; every attempt to re-establish Peace ridiculed and frustrated.

The landed gentry in 1775 were firm supporters of the North ministry. Willingly assenting to an increase in land taxes, they looked forward to a successful war in North America. A military victory, they were convinced, would lead to lower land taxes in Britain. By 1777 they were displeased, disappointed, and dejected with the conduct of the war. The *Public Advertiser*, not normally a spokesman for the "Country Gentlemen," printed the following letters on consecutive days, in criticism of Lord North and his Ministry. Lord North was accused of "political cowardice," of "temporizing Timidity," and of being responsible for a "patched-up" peace that did not represent the advantages expected from an investment of "five and twenty millions":

A COUNTRY GENTLEMAN (*PA* 11/25/77):

Your weak side is well known to be a temporizing timidity which any person who had less respect for you than myself, would not scruple to call downright Cowardice. Do you think that the People will be satisfied with a patched-up Business at the Conclusion of a War which may cost five and twenty millions? Who is among you who dares to treat with the American Congress upon equal Terms? Where is the Man in the Cabinet who will presume to finish the great business of Pacification without giving Great Britain a fast hold of her Colonies?

A COUNTRY GENTLEMAN (*PA* 11/26/77):

You see to what a low ebb your political Cowardice has brought you. You have courted your enemies, and they despise you; you have disobliged your Friends, and they hate as well as despise you; Were the Consequences only to you, I believe few would regret your Situation; but unfortunately you involve your Country to ruin, whilst you disgrace yourself.

A COUNTRY GENTLEMAN (*PA*11/27/77):

I have shown in my former letters into what an abject Condition you are fallen, through your temporizing Timidity: and how much you are despised by those whom you ought to command, as they believe they do not owe their being appointed to you. They obtained their places from your fears for yourselves, and your Treachery to your Country, in endeavouring to sacrifice her Rights for ever to a temporary Quiet.

There was little enthusiasm among scribblers to bear the escutcheon of the ministry in 1777. The letter that did appear in support of the ministry were relatively few in number and lacked enthusiasm. Beset with an unsuccessful war, it was difficult for the ministry or its scribblers to claim mastery of the state of affairs.

A NORTH AMERICAN (*LC* 8/5/77) defended the ministry and the Tea Act. His readers were informed that the duties of a minister must be supported by revenue, and the Tea Act provided such funds:

To regulate trade, to recommend good and wholesome laws, to enforce the impartial execution of them to protect the property and persons of individuals from violence and fraud, to support public and private credit—such are the duties of a minister, which cannot be effected without a revenue, which alone gives life and action to the executive parts of administration. How then is the minister blameable for the tea act? And would he not have neglected his duty if he had tamely looked upon these public abuses of authority, and private disregard of everything just and honest, without exerting himself to correct the one and amend the other: or if he had indulged those apprehension which some of his predecessors had done, who declined the task for fear of burning their fingers with America, and left evils to be cured, which, but for that shyness might have been in part prevented.

The writer BRITANNICUS (*LC* 9/4/77) saw little reason for the colonies to protest: "It is true, my Lord, that the Americans, as a free and privileged people, have a right to defend their rights and liberties, when unjustly attacked; but I do not see in the present case that they have much room to complain; if they have been oppressed, why did not they complain; if they are easy, why have they rebelled."

A FRIEND TO LEGAL LIBERTY (*PA* 8/28/77) complained to his readers of the provocations offered by the Americans:

> With regard to the Americans who are said by some to be cruelly treated and oppressed, I think no reasonable man can justly censure Government. If we consider the various insults and wanton provocations offered by them to the rulers and people of this Kingdom it is a most surprising infatuation that they should have any advocates here. As they have been protected at a most enormous expense, is it not reasonable that they should contribute towards the Public Service?

The use of force was not necessary to bring back the Americans to their allegiance. Thus did A NORTH AMERICAN (*MC* 8/28/77) inform his readers that the people of the rebellious colonists regretted the former times:

> The people [of America] in general curse both the French and their trade, and earnestly wish for old times. . . . The back country people are almost to a man against their measures; and through the whole province all the North Britons in particular, all the Quakers, and a great number of the Germans . . . are against them also. So far from that once happy and flourishing country being the seat of liberty, it is only the place of tyranny, arbitrary imprisonment, and oppression. . . . The innocent part of the people . . . pine at their unhappy situation, and only wait for proper leaders, arms, and ammunition and to see the Royal Standard once displayed.

The letter writer OBSERVATOR (*MC* 10/17/78) shared with his readers the opinion that the ministry had been in general successful:

> Have not our Ministers, in every department of the State, though their measures have generally been widely concerted, and (except in cases of unforeseen accident, which human wisdom could not provide against) eventually successful; run the gauntlet of scurrility and abuse through the channels of our public prints, and through every petty circle, from the pert tradesman (who is scarce known out of the compass of a beer-house-box, except by his creditors, until fraud of dissipation has introduced him to the insolvent list in the Gazette) to the disappointed City Junto.

The year 1778 dawned with the news of Burgoyne's capitulation at Saratoga still fresh in the British memory. As the year progressed, news from America was hardly more heartening. In March the British government was informed that France and America had signed a Treaty of Commerce and a Treaty of Alliances. In April, John Paul Jones aboard the USS *Ranger* captured the British sloop *Drake* off Carrickfergus, Ireland, and struck at the port of Whitehaven, Scotland. Congress had advised the British peace commission that the only acceptable terms would be the withdrawal of British forces and the recognition of American independence. At the battle of Ushant off the coast of France on 27 July, the legend of British naval supremacy was shattered in a indecisive clash with the

French fleet. To further endanger British commerce, a Treaty of Amity and Commerce was signed by representatives of Congress and the Netherlands government in September.

With such a record of failure it was not surprising that the scribblers of the hour found Lord North and his ministry a convenient target for disdain and derision. The ministry was termed pusillanimous vermin, and was accused of ineptitude, of falsehood and chicanery, and of imbecility and folly.

GRATUS (*PA* 1/3/78) accused the ministry of spreading untruths about military victories and conducting the war ineptly:

> I think it is allowed by our Ministers themselves that the national affairs do not wear a very pleasant aspect. They have acknowledged what could not be denied, that nothing has prospered in their hands. They have involved us in a most cruel Civil War; and they have manifested in the conduct of that war an incapacity to be equalled only by the absurd temerity with which it was undertaken. For a time they amused us with accounts of victories and successes. How did these generally turn out? One day we heard of their having taken a town,—Good! Next day we learned that our Army was besieged in that town, and soon after that were obliged to fly from it.

Another writer, INVESTIGATOR (*PA* 1/28/78), wrote of "pusillanimous Vermin" who "cheat the Principles of the Nation and keep their Places":

> It is ridiculous to follow Administration through the dirty windings of their present Conduct. The Nation were manifestly roused by the late Misfortunes; and, to keep their places, Ministry found they must appear to do something. Administration have the Name of spirited Measures; and Care is taken, that those Measures shall not be carried into execution. An excellent Prince, and a great and generous People, are deceived; and a parcel of pusillanimous Vermin cheat the Principles of the Nation and keep their Places.

Cautioning his readers about the falsehood and trickery that characterized the ministry, DECIOUS (*PA* 2/25/78):

> There is one other quality common to every Character of Administration, that should exclude them for ever from being permitted to take a part in any public act that required Sincerity and good Faith. They are utterly devoid of Integrity. One spirit of Falsehood and Chicane runs through all their measures. What insidious Arts have they left unnoticed to impose upon the unsuspecting credulity of the Country? The Americans can have no reliance upon any propositions of accommodation that the present Ministry can offer.

An IMPARTIALIST (*PA* 8/28/78) was far more extensive in his condemnation of the ministry:

> O Britain! Britain! how long is thy Welfare, nay, thy political Salvation to be the Sport of Imbecility, Avarice, Obstinacy, Presumption, or Treason? Or

is it high time, if not quite out of Time to liquidate the few following questions? Does not the actual Rebellion of the Colonies manifestly and principally originate from the general Contempt of a worthless Government? Or did ever any Government incur such a Contempt that did not deserve it? Or can it rationally be, for any Expectation from such a Government, to tranquillise the Public on the Fate of a Country in actual Jeopardy?

TAGES (*PA* 12/4/78) wrote of the folly of the ministry and the fear of an impending war with France and Spain. He ended a moving narrative with a request for the ministry to depart:

The Situation of public Affairs has sensibly proved (what has often been asserted) how peculiarly our American Policy was calculated to produce a War with France: it has proved more; it has proved how dismally that Policy has affected the Success of the War it has produced. A French War is now engrafted on an American one. We are afraid, but we must look forward to the new Appearance of the combined and complicated Wars of France, America, Spain, and Holland, against England; against England, first impaired by the Loss of Thirteen valuable Colonies, and afterwards exhausted by its violent and fruitless Efforts to regain them. All we know with Certainty is, that our Labours increase, but our Strength diminishes. Shall we be more likely to beat the French by being unanimous in wishing our Affairs to be ill conducted? by being unanimous in Favour of a bad Administration? Shall we be more likely to go straight by following the Blind? Will Ruin be less Ruin, because we were unanimous in the Means that produced it? They talk to us as if we really imagined Folly would become less by being divided among a great many; or as if the Merit of Measures and Men depended not upon their intrinsic Value, but on the Number of their Partisans. Will not the Nation rise up at last and stifle in its general Voice the pitiful Quibblings of these wretched Evaders? Will it not cry out to them, Miserable Men! we have given you Riches, you have returned us Poverty; we have given you Armies, you have returned us Defeat; we have given you Honours, you have returned us Disgrace; and do you now ask us for the Revenues you have wasted, and the Confidence you have betrayed? Is it a Compensation for our Misfortunes to insult our Understandings? Go, then; offend us no longer with your hateful Presence. In the Multitude of Calamities you have caused us, show us one Instance of your Love. Do not cling to us forever with an ill fated and deadly Clasp. Give your unfortunate Countrymen one Chance of Salvation. Leave them in Peace to struggle with their Misfortunes.

The accomplishments and effectiveness of Lord North received no greater regard from the pens of the letter writers than did his ministry. A writer who signed his name as A LOVER OF SPIRIT AND CONSISTENCY IN A PRIME MINISTER (*CM* 8/10/78) revealed to his readers that the real problem was not faction or timidity, but the weakness of the prime minister:

That our own body politic is at present greatly disordered, no man in his senses will venture to deny; but men even of the soundest sense will probably differ with regard to the real cause of this national malady. Some think it is owing to the violence of faction; others, to the folly and timidity of the Ministry; but, in my opinion, it ought solely to be attributed to the want of some bold and enterprising spirit, to animate and direct our public counsels, and to give consistency, vigour, and finally success to our national measures. In a word it is entirely owing to the want of a Prime Minister.

GUSTAVUS VASSA (*MP* 1/1/78) reminded Lord North that as chief of the king's ministers, he bore the responsibility for the course of the war:

> The turn American affairs have taken . . . proves that error, or something worse, has operated amongst those who followed, and abetted the system adopted for bringing back to their duty the rebellious Americans. It is a matter of little consequence to the aggregate body of the British empire, whether your Lordship, or Lord George Germaine, or any other is officially responsible for measures immediately issuing from their department in administration; since his Majesty consigns the superintendency of the whole administration to a Premier, your Lordship is that chief of the King's Ministers. It is therefore that no scheme, no plan, nor no measure can meet with approbation, or success, if it be in any way adopted, without your knowledge and concurrence. A time draws near, when a justification of the fatal measures pursued during the course of this unlucky war will be demanded, (I speak not, my Lord, as a modern patriot, for I despise the tribe) of Administration; and I am well aware, Sir, it will be had.

PHILOPOEMEN (*PA* 4/21/78) concurred with GUSTAVUS VASSA that Lord North was incompetent:

> The cause of your Disappointments is to be sought for only in the Imbecility of your own Counsels, and your not knowing how to proportion the Means to the Ends which you desired. The skilful Mechanic knows what Force is requisite to move a given Weight; and the true Politician can judge what Means are necessary to effect a certain purpose. Unless you depended upon Miracles, there was no Reason, from the Measures you took to expect Success. Yet compelled by the Want of every other Refuge, notwithstanding your Miscarriages, you have asserted, with great Modesty, that your Plans were good, but that they had not been duly executed. My Lord, you are mistaken, if you think to escape by throwing off the Blame from yourself and laying it upon your Generals.

The accolades offered to Lord North by the ministerial writers, although fewer in number than those who had denigrated his abilities, soundly favored his conduct and abilities. ARISTIDUS (*MP* 7/11/78) was convinced, after suitable investigation, that Lord North filled his post in an energetic way:

> As you have often been reproached, both within, and out of the Senate, for Indolence, I was determined to watch, and investigate your conduct in the high department you reside, which I have done with the utmost accuracy,

and keenest inspection. I am master of every information possible to be collected, I have had, and from those to whom your manner of filling your appointment, or your general mode of acting in life was totally indifferent; and, upon the whole, I must honestly declare, that there never was a man before, nor can there be one after you, more attentive to, and indefatigable in business, than yourself.

To FIDUS AND PROBUS (*MP* 7/23/78) the "character and abilities" of Lord North were incomparable: "There is one circumstance, during his Lordship's political warfare, that well deserves the public notice; which is, that the keenest and most bitter of his adversaries have not been able, upon some occasions, to withhold the applause due to his character and abilities."

For RETZ (*PA* 1/5/78), the honor due Lord North was for his "conduct and principles":

I have, my Lord, been an advocate for your Lordship's conduct and principles ever since your Lordship has had the Guidance of the Affairs of this Country, on the supposition that you have acted on the firm basis of constitutional freedom, without a design of infringing on any of the invaluable privileges of an Englishman. Whilst you continue to act on this ground, you will find yourself supported by every subject who has any love for his country.

As with the attention paid Lord North, the ministerial scribblers gave due approbation to the conduct and wisdom of the ministry. Their correspondence, although limited, was equally fervent. NOVANGLUS (*MC* 3/21/78) was persuaded of the proper conduct of administration:

Administration are entitled to great credit for procuring and transporting to America an army consisting of near fifty thousand regular troops, in every respect well appointed. This army, which would have been respectable in any part of the world, with the addition of several thousand Provincials, and attended by above a hundred men of war, besides transports, was commanded by Generals from whose former conduct great things were expected. If they have been guilty of misconduct, in God's name, on them let the censure fall. I do not flatter when I say, that Administration appear to have conducted themselves prudently, constitutionally, and firmly, according to the sense and feelings of the nation, thro' the whole of this controversy, and to have candidly and liberally conformed to the exigencies of the different conjectures as they arose, and the reason of their measures having failed of success, may be fairly and evidently traced to the mildness of our Government, the forms of the Constitution, and the distance of the scene of action, and the conduct of our Generals.

In defense of the ministery, CICERO (*MP* 5/7/78) proclaimed to his readers that it would be desirable "that every act of government, tho' attended with different degrees of success, had been planned with that wisdom and universal philanthropy."

The writer OBSERVATOR (*MC* 3/28/78) implored his readers to support the ministers:

> Britons! sons of thy great fore-fathers! whither is thy spirit fled? Where is that ardour, that courage which have so often successfully resisted the power of mighty hosts? Where is that vigour of soul which formerly animated you to the first deeds of glory? Bring it into action, Britons; take fire at the insult offered to your name and your nation; be unanimous in the great cause of your gracious King and your country; be not terrified at the sound of danger from foreign foes, whom you have before chastised, and whom, with union in you breasts, you are still able to repel and defy: Put your confidence in your sovereign and his administration, who, in spite of faction and disappointed ambition, are virtuously, anxiously, and perseveringly devoting their labours to your real interest; then will the clouds of danger be dispelled, circles of glory again brighten in your native land, and union and magnanimity so permanently exalt the British empire as once more to render it the terror and envy of all its foes, and the admiration of the whole world.

The anti-ministerial writers continued their assault on Lord North and his ministry throughout 1779. DEMOCRATES (*PA* 3/5/79) illuminated his readers that Lord North was forced to turn to rhetoric when his plans failed:

> It becomes necessary to grow strong in Words, as he fails in Fact. He thus repairs his Deficiency of Matter by Force of Assurance; and secures the requisite Parliamentary Momentum to move at Will the Purse of the Public.... He promised—But what did he not promise? Nothing is too arduous for his magnanimous Imagination. He promised even the Continuance of the War in America. He pledged his honourable Perseverance in it, because he had studied its Relinquishment thro' every Disgrace to himself and his Accomplices; and he vows Vengeance on the Rebels, because the greatest total Exertions of his Country have been baffled; he promises Success from distracted Efforts, and little Battles; from Operations of less Extent, and Struggles of wasted Vigour. And he defends this monstrous Mass of Absurdity and Calamity, by the Offence of Truth and Honour; by libelling the most honoured Names in the Country.

Although the press was less than kind to the generals and admirals who they believed had been guilty of neglect and treachery in their conduct of the war in North America, there were writers who put the blame for the military failures squarely at the feet of the ministry, as did A MODERATE MAN (*MC* 12/24/79):

> The misfortunes which we feel must have arisen from treachery or impotency of our Governors; or from so providential a disposition of things, that no human discernment could foresee, and no human ability prevent: no one in accounting for our national evils has considered them to flow from the latter cause. Every ministerial writer thinks to recriminate is to justify; and by charging our Generals and Admirals with misbehaviour, attempts to defend

the integrity and propriety of the measures of their employers. If our Commanders have not done their duty, why are they not punished? 'Tis clear to every person, that the calamities of the State have originated from misconduct; and since we may have been equally injured by ignorance, indolence, or imbecility, as by treachery, it is a noble object impartially to consider the history of the Ministry.

DEMOCRATES (*PA* 2/1/79) explained to his readers that both Lord Howe and Admiral Keppel were hampered by the administration:

> Lord Howe, no less than Admiral Keppel, experienced from the first Moment of his Appointment the cold and discouraging Neglect of Administration. That dilatory Distrust which marks the Indecision of little Minds, disappointed the Hopes of the Country and of Lord Howe, in the Effect of the Commission to which he was named. The Powers granted to him were imperfect, as he in vain remonstrated before he went out; and the Delay was fatal, as every Man except the Ministers foresaw. Seven months had elapsed between the declared Intentions and the Appointment of the Commission.

The writer G.N. (*PA* 7/15/79) reported to his readers that the American war was the source of most of Britain's problems:

> The American War is the Broad Basis on which all our Misfortunes rest. There is no reason to suppose, that if Ministry had not rushed so inconsiderately, so unjustly, into this War, but that we had now been in Peace with all the World; enjoying the Fruits of Commerce and Security; united with America; discharging, under a provident Ministry, by Degrees, the oppressive Weight of National Debt; and increasing in Riches, Strength, and Power. But it was their infatuated Policy that we should engage in, and prosecute the American War, contrary to the Sense of the collective Body of People, who on every Occasion appealed, implored, remonstrated against it, as though they as distinctly foresaw, as we now palpably feel, all those Evils with which it has been attended. To silence reiterated Clamour, while Reason, Justice, and Argument were disregarded, the Populace were to be deluded by a Notion, fathered by Ministry, That there would be no Resistance to their Army in America; and that a small Military Power would enforce Obedience to their Decrees. And the Capacity of that Ministry proved contemptible. Their Abilities despicable. And with such Succours granted them, and with such Powers placed in their Hands, as I never desire again to see in those of any Ministry, (for they can never be so placed with Safety to the Commonwealth,) all their Endeavour have been rendered fruitless (except the ruin of ourselves) by America alone, at least, not openly supported by any other Power.

JULIUS (*MP* 4/1/79) used his letter to inform his readers of the situation in North America. He denounced the ministry for the untruths offered to the people about military conquests and noted that with France as an open ally and a threat in Europe, the Americans were in a good military position:

The conversation of the day being, in all companies, the great probability there is of conquering all North America, it may not be wholly unamusing to your readers to consider what reasoning there are for embracing such sanguine expectations. That Ministers, and their dependents speak this language is by no means a reason for its being true; let every one recollect what have been the reports given out at the opening of every campaign; what have been the magnificent promises of powerful exertions; how much the enemy's force has been lessened, and ridiculed; and what animated hopes have been fixed on the great party Government has in the Colonies. This has been regularly the annual cant, and I am amazed to find there are people ready again to listen to such stuff, which has annually proved so deceiving. Georgia is conquered, but by no means thro' the people being averse to Congress. Sir W. Howe conquered Philadelphia; we know very well that it was evacuated as readily as it was taken. Sir Henry Clinton has no force large enough to prosecute the war with vigour; Administration seems, from the very beginning to have fought the battle of the people in America, by making it a war of duration, and disciplining the enemy by degrees. We know very well that all the reinforcements sent to North America do not exceed 4000 men; and I leave it to every impartial man, to judge whether the last campaign did not lessen our force to that amount. It may also be left to the same decision to pronounce whether America, now assisted openly by France, with our power kept in check in Europe by the same potentate, will not this year be able to make as good a figure as she did the preceding? Upon the whole, Sir, the time for triumph is the cool season of review, not the exalted moment of perhaps visionary hope.

By 1779, the ministerial scribblers were indeed hard pressed to find grounds for the defense of the administration. The letter writer OBSERVATOR (*MC* 2/26/79) addressed his readers on the American question in the first letter to be printed in the *Morning Chronicle* on that subject since the 1 January. The success of the British military in the southern campaign provided a bit of light in the abyss of painful news emanating from America: "Much credit is certainly due to the Minister who planned the Southern expedition in America, under Colonel Campbell, since the happy consequences of its success, as, indeed, already appears."

Cheered by the success in the Carolinas, HONESTUS (*MC* 7/19/79) suggested to his readers the need for unanimity with the ministry: "Friends and brethren be not discouraged; do not despair, no doubt we shall still prove a match for them, and perhaps recover America yet. We have got some fruits already; never fear, we shall have the harvest by and by. Do not encourage that wretched spirit of condemning every measure adopted by Ministers, but rather cheerfully strive with them, in your several stations, to repel a common foe."

The measures of administration "have been unfortunate, and therein mixed with failings from which the most exuberant wisdom is not exempt." Thus did A BRITON (*MC* 11/16/79) attempt to exonerate the ministry from its blunders. DECIOUS (*MP* 1/29/79) uncovered other justification for the unfortunate execution of ministry plans:

> When I hear the same measures arraigned by the violence of one party, as unnecessarily severe, and inhuman, and at the same time, by the zealousness of the other, as too lenient and feeble, I am naturally led to conclude, that they are exactly what they ought to be; and then, taking into consideration the different interests of this kingdom, the sense and feeling of the nation, the dignity of government, the clamour of faction, the state of the army, navy, and finances, the disposition of foreign power, and the great variety of circumstances that must have operated in producing the results, that the plans hitherto adopted, however unfortunate in the execution, do honour to their authors, both as statesmen and as men. I suspect it was even necessary that affairs should be in their present train, in order to put an effectual end to the rebellion, and to establish an union between Great Britain and the colonies on a permanent basis.

"Uneasy rests the head that wears the crown." No administration within a democracy escapes criticism. As the North ministry was besieged by an assertive populace and a critical press, so did it generate broad support from the people and the newspapers. Those who have accused the ministry of gross ineptitude in the conduct of the war in North America should remember that there was no precedent for such a conflict. To the credit of the ministry, a disparaging press experienced remarkable freedom for the eighteenth century.

CHAPTER FIVE

Peace or the Sword

The British Parliament offered the rebellious colonies three official plans for reconciliation during the War for Independence: Lord North's Conciliatory Resolution of 1775, the Howe Commission of 1776, and the Carlisle Commission of 1778.[1] All met with failure. The essence of British policy was to govern the empire on the basis of the constitution, which gave primacy to the concept of parliamentary supremacy. George III believed it his duty to uphold those statutes which the Americans had defied, and the British Parliament confirmed that policy in 1775. The government was prepared to wage war to enforce colonial subordination.

Lord North's Conciliatory Plan, introduced on 20 February 1775, proposed that Britain would promise not to tax the colonies if, in return, they agreed to pay the cost of their own civil governments, courts of law, and defense. Parliament thus would refrain from exercising its right of taxation if the Americans agreed to pay their own governmental costs.[2] The ministry won the approval of Parliament for its plan and a peace commission only by portraying the scheme as a means of accelerating colonial submission.

The actions of the ministry, however, were not likely to gain the confidence of the Americans in 1775. Lord North had introduced the New England Restraint Act early in February (the same month as his conciliatory plan).[3] The act declared that "as the Americans had refused to trade with this Kingdom, it was just that we should not suffer them to trade with any other nation." The Conciliatory Plan did little to assure the colonists of the good will of Parliament. It offered a pardon to all colonists guilty of rebellion who would submit within a month and would promise obedience to parliamentary legislation. The requirement of such an explicit declaration robbed the offer of all practical significance.

As the gesture for conciliation in 1775 was short-lived, so was the fate of a similar attempt in 1776. On 3 May 1776, George III placed the new commission charged with making peace in the hands of the recently appointed commanders in chief of the Atlantic seaboard, Admiral Lord

Richard Howe and his brother General William Howe. The instructions
which they received from St. James precluded any hope of a reconciliation
with the rebellious colonies. Rather than exhibiting an interest in conciliation, they attempted to set a new standard of royal privilege and of
parliamentary control of the provinces of Connecticut and Rhode Island.
Their object was set forth as follows:

> To induce such a submission on their part to lawful authority as shall consist
> with the just relation and dependence in which they stand . . . promising a
> free pardon of all treasons and misprisions of treason to any person or per-
> sons who, within a time or times to be therein limited, shall return to their
> allegiance . . . of their resolution to adhere to their loyalty and obedience . . .
> the dignity of our government and the necessity there is from considerations
> of general policy that all our colonies should be maintained in due subor-
> dination to the authority of the parent state. . . . The pretence under which
> the governors of those colonies [Connecticut and Rhode Island] enter upon
> the exercise of their functions before our royal approbation of them can be
> known, and the enacting of laws not subject to a negative by us in our Privy
> Council, are defects which, whether they arise out of the nature of govern-
> ment itself or from a misapprehension or misunderstanding of the principles
> upon which it is established, are evidently inconsistent with the constitu-
> tional relation in which the colonies stand in relation to this kingdom.
> Additional Instructions [More on Connecticut and Rhode Island] . . .
> that they do repeal all such laws now upon their statute books [as] impeach
> our authority to appoint such persons as we think proper to command their
> militia or declare a right in the people to be exempt from the control of Acts
> of the supreme legislature of Great Britain . . . they do submit to such altera-
> tions to be made by explanatory charters as shall be necessary to restrain per-
> sons elected governors of the said colonies from entering upon the execution
> of their offices until approved by us, our heirs, and successors.[4]

The last attempt at conciliation by the North ministry developed in
late January 1778. A commission was to be dispatched to America empowered to negotiate all outstanding points of dispute.[5] The policy affirmed a complete renunciation of colonial taxation rather than repeal of
specific legislation. Presented to the Commons on 17 February 1778 with
an act to authorize the appointment of a conciliatory commission, the
policy's slim chance of success was reduced by restrictions on the discre-
tionary powers of the commission and by the choice of the commissioners.
Among the three men chosen was the inexperienced young Lord Carlisle,
who headed the commission, and George Johnson, an outspoken adversary
of colonial independence. To add to the difficulties of the commission, the
news of the American treaty with France preceded the commissioner's arrival in America. The commission was an utter failure.

There is strong evidence that after the news of Lexington and Concord
and at least for the remainder of 1775, the people of Britain were not wholly
committed to the war. The letter writers were convinced that a reconcilia-

tion was necessary, an understanding resulting from a mutual endeavor. Whether the responsibility for the disagreement lay with the ministry or the Congress, with Whigs or Tories, the scribblers believed it behooved all to seek an amicable settlement to the dispute.

AURELIUS (*LC* 7/20/75):

It behooves every Englishman, every Briton, every American to endeavour to throw down these odious distinctions, which serve only to distract us and render us less respectable in the eyes of our enemies.... Let us not ask who are Whigs or who are Tories; let us ask who are honest men and patriots, whether of this or the other side of the Atlantic.

CLYTUS (6/17/75):

The blame for the present crisis lies both with the Colonists and the Government. The former have shown this by an extravagant zeal for liberty, without considering how it should be nourished and maintained, without considering that nothing is so essential to that purpose as a due obedience to the government they live under.... On the other hand, government have been equally blameable; they seem all along to have had more confidence in the strength of their army and navy, to bringing the Americans to a sense of duty, than to the strength of arguments.

BY-BLOW (*MP* 10/11/75):

Seek accommodation rather than conflict. Every dispassionate Briton must acknowledge there are great errors on both sides.

There were writers who simply advocated mutual love as the solution to the crisis. OBADIAH JUST (*MC* 11/1/75) wrote, "Love thy neighbour as thyself." Another writer, H. MORNAY (*LC* 7/4/75), suggested: "Let us do as lovers do; if we must quarrel, let us kiss and be friends, but not break off forever; let our quarrels cement us the more."

Some writers believed the responsibility for conciliation was an obligation of the mother country. A DETESTER OF TYRANTS (*MP* 11/30/75) considered that responsibility was the duty of the king and so advised his readers: "To Him whom it most concerns: ... Sheath your sword now drawn against the Americans;—Turn away your corrupted and diabolical servants;—punish the guilty;—Do justice to the oppressed.—By these means you will not only regain, but truly deserve the title of Father of your country."

It was not the king, however, but rather Lord North who carried the main burden of responsibility and criticism, as ENTELLUS (*MP* 7/29/75) suggested:

At a time like this, when every circumstance is big with alarming consequence of a civil war with our fellow subjects and brethren in America, would it not be more praise-worthy and becoming a wise minister to advise the exercise of conciliative measures rather than the irritative, oppressive and unjust ones? How it ever could be presumed that so brave a people would silently yield to such a yoke ... [that would] at one and the same time rob them of their trade, religion and liberty. Can it be expected that the Americans will be without the feeling of Englishmen?

When Richard Penn was in town, DETESTER OF HIS ENEMIES (*MP* 11/29/75) apprised his readers: "Penn and (General) Gage are in town.... If Parliament is in earnest, and wishes a reconciliation now is the time. May it be accepted and effect an union that may be everlasting! May trade in consequence flourish and peace abound."

Although it was still early in the war there was an awareness, which continued throughout the conflict, that Britain could not subdue her rebellious colonies in North America. Two writers for the *Public Advertiser* again counseled reconciliation:

UNBIASED PATRIOT (*PA* 10/7/75):

However contemptuously some may affect to treat this injured people, surely by this time we must be convinced that they are not to be subdued by force; and even supposing they could, what should we gain by the conquest? Their irreconcilable hatred, the ruin of manufactures, and at length the loss of our own Liberty.

VESPUCIUS (*PA* 12/5/75):

As no advantage has been gained over the Americans, as the inability of this Country to subdue the Americans is evident, and as the Ministers, from Menacers of Vengeance, are turned supplicants for Peace, no man can wonder if the Americans, who treat sword in hand, and backed by powerful armies, are determined to maintain their Liberty as obstinately in Negotiation as they have done in Arms. They cannot Fear, Love, or Esteem the present Administration, who have asserted the highest claims in the most contemptible manner: and though the Americans desire re-union with England, they will treat like one great Nation with another; and as they have not been frightened or beaten out of their Rights, they will take care not to be duped out of them by Ministers, whose capacity and integrity they scorn alike.

Some of the British populace believed that certain items should be nonnegotiable in any contacts with the Americans. Reflecting that opinion, scribbler A.B. (*MC* 11/17/75), being mindful of parliamentary supremacy, sought a "permanent union between Great Britain and her Colonies on a constitutional basis." The *Morning Post* published an unsigned letter (6/15/75) which accepted reconciliation, but on the basis of a continuing trade monopoly with America.

CRITO (*MP* 9/6/75) reported much the same to his readers. He suggested the ministry make concessions to induce the Americans to return to their duty:

We are at present fighting for dignity alone; and, as there is no dignity in being beat, our ministers will show their wisdom more in reconciliation than in arms ... [and] repeal the acts of punishment in consequence of the Americans returning to their duty, and let the Declaratory Act be repealed at the same time ... [and] insist firmly on the exertion and regular practice of taxation as a regulation of trade.[6]

The superiority of Parliament was not negotiable, and it was most important that the rebellious colonies recognize and submit to that supremacy. CORNELIUS (*MP* 8/28/75) was in favor of "granting all that I can in reason and prudence to the American subjects of Great Britain, yet I must insist on the natural and necessary dependency of our colonies." The *Public Advertiser* published an unsigned letter (10/10/75) suggesting a reconciliation; again, the superiority of Parliament was to be acknowledged by the colonies: "so as not to be inconsistent with the superiority of the Mother Country over the Americans, in such matters where a superiority ought to be, according to the constitution subsisting between them."

The North Conciliatory Plan of 1775 failed to titillate the scribblers of the press, and their writings were sparse. Most appeared in the *Public Advertiser*, and an even-handed policy by that newspaper provided a platform for all persuasions.

CINCINNATUS (*PA* 8/15/75) informed his readers that since the provinces had spurned the conciliatory offers of Parliament, England should pursue a firm course:

> Conciliatory terms were offered by Parliament and stated the Colonies were to raise a certain sum equal to the expectations of Parliament for the common service of their common government, [and] to leave the mode of taxation wholly to the Colonies. The Provinces spurned this proposition, declaring they would only contribute in such proportions as they judge proper. . . . The blood and treasure of this Kingdom have been lavishly shed to acquire the colonies; we must therefore neither shudder at Danger, not murmur at expense to preserve them.

PACIFICUS (*PA* 10/6/75) could find little fault with the North Conciliatory Plan. He reminded his readers that "the throwing of Teas into the Ocean belonging to British subjects, is in consequence the cause of the war."

In defense of the colonies, CATO (*PA* 10/9/75) advised his readers that the Conciliatory Plan of 1775 stopped short of offering the Americans necessary assurances:

> The Colonies are reviled for taking so little notice of the vague Motion which passed in the House of Commons, on the 20th of February last, by which no assurance is given them that they shall be allowed to raise taxes by their own general assemblies in the same free manner they have hitherto been ac-

customed to; nor shall that the late Acts of Parliament complained of should be repealed. On the contrary, these Acts are to be kept hanging over their heads.

The paucity of printed comment on the Conciliatory Plan of 1775 did not carry through to the scheme for reconciliation in 1776. Letters for and against abounded in the newspapers. The *London Chronicle* printed an unsigned letter (3/30/76) cautioning its readers against supporting concessions to the colonists:

> Any offer then of accommodation or treaty, . . . even the discussion of any terms of agreement in the present circumstance would be not only dishonourable and dangerous, but altogether unavailing and without effect. There is plainly no way left but to press the war with all possible celerity and vigour if we desire to see order and tranquillity restored, and a just submission yielded to the supreme authority of the state.

It was not until the last quarter of 1776, and well after the American Declaration of Independence had become public knowledge in Britain and the Howe Peace Commission had been rejected, that the scribblers found their pens. Rather than commenting on the Commission itself, letters reflected an uneasiness that concessions that might be offered to the rebellious colonies. PACIFICUS (*MC* 10/16/76) warned his readers that Congress had different goals than Britain:

> The cause of Congress can never be the cause of Britain or of America. The object of the Congress is the gratification of ambition, republican fanaticism, the pursuit of wealth obtained by private plunder, public devastation, and unheard-of-cruelties to the loyalists in the different colonies, who refuse to renounce their allegiance to his Majesty. Commissioners have been appointed with the manifest purpose of sheathing the sword, if possible, and of giving the Americans every security that their rights and liberties should not be invaded. Lord Howe, more zealous to restore peace than to acquire military fame, by shedding the blood of his fellow subjects, accepted the command of a fleet upon condition that it should be accompanied with ample power to terminate, in an amicable manner, a most unnatural quarrel; but his terms, though generous perhaps to a fault, have been treated with an indignity not less preposterous than insolent, and must create indignation mixed with contempt, in the mind of every honest Englishman, when he reflects on the dastardly conduct of those rebels, who thus presume to spurn at proffered peace.

The letter writer PHILO-PATRIE (*MP* 11/5/76) informed his readers of the new independence of the rebellious colonies. The Americans had rejected the offers of the brothers Howe: "The Americans have rejected with circumstances of indignity and insult, the means of conciliation held out to them under the authority of his Majesty's commission; and presumed to set up their rebellious confederacies for independent states."[7]

Congress having rejected the peace initiative of the Howe brothers, there was good reason not to offer America terms of a compassionate reconciliation. Nothing more should be offered to the Americans wrote OLD ENGLAND (*MC* 11/22/76) but pardons for those who accepted the king's authority. He argued that the English military operations should be continued until the colonists were vanquished:

> We have been repeatedly assured by the Ministry that the brothers had power only to grant pardons to such as submitted themselves to the King's authority; but we now find that they are invested with much more extensive powers—powers sufficient to ruin the kingdom. Our arms at present are in a fine train of success, our men consequently in high spirits; why then should we not seize the golden opportunity of bringing the Rebels to reason and justice? Let us first, by force, compel them to lay down their arms, and give up their tyrannical Congress, Conventions, Committees, etc. and then let us, with true British generosity, grant them the utmost constitutional indulgence.

There were writers who lent their support to the rebellious colonies. Governmental instructions to the Howe brothers were not available to the readers of the press, but to compensate, MICROMEGAS (*CM* 7/29/76) suggested the "Commissioners address the parties as follows":

> Countrymen and brethren, ye are all Britons alike; your first right is freedom; no deduction is to be made there from; no partiality or notorious inequality can be allowed among freemen; Americans and Irish are not to be treated as Britons one way, and as foreigners another; both justice and policy forbid it. The line was happily drawn between you, therefore return to your former state. The infancy of America is ceased; 'tis not a mother and a daughter; Britons on both sides of the Atlantic are brethren; let each be the supporter and each the supported, till millions constitute the greatest commercial empire the World ever knew.

The writer who signed his name A CONSTANT READER (*PA* 10/18/76) rested his desire for peace with the clemency and disposition of the Howe brothers: "From the known clemency and disposition of General Howe and his Brother, I believe every opportunity of bringing about a Peace would and will be taken hold of. If such an opportunity is offered after the engagement on Long Island, why not try it? They are sent for the purpose of Peace as well as War."

There was a belief among the people and the scribblers that the administration was sending the commissioners to America to arrange terms with the colonists when they had been subdued by British troops. CRITO (*MP* 2/1/76) wrote:

> As Administration have continued to give out even to the present moment, that the only means to be used to bring the Colonists to reason is by coercion; and that the plan of sending commissioners to America is to be considered

merely as an attendant on the success of the field to receive submission, and to offer protection, we may fairly conclude that the fixed design is that of force and nothing else.

Lord George Germaine, as American secretary and a firm advocate of the need to subdue the rebellious colonies, was considered a suitable target for those writers wishing for an accommodation with America. METAPHOR (*PA* 3/2/76) issued this warning to him:

> In terms of decency and respect you are called upon for a plan of accommodation, or to assign the reasons why this work (officially in your Department) is not in equal forwardness with our fleet and army. Should the idea of accommodation be totally set aside, and neither terms nor Commissioners sent or appointed, remember these emphatic words of Macbeth, "Blood will have Blood"; and that those who in the fullness and wantonness of power unnecessarily shed a Nations Blood in the fullness and strictness of Justice must be accounted for it.

AN IMPERIALIST (*PA* 12/24/76) could feel only pity for the brothers Howe and scorn for the ministry:

> I could not help sincerely pitying the two Howes, that noble pair of brothers. If ever there were subjects of untainted principles, unquestioning Probity, and strict Honour, the Howes had every title to a rank in that class. But all this is, in the actual state of things, against them. They have been pressed from an irresistible quarter, they have been betrayed by their own good intentions into a service in which no one has hitherto gone. . . . At the expense of theirs they will probably find, that on a false bottom every thing is false. Their Mission has precisely taken place, with so much Crudity, so much Improvidence, and especially under so total a want of political views, that every hope for them of an honourable success is out of the Question, whether in point of negotiation or in the issue of War. . . . A Nation under a Sovereign, deplorably abandoned to the direction and pillage of a few personages totally incapable on making any but the worst use of their disastrous influence.

Whether it was to be implemented by the good offices of the Howe brothers or not, there was a general appeal for reconciliation. CRITO (*MP* 1/4/76) counseled his readers that there were more desirable options than the one suggested by Lord Mansfield:

> An Argument in Answer to Lord Mansfield's famous Defence of the present Measures: Re: Prohibitory Bill—
> Mansfield: . . . In the present state of the quarrel, we must of necessity use coercive measures, or America will be independent, seize our fisheries and sugar islands, and become a formidable naval power.
> Crito: Why not treat with them? What sort of a war is it to which no end can be put by treaty?

The writer NO CREOLE (1/11/76) reminded Lord North of a letter he,
NO CREOLE, had written six months earlier suggesting that Britain withdraw
all troops from America:

> Further, to publish a general and unrestricted pardon throughout America
> and you will prove immediately that every man will lay down his arms and
> return to his employment; for those who have nothing to lose may have
> something to fear; and those who have much to lose will have everything to
> fear; therefore, what one will do for his personal security, another will do
> from positive necessity.

Appealing to the good sense of the ministry, NEUTRALIS (*PA* 11/22/76):

> It is time to come to our senses, and abandon our wild Chimeras. Could we
> conquer America, which the experience of three years has proved imprac-
> ticable, the effort would totally ruin us. During the contest our merchants
> are undone, our ships are rotting in those inhospitable seas, our Armies
> moulder away by the Climate, without reckoning the loss by the Sword. Can
> we retain such wide and now hostile regions but by Armies? or by extirpating
> the inhabitants? We for years have been complaining of emigration to
> America. Are we to repeople it hence? or is it to ease our Taxes by being
> destitute of Inhabitants? Oh! fatal delusion! Oh! my Countrymen, awake!
> Make use of your natural good sense, and take the only method of avoiding
> three wars at once by ceasing to persist in carrying destruction into your own
> vitals. America may be reconciled, if temper and prudence preside; but the
> more we waste ourselves in that part of the world, the easier a prey we must
> be for our European Enemies.

Britain was a trading nation, and the exclusive trade with America was
an integral part of that country's economy. Hence the working scribblers
presented a wide range of options to their readers. Suggestions ranged from
unconditional control of American manufacture and commerce to the
drastic alternative of ridding Britain of the rebellious colonies.

AMOR PATRIAE (*MC* 2/17/76) suggested a "plan for peace and reconciliation." It was a scheme so absurd as to be ludicrous. Among the
conditions listed was parliamentary control of American taxation, manufacture, and commerce. It was a strategy which was highly unlikely to
be accepted as a basis for reconciliation by the colonies because it suggested:

> One half of the land tax [is] to be the American portion; that they be allowed
> to manufacture for their use only, Province by Province, but not to transport
> without being liable to such limitations as Parliament shall judge needful for
> the good of the whole; and also that the Colonies may be allowed to import
> certain foreign articles, as wine, currants, etc., from foreign European coun-
> tries without first bringing to England on paying a duty of ten per cent on
> the parliamentary rates.

RORERY MACCROWDEY (*MP* 5/21/76) was less demanding and proposed a way to settle the entire dispute:

> I think we ought to restore them the privileges they enjoyed in 1763; withdraw our forces—they want no protection nor support from us—they are willing to support themselves; let the accounts of the last war be fairly stated and I have no doubt they would be willing to discharge it. . . . England then ought to be satisfied with the advantages of their trade and the power to regulate it.

A writer who signed his name ANTI-MELA (*MP* 9/19/76), a ministerial scribbler for the *Morning Post*, warned his readers of the dire effects of a parliamentary victory for the Opposition, a triumph that he thought would spell disaster for Britain. It is universally true that in a democracy the party in power, if besieged, will attempt to discredit the opposition, as did this writer:

> Their [Opposition] great cry is reconciliation with America; to be tolerably consistent therefore, they must effect it at all events; this perhaps they would do; and I will venture to say, they had better lose America than give us a rotten peace with it, just sufficient to burthen us with the old American expenses but give us none of the old benefits; we should have the navigation act trampled under feet. The Americans would feel what they had obtained by resistance and would laugh at our restrictions; they would have free trade with all the world; the profit of our monopoly would be gone; the expense remained.

Two causes for the "present rebellious conflagration" were presented to the readers of CICERO (*MP* 10/4/76). The first was the desire of the American merchant to rob their counterparts in Great Britain of the debts owed her. The second arose from the nefarious working of the Opposition:

> The present rebellious conflagration that now rages with such violence on the American continent owes its baneful rise to two causes: A desire of the American merchants to cut asunder the commercial chain between the two countries, in order to rob Great Britain of nearly four millions of money which they were indebted to her and the parliamentary countenance shown to their first overtures of rebellion, by an interested minority in the British senate, who, regardless of the national consequences to either country, joined in the sacrifice of both, to overturn if possible a Minister who was respected by his King and every day rising in the estimation of the public.

The year 1777 brought a change in opinion regarding the conciliatory efforts of the Howe brothers. There was a significant disapproval of their endeavor. COURAGE SANS PEUR (*MC* 6/9/77) wrote in resentment: "We are lulled asleep by an ignominious patched up peace; an olive branch, forsooth offered by the first empire of the world, to a rascally Banditti in the Colonies, at the same time in actual rebellion against a lawful Sovereign." IMPARTIAL (*PA* 12/8/77) laid the blame at the feet of Lord North: "Your humiliating Concessions to the Americans rendered them insolent: your Proposals of Conciliation gave them Presumption and Courage."

The writer VIGILANS (*MC* 2/11/77) launched a tirade against those who sought reconciliation, and he was one of the few writers who brought the plight of the Loyalists before the reading public:

> We have done little more than follow the example they [Americans] have set us in all things but running away, in which I hope we shall never copy them. Do we make a law restraining their commerce? We only follow the example afforded us by their associations against trading with us. Do we make a law to grant letters of marque and reprisal? The number of privateers they had fitted out, and prizes they had taken from us. . . . Suppose the late terms proclaimed by the brothers had been accepted by the Rebels, would not the firm adherents of government have the most aggravated reasons of complaint? There are many instances of men in America who have stood boldly forth for their King and country, and have suffered on that account with an integrity and firmness of spirit which would have done honour to an ancient martyr. I am not of Renault's disposition, who says, "Let there be blood, blood enough," far, far from it. But, perhaps, I may think, that after so unprovoked and wicked a rebellion, the people may be taught by the capital example of some of the most flagitious of their leaders, that such daring excesses are not to be looked upon in the light of a common frolic, and that they not be repeated with impunity. Justice requires that the friends of government should be rewarded. . . . It must be wretched policy in any government to make it the interest of the subject to rebel. This proclamation has its advocates among those who call themselves moderate men, the idea of reconciliation pleases them; but of this I am convinced, that he who hopes to conquer the strong aversion, and gain the friendship of the Congress and other leaders of the rebellion, by such means as these, acts as wisely as one who would sow the sea with corn and expect an harvest.

In 1777, there emerged writers who suggested that a lasting peace, a peace based on terms favorable to Britain, could only be secured by vanquishing the rebellious colonies. DETECTOR AMERICANUS (*MC* 12/9/77) remained convinced, and so counseled his readers, that peace with America would come only when the colonist's ability to fight had collapsed:

> But before we clamour so much about making peace with America, let us enquire what reason we have for thinking that she wishes to make peace with us. Nothing at present will bring about peace with America but the utter inability on its side to contend. Line their coast with our ships, and burn every place that fitted out pirates. I would have left them the enjoyment of their paradise; but they should have no pretence for forming armies, and no impunity on becoming pirates.

NUMA (*MP* 5/3/77) rested his hopes for advantageous terms on a military victory in the next campaign: "I think there is the greatest possibility that we shall open the new campaign with so much eclat, that the Americans will be very glad to come to such terms as may be very advantageous to this country to grant."

An INDIGNANT ENGLISHMAN (*MC* 12/19/77) had only scorn for "these demagogues" who urged overtures to the colonists: "To try your patience a little further, know, my fellow countrymen, that these demagogues not only avow their intention in private, but they proclaim it in their solemn orations. Their language is, withdraw your troops, make overtures, and, perhaps, the colonies may hear you. What a combination of insanity and impudence!"

Such were the writers who were advising their readers to reject conciliation with America. There were many, however, who favored a harmonious accord to end the war. Contrary to those scribblers advocating the need for military success to acquire proper terms for peace, PEACE! PEACE! (*PA* 7/11/77) suggested an accord founded upon mutual interests and affection:

> Should any one urge the Necessity of Peace with America, there is not a man who would not agree with him in that Necessity to the Honour and Interest of this Country. It [peace] ought to be a Cordiality and Union of Interests; it ought to be maintained by a reciprocal sense of public Honour, and a general and impartial Welfare; it ought to be founded in affection and not in force.

Peace and reconciliation, wrote the scribblers of the *Public Advertiser*, must be achieved without the slightest hint of coercion. Force had been the cornerstone of the unsuccessful policy of the ministry:

AN IMPERIALIST (*PA* 3/31/77):

Unhappily, it must be confessed, the Cabinet-Regents, departed on this occasion from the only true national system, that of keeping as clear as possible from any appearance of coercion; or at least from that mode of coercion which they have pursued, they whose weakness, whose absurdities, had been principally the cause of all the mischief rising to that height at which we see it. It will not then be by means of coercion, so injudiciously employed, but in spite of the coercion, that a conciliatory termination of this infernal embroil can ever be expected; when the storm that will have desolated our country in America, and surely not unfelt here, may be overblown, the swell of the surge subside; but, alas, the damage sustained from it will scarce be soon or easily repaired.

PACIFICUS (*PA* 6/4/77):

America has supplied the Ministerial Faction with the principle they were in search of which does and must continue them in Place and Profit. Their Power and Profit is the true object of the War. (Quoting Edmund Burke): "Civil Liberty is not . . . a thing that lies in the depths of abstruse science. It is a Blessing and a Benefit, not an abstract Speculation. . . . Liberty is a good to be improved, and not an evil to be lessened. . . . It would be right to reflect that the American English can, as things now stand, neither be provoked at our railings, or battered by our instructions. All communication is cut off between us. But this we know with Certainty, that though we cannot reclaim them, we may reform ourselves. If Measures of Peace are necessary, they must begin somewhere; and a conciliatory temper must precede and prepare every Plan of Reconciliation.

WARNING (*PA* 10/10/75):

We will not examine whether his Majesty turns pale and is frightened when he receives news from his Generals and Admirals in America; but this we can honestly assert, that the Nations's Eyes are opened; they are tired of this cruel, unnatural, and ruinous war. Plunged as we are in a variety of difficulties there is yet time to extricate ourselves from them by the only method which is left us. Withdrawing our Forces, and leaving Americans to themselves. If a Union between the Colonies and Great Britain could be brought about, nothing would be more warmly desired by every lover of this country. But I fear the hatred which our unhappy conduct has rooted in the hearts of the Americans will never be obliterated.

PEACE! PEACE! (*PA* 10/20/77):

We have waged War against Americans in a spirit and manner that we shall one day or another be ashamed of: Let us now do that which ought to have been done at first, and which has not yet been done; let us endeavour to establish Peace by Negotiation and not by War: Such a Peace will be permanent, honourable, and is necessary for us.

A review of the manner in which the administration had conducted the war in America would show a long series of mistakes, according to A BRITON (*PA* 6/30/77). The guilt, however, was to be shared by the rebellious colonies. He wanted the colonists to confess their mistakes and their misunderstanding of the intentions toward them in the mother country:

It is nothing but true to say, and right easy to prove, that the whole history of the conduct of the Administration, relatively to this fatal Embroils, would exhibit nothing but one unbroken series of the most egregious Blunders that ever dishonoured the name of Politics, or the Authority of Government. I should not have despaired of seeing the Colonists subdued in the ONLY way I wish to see them subdued, by the true dignity of their own spirit, confessing their Error, confessing their Mis-apprehension of the intentions toward them of their Countrymen here. In the cool of their minds what pardon would they not have to ask of themselves for their having suffered such wretches as their deceivers at once to rob them of their Tranquillity, Concord, Loyalty, and Liberty, and to plunge them into the depths of the foulest Treason, and of the Blackest Ingratitude? And what a punishment has that Country prepared for them which they have been led to renounce! A Reintegration of them in all their Rights Privileges; Satisfaction in any REAL Grievances; a Re-incorporation of them to the great British community, with all the Advantages of a fair and honourable Pacification; for all which they should neither acknowledge nor have any obligation but to the SPIRIT of the LAWS of their Country; Laws which breathe nothing but Goodwill to them, and which, if faithfully consulted would render such a PEACE AS EASY to negotiate, as it would be happy on BOTH SIDES to obtain it.

The *London Chronicle* (9/13/77) managed to put the need for mutual reconciliation in verse:

> When brothers fall out about trifles of state,
>> And wrangle, and quarrel, and fight,
> And in rage with each other they seek their own fate,
>> And act wrong from false notions of right:
> It were well if a moment's reflection could show
>> That neither can e'er get their wishes;
> But that both will be losers by every blow,
>> While they fight for the loaves and the fishes.

The year 1777 ended and 1778 dawned with the blackest of news for British efforts in North America. Burgoyne had surrendered his army at Saratoga in November 1777, and the French had formalized their relationship with America by signing two treaties with the rebellious colonies in January 1778. Such was the background against which the North ministry proposed the third of its conciliatory plans.

America had declared its independence some two years earlier. Now, with the additional support of the French, it was obvious that there could not be a rapprochement unless Britain acknowledged the reality of independence. Most writers agreed to accept such a reality, but with limitations. Trade with America was of critical concern. AMOR PATRIAE (*MC* 9/19/78) advised his readers that the time had come for the British government to allow the Americans to be independent, and he then outlined a series of limitations to protect British investment and British trade:

> I am of the judgement that the very wisest and best method the British Government can now take is, to suffer them to be independent, under wholesome limitations, and make it safe to the Parent Country, and consistent with justice respecting the property of the King, and private sufferers, in regard to quit rents, confiscations, etc. and that they may not build, or purchase, or navigate any men of war, other than such as in time of war, or imminent danger. Great Britain might furnish at their request, and they paying an equivalent for the same, and withal solemnly engaging to impose no duties on imports from or exports to Great Britain. It will be the best way of making retribution of rewards and punishments, in lieu of confining them by Acts of Parliament to merchandise with Great Britain.

The writer who signed his name PEACE! PEACE! (*PA* 1/19/78) apprised his readers that sovereignty over America was already lost de facto. Peace would, with other advantages, relieve Britain of the burdens of colonial America, assure the continuation of a very desirable trading partner, and provide for a powerful ally in time of war.

> Nothing less than open and immediate acknowledgement of the Independency of America can break the present connection with France and restore the former happiness of England. Should it be asked, What will be the gain of this disclaimer of the Right of Sovereignty? It may be answered by another question, What will she lose: The Sovereignty is already lost de facto. There is no prospect of a recovery but by War; and War, in the present state of things, must be fatal to her existence as a power in Europe; but she will by this measure gain Peace, which is essential to her; she will gain besides real strength and honour. The Americans being acknowledged independent, and all the causes of jealousy and distrust thereby removed, they will eagerly, and with the greatest cordiality, enter into the closest bonds of amity and union; being now able to defend herself, as has been proved, she will no longer be a burthen to this Country, and therefore the pretence of Taxation be removed. She will supply you with many of her raw materials; take your Manufacture in preference to others; will contribute a certain quantity of Naval Stores for the use of Government; oblige herself to keep up a given number of ships for the general defence; afford protection and support to the West India Islands, and engage not to interfere in your settlements in the East. These, among other stipulations might serve as a basis of Union, and are worth the attention of those who cry out with me, PEACE! PEACE!

The letter writer who signed his name "H" (*MP* 3/16/78) perceived American independence as the most desirable option for Britain, with mutual agreement regarding trade that could lead to an offensive alliance against France:

> Repeal all the acts America complained of; allow her Independence; form with her an alliance, offensive, and defensive for ever, and a mutual agreement with regard to trade. France has used her ill, as well as us, and for every seeming favour, has extorted from her the goods bartered for warlike stores, at her own price. Let us jointly attack France with our whole force, which the united world could not withstand. The West Indies must fall! France be humbled! and England, and America, flourish jointly, amid the ruins of the House of Bourbon! Nature has pointed it out, that America should be allies; and wisdom should ratify what so strongly appears our mutual interest.

By the end of 1778, the fear of an invasion of the British Isles was both real and frightening, as A FRIEND OF GREAT BRITAIN (*MC* 12/1/78) wrote:

> Considering the train of disappointments we have experienced in the course of this dispute; considering too the fate of France, when contending in America against the united powers of Great Britain and her Colonies, the chance of war seems greatly against us: but allowing it to be in our favour, still it may be doubted whether any terms of peace, purchased at an additional expense of blood and treasure, will be preferable to those the Colonists

may now be induced to grant, on the condition of acknowledging their Independence, and withdrawing our troops. Thus, in every point of view, the continuance of hostilities against the Colonists seems impolitic: It is destructive of the strength of Great Britain, ineffectual either to the conquest or devastation of America, and vain and delusory as to hope of an advantageous peace. But there is another, and more cogent reason still behind. By transporting out of Great Britain the few regular troops yet remaining, we deprived both ourselves and Ireland of a necessary means of defence. But it is answered, no: the protection of both kingdoms is effectually provided for by our navy and militia, and the stipulated assistance of allies. There has been a time when the naval power of this country, by its manifest superiority, was sufficient for the purposes of home defence. That time is past. In a late encounter at sea, when France engaged us on equal terms, the advantage we gained was scarce perceptible; and it may happen, from the vicissitude of war, that, on some future day, victory shall be hers.[8] In this situation, a militia that never trod the hostile field, and a body of mercenaries, with interest separate from ours, will prove our only resources against a numerous and skilful enemy. How impotent such resources, I leave to the imagination by my fellow citizens.

The *Public Advertiser* as usual considered the ministry fair game for criticism. The writer G.N. (4/11/78) wrote a moving rebuke of the war and of those in power who failed to avoid such a conflict:

War may have Charms for those who are not immediately engaged in it. To read of Battles and Slaughter, and the storming of Towns and the taking of Prisoners, with all the horrid Din of War, may captivate the Vulgar, and nail down the Ear of Ignorance in the motionless Attention to the News of the Day, though the Party may have no clearer Idea of the Seat of War, the Powers engaged, and the Interests concerned, than if those Transactions were carried on in some remote District of the Moon. But Men of reputed Abilities should not give into this Foible so natural to the Inconsiderate and Vulgar; these ought to reflect on its dreadful Concomitant; to persuade and dissuade Mankind from introducing so dire a Calamity; and to stifle and suppress every Breath that may kindle into Flame, and revive the dormant Embers of so ravaging a Conflagration. I shall ever consider such Men of Abilities, who on every trivial Cause shall declare abruptly for War, as having a mean Self interest in promoting it; and whether he be Minister, or General; Civil, Military, or Ecclesiastic; he shall not under the specious Artifice of false Pretences lurk in Disguise, and escape Animadversion. We are in no Condition to enter into War. Nor yet to be plundered by the rapacious Hands of our Fellow Citizens in Power. And he must be very Ignorant, or what is worse, a crafty Enemy of his Country, who should at this Time, and in our situation endeavour to promote it.

Frustrated by the lack of success in America and the news of the Franco-American treaties, many Englishmen made renewed demands to reduce the rebellious colonies. The situation was further exacerbated by the news in mid-1778 that Congress had rejected the peace offers of the Carlisle

Conciliatory Commission. America was demanding independence, the acquiescence to which would be the destruction of the British Empire. Independence could only be averted by conquest.

To writer QUERIST (*MC* 1/3/78), independence would mean the loss of a secure market. And so he briefed his readers that there was little alternative to a continued attempt to conquer the Americans militarily:

> Is there any reason to suppose that the revolted provinces will accept any terms from this kingdom, short of absolute independence, unless they be first reduced by arms? Would not the offer of terms at present be construed into timidity, and serve rather to confirm the Colonies in their rebellion, than to detach them from it? Were not the Colonies a sure market for our manufactures, and a constant nursery for seamen? Is there a power in Europe, of equal ability with this kingdom, that would not long ago have suppressed a similar rebellion, or that would not still suppress it and punish its abettors?

A FRIEND TO GREAT BRITAIN (*MP* 6/11/78) warned his readers of the dire consequences of independence before urging forceful military action:

> As we early next month expect to hear some account from the Commissioners sent over to America, and as I make not the least doubt but the terms offered will be rejected; and as many people then imagine Independency must be granted them. I think it is a duty incumbent on every man to endeavour as much as lies in his power to prevent so dangerous a plan being put into execution. If Great Britain once gives them up to themselves, every thinking man ought seriously to ponder on the consequences. . . . What will become of our West India Islands? What will become of our valuable Newfoundland fishery? What will become of the Floridas? What will become of our East Indies? There will not be a single loyalist to be found in all these places, if this is given up, the American ones having so little encouragement for their steadiness to this government. And, lastly, what will become of poor old Britannia? If the Americans alone have made descents on our coasts, what will become of us then? Indeed, the consequences are so fatal, that it behooves every thinking man to stand up against so dangerous a proposition; the man who wishes for it is certainly guilty of treason against his King, his country, and himself. Britons! strike home, revenge your country's wrongs, or else you are undone!

Another writer who simply signed his name "F" (*MP* 4/30/78) reported to his readers that no orders had been issued to the conciliatory commissioners, nor were the commissioners likely to accept the independence of the rebellious colonies. He was convinced that the Americans would be forced to return to their subordination:

> The fatal consequences of the independency of the revolted Colonies are sufficient to induce every man to believe that, without the least necessity, it will not be admitted. The public declarations against this independency by

one or more of the Commissioners, as well as by Ministers, must leave us without doubt, that there are no orders given which will admit of its being conceded to. Until this concession is made, I never will despair of the return of those colonies to their allegiance to their Sovereign, and to a subordination to the supreme authority of the British dominions; they will rather be a burthen to the rest of the empire, if they are brought to an acknowledgment of the sovereignty of the British crown, the nature, or degree whereof they will eternally be disputing, and are left to an independency on the legislative power of Parliament. What degree of severity will be necessary [to subdue the Americans], it is not in my power to say. I always abhorred the cruelty of fox-hunting; and I would not kill a fox, nor a wolf, if it was not for the sake of my chickens, and my sheep. Much less can I delight in injuries to my own species, and I wish destruction to the lives and properties of rebels, so far as shall be necessary for the preservation of the lives and properties of loyal subjects and no farther.

To MENTOR (*PA* 2/14/78), the conquest of America was to be the means of last resort. In the spirit of true negotiation, he briefed his readers, Britain should repeal the "obnoxious Acts of Parliament" and America should follow by relinquishing its claims to independence. If America refused to relinquish her claim to independence, MENTOR made it clear that Britain should pursue all-out war:

Who shall be the first to desire Reconciliation, or show (if it should be so expressed) Signs of Submission? Certainly that Party which is most valiant and magnanimous. For it is many Times truer Fortitude to despise, in a right Cause, the Reflections of the Proud, and dare to humble ourselves, for the Public Good, before a weaker Foe, then to be bold and fearless amid the Shock of Arms. Let Britain, therefore, begin in the Repeal of the obnoxious Acts of Parliament, and America will probably follow in the Repeal of the more obnoxious Independency. If they do not, and we must fight to the Death, we shall at least have the consolation to know, that we resolve to conquer, or die, for something.

A writer FRIEND TO TRUTH (*MC* 1/23/78) prayed for reconciliation but believed such a desirable event could only be accomplished by British determination to force the colonies to accept subordination:

It is my constant and fervent prayer that a speedy and permanent reconciliation may take place between Great Britain and her Colonies; but before that most desirable event can be accomplished, unanimity must influence our Councils at home, and the most animated vigour direct our operations in the field. When every department appears equally determined to enforce a just subordination, the calamities of war will quickly be succeeded by the inestimable blessings of peace and freedom.

Another writer who called himself A NORTH AMERICAN (*MC* 2/20/78) was not persuaded that reconciliation could take place without total destruction of the American army and Congress: "As much has been lately said about a reconciliation between Great Britain and her Colonies, I would be glad to be informed how such an event can take place, without annihilating both their army and Congress."

AN INDIGNANT ENGLISHMAN (*MC* 1/20/78) also outlined a bellicose proposal to his readers:

> You must immediately exert yourselves with your wonted spirit; let every individual of you determine within himself thus: These American ingrates shall not withdraw themselves from us, who have, at the expense of more blood and treasure, than we in justice to this country could spare, planted, cherished, protected, and made them a people; they shall not break through every tie, by which they are so repeatedly and solemnly bound to us; they shall stoop to reasonable terms, which is all we demand, or the just vengeance of this much injured country shall crush them. May you be virtuous and conquer.

A ROYALIST (*MP* 1/1/78) briefed his readers that a force which would terrify the rebel colonies would bring about a reconciliation:

> The present situation of affairs, calls for extraordinary supplies for the current year, so as to enable Government to send such a force abroad, as may strike terror in the rebel colonies, and bring them to a due sense of their past errors. Were we to augment our forces to 30,000 more than we now have in America ... the appearance of such an army in the field, would not only be the means of preventing the shedding of much blood, but be the happy cause of bringing about such a reconciliation as would tend to the mutual advantage of the belligerent parties.

Although British arms were not meeting with wide success in 1778, and the French had already declared for the rebellious colonies, the Carlisle Peace Commission met with only limited approval in Britain. Fear persisted among the scribblers and their readers that terms of reconciliation had been offered to the Americans, or were about to be offered, which would lead to the ruin of Britain. There prevailed a wide distrust of the ministry, the commission, and the ability of Great Britain to obtain favourable terms from the rebellious colonies.

The writer CONSTANT READER (*CM* 3/23/78) suggested to his readers that they reject the conciliatory plan totally and unconditionally: "First that the conciliatory plan is derogatory to the honour and dignity of Great Britain. Secondly, that it is ill timed. Thirdly, that the probability is, it will not have the desired effect. And lastly, that the consequences may be fatal to the kingdom."

Why consider unfavorable terms when the success of the British military was about to unfold? FIDUS VETERANUS (*MC* 9/7/78) was satisfied, and so assured his readers that General Clinton, the new commander in chief in North America, with additional troops and the help of Loyalist

Americans, might so reduce the rebellious colonies that they would beg for dependence on the crown:

> I cannot entertain the least doubt that this General [Clinton], these officers, with 25,000 troops from Great Britain and Ireland, the Hessians recruited, together with the Loyal Americans, who have already taken and in future will take arms in the British cause, but that in this and the next campaign, the Rebels may be reduced in humility to implore that dependence on the crown, which they now so arrogantly reject.

GUSTAVAS VASSA (*MP* 3/10/78) could only foresee great benefits from unrelenting military pressure and consequently voiced dismay at the "tacit acknowledgement" by Lord North that the colonists were invincible:

> At a moment when the torrent of good fortune was breaking in upon the efforts of your Sovereign, to bring back to their duty a race of unnatural, and ungrateful bastards, in order that they might in due time be legitimized; at such a crisis to offer, in the face of a British Parliament, terms of humiliating reconciliation, beggars, my Lord, in my mind, all descriptions of pusillanimity if not depravity in the management of the public cause. The bill you have brought into parliament, as a measure of reconciliation between Britain and her revolted colonies, lays down a precedent for them as an independent people, confessing by your own tacit acknowledgement, that they are invincible. It was all they wanted, my Lord, and they will speedily show you that they have the wisdom, and gratitude to despise your measures, notwithstanding they are sanctified by the consent of parliament.

On 2 March 1778, the *Morning Post* published a letter from OBSERVATOR which was then reprinted by the *London Chronicle* the following day. This writer made it clear to his readers that all the threats to vanquish America were meaningless boasts. It was absurd to insist on a right without the power to enforce it:

> Since Lord North's Conciliatory Motion, the public have been frequently informed, that the Senate of the nation has been engaged in considering their right of taxation. It would seem that this point has already been sufficiently debated, discussed, and concluded. Every sensible man acquainted with the constitution, who considers the point impartially, must acknowledge the Parliamentary right of taxing all subjects of the Empire, who depend on its laws, and power, for protection; but, at the same time this right is acknowledged, it must be confessed by all that things may be so circumstanced, as to make the affecting of it not only incompatible with, but diametrically opposite to political wisdom.... Wherever there subsisteth any right of commanding, that right is always best acknowledged, when it floweth from respect, and not when fear is the motive; mere forced obedience, separate from other motives, is so imperfect, as to be scarce worth having; so that, to gain the love, or the good will at least, of those from whom we expect it, is consistent with the truest wisdom, and, to insist upon it,

notwithstanding our claim to a right of commanding, where there is any
want of sufficient power to force compliance, must bear the aspect of folly!

The *Public Advertiser* continued its role as an ardent critic of the
ministry. OLD MAN (*PA* 3/24/78), in the tradition of scribblers disclaimed
being of any consequence but then did not hesitate to advise the ministry
on the proper qualifications for the conciliatory commissioners. His
criterion for a suitable commissioner disqualified the nobility but promoted
ordinary men:

> Surely if the Minister is not predisposed to make his Negotiation with
> America ineffectual, he will be very careful whom to recommend to his Ma-
> jesty for Commissioners; I am but an unimportant individual in the State,
> and yet I declare to God I feel so much for the future consequences of the
> Minister's Choice in this business, that I am not easy of Mind till I find the
> Choice announced to the Public, and till I find the Public approve it. I pro-
> test against Lords or Earls in this Business. I would send plain, sensible Men,
> such as the Americans would think on a footing with themselves. I often
> thought that a man of good heart and real affection for his country and her
> children might settle the American Dispute with Mr. Washington and Mr.
> Gates in a very short conversation. But alas! Men rise to be Ministers in our
> Nation without studying the Nature of Men or of Society. Parliamentary In-
> fluence has brought us to this Distress.

AUGER (*PA* 8/7/78) taunted the ministry and Lord North for their
choice of members for the Carlisle Commission and for their entire conduct of the war:

> So you are astonished to hear that the Peace Commissioners are at War with
> one another! Indeed, my Lord, you are a provoking Joker! You have joked
> us out of our Money, Reputations, and Dominions. When you wanted to
> carry on the War, you sent out the boisterous Sir William; when you want
> to make Peace, you make the Choice of the Lamb-like, meek-eyed Governor
> J—ne. The Event has answered your most sanguine Expectations. You did
> not wish to succeed by War, and you have had your Wish; you did not want
> to obtain Peace, and your "Will is done." You have left us in a pleasant
> Degree of Uncertainty. We get no Laurels in the Field, and we obtain no Ac-
> commodation in the Closet.

The year 1779 brought Great Britain no closer to conquering the
rebellious colonies. Spain had become an active partner of America, and
British arms were yet to achieve marked success. The Carlisle Conciliatory
Commission had failed to gain its objectives in America, and the scribblers
bathed in postmortem conjecture.

Neither the commission nor the ministry could escape the wrath of the
press—the ministry for its conduct of the war and its instructions to the
commission, the commission for being little more than the dupe of the
ministry. POLICRITES (*PA* 2/1/79) had little sympathy for either:

Happy had it been for Great Britain, happier still had it been for the British Colonies in North America, if the Superintendent Power, and Supremacy of the Parent State, which necessarily involves in it, and implies a Right of Taxation, had either been renounced from the Beginning, or had not been equivocally asserted. We have seen the American War conducted in the same manner as a gallant Lover plays a Game of Cards with his Mistress, when, with the winning Card in his Hand, he politely throws away the Game without presuming to play it. The late Commission to treat with the Americans, seems to have proceeded from a consummate Ignorance of human Nature. Concession and Submission are too apt to intoxicate the best disciplined and best informed Mind, and perhaps too much for the imperfect and depraved State of human Nature to bear. What Returns then of Contempt and Insolence might they not have been expected to produce in uncultivated, brutal, and barbarous Minds?

If POLICRITES found the ministry offering too much to the rebellious colonies, and he did, the *Public Advertiser* in an unsigned letter (7/26/78) expressed an altogether different fear. The concern of this scribbler was that the concessions to be offered by the commission on the instructions of a profligate ministry were "unreasonable and disgraceful":

The French Camp is announced to us by the King's Authority. We know the Danger; we know who brought us into it. It is high Time to ask ourselves by what Men and what Means we are to get out of it? I believe it would be hard to find Men in this Country, or in any Country, who could contrive to make Concessions so unreasonable, so disgracefully, and so ineffectually, as those who sent out the late Commission to America; and no Men that might be entrusted with the Direction of the Force of this Country, could have so ably exerted that Force to its own Destruction, or have carried on a War so successfully, to the certain Loss of all its Objects.

The writer who signed his name Y.Z. (*PA* 2/22/79) briefed his readers in a similar fashion, asserting that the absence of good relations with the colonies was entirely due to a ministry that lacked any common sense:

If the Ministry had three Grains of Common sense left they would on the Conquest of America (which at a certain Crisis might have easily been effected) have settled an equitable Plan of Government on generous and liberal Principles, which might have regained the Confidence and Affection of the Colonies. Such a Plan, not extorted by Fear or Compulsion, (as the humiliating Terms lately offered by our Commissioners) would then have had the Merit of an Act of free Grace, and formed the basis of a permanent and amicable Connection.

CHAPTER SIX

The Sword Unsheathed

There were seven campaigns during the American War for Independence which animated the letter writers to the British press: the clash at Lexington and Concord in April of 1775, the battle of Bunker Hill in June of the same year, the seige and evacuation of Boston in the years 1775 and 1776, the battle of Long Island in August of 1776, the surrender of General Burgoyne at Saratoga on 13 October 1777, the southern campaign during the year 1780, and General Cornwallis's surrender at Yorktown on 17 October 1781.[1]

The Battles of Lexington and Concord

On 19 April 1775, Lieutenant Colonel Francis Smith's advance guard, under Royal Marine John Pitcairn, arrived at Lexington at dawn and found some 70 armed Minute Men under Captain John Parker on the Common. The Minute Men began to disperse in response to the repeated commands of Pitcairn: "Disperse ye Rebels!" However, an unidentified shot, "the shot heard round the world" (Ralph Waldo Emerson), brought a series of volleys from the British. The Americans returned a few shots. After the brief action, eight Americans lay dead and ten wounded. One British soldier was wounded. Pitcairn's force moved on to Concord, four miles away, followed by Smith and the main body.

At Concord there were brief skirmishes between Smith's troops and the militia encircling the village. After pillaging what few supplies had not already been removed or destroyed by the colonists, Smith's troops returned to Boston. All along the way, they were constantly harassed and attacked by militiamen. On the way back to Lexington, they met with reinforcements sent by General Gage, a force of over 1,000 men under Brigadier General Earl Hugh Percy. The combined force returned to Boston, harassed every step of the way. At the end of the day, some 1,800 British regulars had met about 4,000 disorganized but determined coloials: 65 British were dead, 173 wounded, and 26 missing; 49 Americans were dead and 46 were wounded or missing.

Early in June 1775, before the official version of the skirmish at Lexington and Concord appeared in the *London Gazette* and before the scribblers unleashed their pens, the *Caledonian Mercury* (6/3/75) published its exclusive version of the affair at Massachusetts Bay:

> The following is the substance of the account of the before mentioned affair, which is handed about at Lloyd's and Garraway's. General Gage having heard that the insurgents were drawing some cannon a few miles from Boston, he dispatched an officer, with some troops, to demand them to be delivered up, which the insurgents refused to comply with. A second message was sent, when the officer informed them, that he must obey his orders, which were, in case of refusal to surrender them, that he must fire on those that surrounded them, but which he hoped they would prevent, by immediately relinquishing them. This they absolutely refused to do; on which the troops fired on them, and killed about sixty. On this the country arose, and assisted the insurgents to load the cannon and directly fired on Gen. Gage's troops which did great execution, near one hundred killed and sixty wounded.

By the middle of June, the British people had the opportunity to read the official version of Lexington and Concord and that of their American brethren printed in the *Essex Gazette* of Salem, Massachusetts. That these country people resisted the might of British arms was inconceivable. Little wonder that the scribblers bellowed their disbelief. In the *Caledonian Mercury* (6/12/75), the author of an unsigned letter assured his readers that it was all a fabrication:

> The English nation are generous, so very generous, that to be unfortunate is with them to be faultless. The Bostonians are now the favourites of all people of good hearts, and weak heads, in the kingdom. Their faint-like account of the skirmish at Concord had been read with avidity and the impudent falsehood that they have defeated the King's troops believed and rejoiced in. If the Americans really vanquished the King's troops they will be in as comical a situation as the most sanguine saint could wish for, viz. Sheep who had not been lost, but run their heads against and killed their Shepherd.

An ENEMY TO IMPOSITION (*PA* 6/10/75) refused to accept the entire episode as a battle, much less as a defeat for the forces of General Gage:

> Of the skirmish at Concord ... a parcel of country people, under the direction of some arch-patriots, in the secret, had the impudence to fire upon a party of his Majesty's troops as they were marching through the Town of Lexington. Some of the soldiers were murdered by these means; and the troops in their own defence, set fire to some of the houses from which they had been annoyed. The Regulars marched quietly back to their quarters. The attack made by a few assassins was magnified into a battle; and the marching of troops to their quarters was construed as a defeat.

The writer JOHN STAPLES (*CM* 6/10/75) acknowledged that fighting had developed but asserted that the king's troops had quickly mastered the situation: "The rebels who durst not face the regulars fired on them out of windows as they passed, which so irritated the King's troops that they fired and burnt every place that harboured such cowardly miscreants."

Horrified at the actions of the New Englanders, ARISTIDES (*PA* 6/7/75), imparted his distress to his readers: "There needs no other proof of this disposition, and of their good will to this country in general, than their cruelty to our wounded in the late affair near Lexington; of which they were not ashamed to publish so false an Account . . . the complicated baseness of the New Englanders . . . their double felony in murdering and mangling our Soldier's reputation as well as bodies."

The skirmish at Lexington and Concord brought forth countless letters to explain the reaction of the rebellious colonies. The *London Chronicle* (6/3/75), the *Morning Chronicle* (6/5/75), and the *Public Advertiser* (6/5/75) all reported that "when people of New York learned of Concord they seized arms stored for the troops and did the same with two vessels in the harbour."

The *London Chronicle* (6/10/75) further reported that "in all parts of America the inhabitants were fully determined to defend their rights and liberties, at the hazard of their lives and fortunes." The *Morning Chronicle* (6/13/75) was less enthusiastic over the happenings at Lexington and Concord and noted that freedom of expression for those who remained loyal to the king was being severely curbed: "The inhabitants of New York called a sudden meeting after hearing of Lexington. . . . The majority for resistance was so great that those who wished well to Government, dared not fully open their minds and assert the right of the Mother country to their obedience and submission."

The Battle of Bunker Hill

On 16 June 1775 an American force of 1,200 men under Colonel William Prescott had initially been sent by General Ward to fortify Bunker Hill. By mistake, in the darkness they began to entrench Breed's Hill, a lower height that was closer to Boston and more vulnerable to fire from artillery in Boston and guns of British ships in the harbour.

On June 17 General Gage sent General William Howe with 2,200 men in an amphibious attack on Charleston peninsula and the fortification. After being twice repelled, Howe's force, reinforced by Sir Henry Clinton, was successful in a third bayonet assault when the defender's ammunition supply became exhausted. The British lost almost half their starting strength, suffering 1,054 casualties. American losses numbered 100 dead, 267 wounded, and 30 captured.

The exceptionally high casualties to the British army provided most unwelcome news for the British people. Few scribblers, ministerial or Opposition, could find the slightest evidence of a British victory. The letter writer OBSERVATOR (*CM* 12/4/75) made a feeble and fruitless attempt to slander the American troops rather than to claim a British victory: "There was a running kind of bush-skirmish near Lexington, and a battle at Bunker Hill, in which the rebels seemed obstinate in nothing but running away as soon as the King's Troops got to them."

NUMA (*PA* 7/28/75) managed to couple an attack on the press with a claim for a British victory at Bunker Hill: "That any one Englishman who professes either a public spirited regard for his country, or entertains a prudent consideration for himself, should look upon the triumph of the King's troops with regret is a circumstance of astonishing absurdity."

The unusually high casualties for the royal troops at Bunker Hill provoked shock and astonishment.

AN ENGLISHMAN (*MP* 8/4/75):

An irregular mob of undisciplined troops . . . cut off in the last engagement the flower of the British army.

AN OLD SOLDIER (*PA* 7/29/75):

I never before heard of so many men, in proportion to the number, being killed and wounded from redoubts made in four hours, and from six pieces of cannon only in those redoubts to oppose above one hundred pieces.

WILLIAM TELL (*PA* 7/31/75):

One thousand sixty four of the troops killed and wounded to destroy a redoubt thrown up overnight. Provincial losses considerable—yet eight days after 100 buried and thirty wounded.

The Siege of Boston

The circumstance of the British troops in Boston was precarious after the battle of Bunker Hill. The siege had begun with the British retreat from Concord on 19 April 1775. The old fortifications on Boston Neck had been strengthened and added to in September 1774. A deep ditch was dug into which the tide flowed at high water, turning Boston into an island. By 20 April 1775, just after the battles of Lexington and Concord, Boston was besieged by provincial troops whose numbers eventually grew to 15,000. The rebels withheld supplies of every kind. There was no fresh meat, no flour except a little from Canada, no straw for bedding. The coast was policed by Nantucket whalers to prevent the fishermen from supplying the garrison.[2]

Despite the deprivations faced by the British forces in Boston, "Q" (*MC* 2/1/76) informed his readers that all was well:

> Good clothing, bread, salt beef, pork, water, with many of the luxuries of life and good housing, are not wanting in Boston, and barracks very sufficient for sheltering the men from weather. I further speak from the last information, that thirteen thousand bushels of wheat lay untouched in the town when the last ships left there the 16th of December. . . . The men were getting hearty and in high spirits.

Meanwhile, a formidable military force was assembled within the town. Tents covered its fields, cannon were placed on the hills, and troops paraded daily in the streets. It was a welcome sight only to the adherents of the British ministry, for it was one place in Massachusetts where the governor was in authority and where the laws of Parliament were still in force.

The strategic importance of Dorchester Neck had long been recognized by Washington in formulating his plans for dislodging the British from Boston. He was convinced that by occupying Dorchester Heights and preparing to attack simultaneously from the Cambridge side, he would precipitate a battle. Two thousand men together with 350 carts of tools and prefabricated defenses were therefore marched across the causeway to Dorchester Heights on the night of 4 March 1776. By daylight the following morning, two fortifications had been erected. Howe is reported to have said that the provincials had done more work in one night than his whole army would have done in six months. The safety of the troops in Boston and of the ships in the harbor was directly threatened. Howe decided to attack Dorchester immediately: 2,400 men under the command of Lord Percy were ordered to Castle William, whence the attack would be launched, but bad weather prevented the British forces from reaching the rendezvous. By the time the storm had cleared, the American forces were almost impregnable. Howe's only recourse was to evacuate Boston, which he did on 15 March 1776, after a siege of nearly 11 months, with 6,000 troops plus some 1,000 Loyalists.

With little to celebrate during the siege of Boston, the letter writers now applauded the evacuation of that city. The *Public Advertiser* favored their readers with two unsigned letters, the first on 10 May and the next eleven days later, congratulating General Howe on his generalship:

> The late embarkation of the troops from Boston without the loss of a man in the face of a hostile Army of above twenty thousand men . . . a great piece of Generalship.
>
> I shall still persist in my assertion that a greater piece of generalship was never displayed by any commander . . . than by General Howe.

To further confirm the "victory" of the evacuation and to deny any rumor that General Howe had left military supplies behind, TRANS-ATLANTICUS (*PA* 6/26/76) informed his readers that "only three cannon were left and they were spiked." Not all scribblers, however, considered the evacuation of Boston a victory or a mark of great generalship. AN OLD OF-FICER (*PA* 5/8/76) could discern little to celebrate. His wrath was directed at Lord George Germaine, home secretary and architect of the American operation:

> Give me leave to congratulate your Lordship upon the success of your Arms. The wretched remains of eleven thousand of our best troops which under your secret and avowed auspices were to conquer America are now the sport and prey of famine, winds and waves.... Your Gazette [*London Gazette*] tells us that it was a voluntary, premeditated movement.... If the infatuation of this devoted people should suffer them to continue any longer under such guidance as yours, our bitterest enemies cannot wish us a punishment more grievous than we shall suffer from this war of Folly, Ruin, and Reproach.

MACHIAVEL (*PA* 5/8/76) wrote of the evacuation of Boston with utter dejection: "Boston is evacuated; New York possessed by the Americans; Philadelphia not well inclined to us; in short there is no place on that continent to which a land army can be sent."

The Battle of Long Island

General Howe, joined by General Clinton, landed 20,000 men unopposed on Long Island between the 22d and the 25th of August. Washington faced him with 9,000 men of uncertain quality; their inexperienced leader had erred in sending a further division into a potentially dangerous position and now failed to spot that the American left flank ended in open country guarded by only five men. Howe, at Clinton's suggestion, engaged the American center and right while skillfully outflanking them on their left. Only Lord Sterling on the right offered prolonged resistance, and soon the Americans were fleeing in confusion to their Brooklyn entrenchments. General Howe now erred in preparing for a lengthy siege instead of overrunning the American entrenchments. Admiral Howe, intending to entrap Washington by occupying the East River, was forestalled by contrary winds, and on 29 August 1776 Washington ferried his men to Manhattan at night in a thick fog. American losses were 1,500, British losses less than 400. The battle of Long Island was the first major and unblemished victory of British arms in the American War for Independence. It was a time for the scribblers to celebrate, and celebrate they did. In the Scottish *Caledonian Mercury* (10/21/76) the author of an unsigned letter rejoiced: "with the agreeable advice of the defeat of the deluded and rebellious Americans on Long Island by his Majesty's army under the command of General Howe, the inhabitants of this place [Inverary] gave the amplist testimonies of their real satisfaction and joy. . . . Such is the attachment of the natives of this quarter to his Majesty."

To AMICUS (*MP* 10/23/76), the taking of Long Island would result in good quarters and fresh provisions for the troops: "How very trivial the taking of Long Island may appear to the friends of America, it is indisputably of great advantage to our troops, who now have the happiness of enjoying good quarters and fresh provisions; not to speak of the advantages arising from being so near New York."

A LOYALIST (*MP* 10/28/76) could only rejoice at the "matchless bravery of the King's troops, and the cowardice of the traitorous Yankee rebels at Long Island."

The military success on Long Island was not without blemish. The Hessians were accused of the massacre of colonial troops after they had surrendered and were disarmed. Condemning the Hessians for this heinous crime of massacre, CAIUS GRACCHUS (*MP* 10/29/76) wrote:

> But to speak of the gallant feats of arms performed at Long Island, where three and twenty thousand of these heroes put to flight six thousand Provincials, and where, be it said in particular, to the honour of the valiant Hessians, that after they had surrounded about one sixth of their own number (who immediately threw down their arms and implored quarter) they very humanely murdered them.

Cautioning his readers about the future of the conflict, MEMMUS (*PA* 10/22/76) wrote:

> Prosperity is to a Proverb more difficult to bear than Adversity. This was never more strongly evinced than in the behaviour of the Ministerialist upon the late success on Long Island. The prospect of continuing to enjoy the plunder of this infatuated Nation, throws them into transports of Joy totally ridiculous ... the most sanguinary inflictions of all kinds of cruel punishments upon the already subdued Rebels, and a total confiscation of their Estates among the King's friends. All these are vicissitudes which every sensible man expects in war. It remains yet to see what will be the event of attempting to reduce two millions of people to Slavery, at a distance of three thousand miles. It is a long journey. But this is certain, that the taking of Long Island and New York, is scarce one step in that journey. It may serve indeed to keep the present Ministry and their Dependents a little longer in a situation to plunder, which they consider much more than the prosperity, or even the safety of the Kingdom. Certain, however, it is, that they cannot be more Knaves than the People are Dupes.

HUMANUS (*LC* 10/17/76) wept for the oceans of British blood shed at the victory of Long Island and the horrid scenes rendered by this unnatural war:

Of the late battle on Long Island ... I sincerely weep over every victory that can be gained in this unhappy contest, on account of the oceans of British Blood with which they are purchased; for which ever side may happen for the time to obtain the superiority, still it will be only the parent having cut the throat of a child, or the child that of the parent; and he that can derive any pleasure from such a horrid scene must have a heart destitute of every tender feeling.

The search for a scapegoat, a whipping boy, increased steadily as the war progressed. No one in government was exempt; ministry, Parliament, the Crown, and, of course, generals and admirals. The frustration of the people and their scribblers spilled over into a profusion of letters.

ODDO (*MC* 1/18/76) held Lord North responsible for the failure of his generals: "Tell me, my Lord, of one operation against the American rebels that would not disgrace the conduct of a school-boy.... Weakness, pusillanimity and contradictions appear in all your schemes, and you seem happy at projecting blunders."

Accusing Admiral Graves and the British navy of "carousing" and thus permitting the Americans to acquire gunpowder, LUCIUS (*MC* 9/7/65) wrote:

How did the Americans acquire gun powder? I must take the liberty to aver that they [British navy] did not do their duty, and that all America was astonished to see arms and ammunition pouring into their creeks and rivers without let or molestation, whilst Admiral G____ lay idle at Boston with a formidable fleet: and almost all the commanders on station spent their time carousing.

MEMMUS (*PA* 10/17/76) found the victory on Long Island tainted by the failure of General Howe to crush the rebel forces. Such negligence cast a shadow over future operations of the war:

One is rather inclined to wonder how a Force [American], so very inferior, with so large a tract of Country to defend, could resist a very superior Army for four days, and then retreat with the loss of only 2000 men. Now, however, we find that General Howe did not think it prudent to attack them with less than four times their number, and that with every aid and precaution that could give them an additional advantage. Under the circumstances there is no great reason for triumph on this success; nor does it promise much as to the future operations of the war. Even taking New York, with as much facility, would be of little consequence in a general view. It is only a Post, as that of Long Island. There are other Posts ... and when these are carried, the grand Army, equal at least in number remains to be assailed. What mighty things were promised us from the possession of Boston. Yet how have these hopes been fulfilled. A cool observer of these proceedings, Sir, cannot help fearing that it is a Visitation from Heaven which has marked us for Destruction.

The British Surrender at Saratoga

General Burgoyne's forces for the Saratoga campaign, which many historians date from the middle of June 1777, consisted of 500 Indians, 650 Canadians and Loyalists, and 6,000 regulars, of whom 3,000 were foreign mercenaries. On August 16, a strong foraging party of British and Hessian forces was defeated in the battle of Bennington, Vermont. Burgoyne then crossed the Hudson River on 13 September and engaged the American forces on 19 September in the first battle of Saratoga at Freeman's farm.

Burgoyne's attack on the Americans left was repulsed with 600 casualties; American losses numbered 300. The second battle of Saratoga developed on 7 October at Bemis Heights. Burgoyne, attempting to drive south, was decisively repulsed by Americans under the command of Benedict Arnold.

On 8 October, Burgoyne retreated to Saratoga (Stillwater), New York. His condition was desperate. Short of food and ammunition, he could not reach Ticonderoga, nor could supplies reach him from that fort or from Canada.

On 13 October, Burgoyne requested a cessation of hostilities, and on the 17th he signed the "Convention of Saratoga" which stipulated that the British army of 5,700 men were to be marched to Boston and shipped to England on parole. A condition of the parole specified that the surrendered troops would not again serve in North America.

When the news of the capitulation of Saratoga reached London, it was met with significant skepticism. The letter writer OBSERVATOR (*MC* 12/1/77) warned his readers that the reports of the defeat of General Burgoyne's army originated in infamous sources:

> The seditious declaimers have again sallied forth in order to make a vigorous attack on the breastwork of the main body of our belief, and to oblige us to admit the certainty of General Burgoyne's whole army being either cut to pieces or in the hands of the rebels. Britons! be firm, be loyal, and deserve your NAME. Resist those mischievous impressions which the agents of darkness would fix on your intelligent powers. Detest the man who has the rebel spirit of audacity to assert that the contents of the accounts handed to you, from the direct channels of infamy and falsehood are true.

Lest his readers had failed to read his letter of 1 December, OBSERVATOR followed it on the eleventh of that month with a suggestion to his readers that the news of Burgoyne's capitulation was totally improbable: "Whatever opinion our rebel partisans may indulge to the contrary, it must be clear to every unprejudiced reader, that the accounts of General Burgoyne's surrender lose every day the strength of probability; and the conditions of his capitulation, now published, (which appear pregnant with forgery, when circumstantially considered) exhibit the most monstrous improbability."

Faced with undeniable proof of the capitulation at Saratoga, many writers felt the need to underplay the American victory. "The brave General Burgoyne [was] entangled in the woods and forced to surrender to Arnold (the horse-trader) for want of provisions" wrote SOLOMON DOUBTFUL (*MP* 12/6/77). FIDUS VETERANUS (*MC* 8/29/78) informed his readers that General Burgoyne was "obliged to surrender to the mandates of famine" rather than to the American forces.

Having accepted the loss of the army at Saratoga, A VETERAN, whose letter appeared in both the *Morning Chronicle* (1/21/78) and the *London Chronicle* (1/22/78), challenged the view that General Burgoyne had lost a "whole army" and maintained that Burgoyne had dictated terms to the Americans:

> Now [that] the consternation of the loss of the army under General Burgoyne is a little subsided, I beg leave to ask what mighty loss we have sustained? Great stress is laid upon a whole army being cut off. Pray, what was this whole army? Not more than sufficient to cover a foraging party, or for an escort of provisions in ordinary services. Attend to a plain narrative of facts: General Burgoyne with four, say five thousand troops, marched into an enemy's country, abounding with mountains, lakes, rivers, woods, and every difficult defile, where five times his number could, within a few days, be brought to oppose him, without having established a line of posts, or any communication whatever, with Canada or his magazines. If there is a possible situation where every circumstance shall conspire to give the rebels a superiority over our troops, it was that of General Burgoyne; and yet he was able to dictate terms to above four times his number, and by the convention, which does him honour, his whole army are at liberty to serve in any part of the empire, except the rebellious provinces.

Assuring his readers that Saratoga was only a temporary defeat, ANGLICANUS (12/8/77) wrote:

> The late defeat and capture of General Burgoyne will afford a triumph to those enemies of their country who are distinguished by the appellation of Patriots.... Let me answer an assertion which appears fallacious—that the resources of this country are exhausted. What has been may be. The troops of Britain have on former occasion been defeated in the American deserts and that defeat has been remedied. Gentlemen, be not dejected; let not the dark cloud of despair overshadow your spirit.

A writer signing his name as A MERCHANT (1/21/78) assured his readers that the "little army" would soon be replaced: "The voluntary offers . . . of troops cannot fail soon to replace the loss of men sustained by the surrender of the little army under the gallant Burgoyne."

Can you not shed a tear when you view Burgoyne's "little army"

resolved to seek death to preserve the honour of the British frame? So A
BRITON (*MC* 2/9/78) queried his readers:

> My countrymen, when you view your General environed, hemmed in on
> every side, animating his little army, intent to renew the fight, bravely re-
> solved to seek death, which appeared in view in horrid dreadful name, or
> preserve the honour of the British frame, can you withhold a tear? Can you
> look on this brave man, and his chosen few, struggling in the storms of fate,
> a fight worthy of the attention of Heaven itself, and not weep? And if weep,
> will you not rouse with reanimated vigour, and unremitting speed, to
> revenge the ill fortune of your General, as the Romans did that of their
> General Varro? Yes, I know you will; me thinks already I see you panting
> for the field, my brave fellows, and each striving with the other who shall
> be foremost to renovate the lustre of the British arms, and do honour
> to the behaviour of your General Burgoyne and your countrymen, who
> should be recorded in the annals of England for their signal bravery at
> Saratoga.

The defeat at Saratoga was no cause for despair to DEMOSTHENES (*MP*
12/10/77): "It is observed that the panic terrors of a warlike people instead
of settling into despondency ever turn to rage and revenge! Now is the moment for these symptoms to appear, and I swear by the shades of those
brave heroes whose blood is now soaking on the plains of America!
You have no cause of despair! Rouse Britons! rouse and assert your
rights!"

The letter writer signing his name as COMMON SENSE (*MP* 12/24/77)
repeated this advice to his readers, stating that although the statesmen and
generals had committed notorious blunders, Englishmen would rally to the
cause:

> The Campaign of 1777 In America Stated: We began the campaign this year
> with fifty-five thousand men and at sea ninety ships of war. The Rebels had
> not, on the whole, fifty thousand regular, or Continental troops; and, includ-
> ing their militia not seventy thousand disciplined men in all America. Their
> navy was totally contemptible. Out of this number, each side had forts, and
> garrisons, to defend: and neither party could bring into the field fifty thou-
> sand effective soldiers. At the close of the campaign, however, we find
> ourselves shamefully defeated, and one of our armies taken prisoner. What
> is the cause of this imbecility and disgrace? Is it owing to superior military
> prowess? No, quite the reverse, our soldiers hold the Americans extremely
> cheap. Is it solely to blunders, notorious blunders, in our Statesmen, and
> Generals? Judge by facts alone. They are much better proof than all the
> rhetoric of St. Stephen's. It is undoubtedly a galling misfortune, but like
> many other misfortunes it has produced some good effects: interest, policy,
> and national honour demand that we should redouble our exertions. Britons
> are roused in good earnest! fire, and indignation are kindled in every breast;
> and destruction already impends over the heads of those who presume to
> pluck the hoary laurels from this isle. . . . In this cause whenever it become

necessary, I shall with pleasure exhaust the last drop of blood in my veins and arteries.

BRITISH LEGION (*MP* 12/30/77) had a warning for Lord North and his moderation:

> Our present situation with America shows us how much we have been disappointed and should inform you that a very different exertion is necessary for the enforcement of our supremacy over the colonies. We know that you still intend to make the appeal to the sword. The longest must now decide the contest, and superior exertion alone can make it triumphant over Faction and Rebellion; for the indignant spirit of the colonies means no more to court the protection of this country, but arms, and bids defiance to its power. Active measures must retrieve us from that unhappy frustration which a mistaken moderation and feeble effort have plunged us into.

There were many scribblers who gave a lie to "Pro Patriae Mori" and sought a way out of the bloodshed. The ministry was attacked for its invention and distortion of the news from America and for the continuation of the ruinous and unnatural war against "our brethren":

POPLICILA (*MC* 12/25/77):

The Ministry, notwithstanding the misfortune of General Burgoyne, continue to employ their emissaries to mislead the people, and still appear fixt in bringing this nation to inevitable ruin sooner than offer terms to America.

J.A. (*PA* 12/10/77):

As this cruel Devastation and Ravage were begun in Deception, so has every Measure been prosecuted in the same Way, until we have made ourselves hated by America, and scorned by all Europe. To fill up the Measure of our Folly and Wickedness, we invent Falsehoods to deceive the Nation, and enable Stock-jobbers to rob Individuals; while regardless of National Character, Persons in the Department of Ministry not only raise the cruel Lie, but propagate it by Means of every Clerk in Office.

J.A. (*PA* 11/14/77):

How long shall we be blind to our Danger? How long shall the Measures, which not only ruin us daily, but have made us contemptible in the Eyes of all Europe be pursued with unabated Asperity? General Burgoyne's Disaster has been made worse by the fabricated Lies, to take off the Nation's Attention; and to the Loss of his Army, we have added the Loss of National Character. Since the 1st of September it is now 71 Days; no Dispatches are arrived; if any have, they are from New York; and this bombastic Gasconade will be followed with a Description of the masterly Manner of Sir William Howe's Retreat; few other Narratives of his Proceedings have appeared. As this unhappy War was eagerly entered into, from its being apprehended an easy Conquest; and, as at Boston, the Military Men who affirmed the Practicability of subduing the Colonies with 5000 Regulars, well knew the impossibility, it appears to be the Consequence of Artifice or Folly.

The defeat at Saratoga entailed a dramatic change of military strategy by Britain that involved the evacuation of all provinces but New York and Rhode Island. This was a switch from a tactic designed to strangle New England to one intended to play to the strength of Loyalism in the South. Philadelphia was evacuated, Sir Henry Clinton replaced Howe as commander in chief. New York was to be retained as the chief British military base, and the British offensive would be shifted to the southern colonies.

The Southern Campaign

In accordance with the new British military strategy, a detachment of 3,500 men under Lieutenant Colonel Archibald Campbell embarked at New York for Savannah, Georgia, on 25 November 1778. On 29 December 1778, British forces under General Campbell captured Savannah, and on 29 January 1779 they possessed the city of Augusta. The delight at these military achievements was quickly reflected in the scribblers' writings.

The letter writer ONE OF MANY (*PA* 3/3/79) shared his enthusiasm with his readers and mirrored British expectation of Loyalist support:

> The Province of Georgia is our own; Gen. Campbell, after attacking and defeating entirely the Troops assembled to defend it, took Possession of Savannah, the Capital of that Province where he was welcomed by many loyal Subjects. He has since penetrated the Country with little opposition, is received by the People with Gladness, and is in complete Possession of that whole Province. The Men and Officers of Frazer's Highlanders, which he has with him, have many Thousands of their nearest Relations ready to join them in the interior parts of the South and North Carolina.

DION (*MP* 3/26/79) could see little hope for America and was pleased to so inform his readers. The British had defeated the French fleet off the West Indies and conquered the French island of St. Lucia. Those achievements coupled with the discontentment of the Americans were all indications that the war would end in victory.

> What must that essence of faction and rebellion, the Congress, think of the turn of affairs took at the close of last year? Having signed a guarantee of the British sugar islands to France, to see St. Lucia in the hands of England, D'Estaing driven with infamy away, and in expectation of total destruction.[3] Georgia conquered, and South Carolina vigorously attacked; discontents and murmurs against their government through all the colonies; and to convince them of the universal weakness of the ally whereon they lean for support, the French driven out of the East Indies.

As success continued to shine on their cause in the southern colonies, the British commitment to that theater increased and their victories continued. On 23 November 1779, 3,000 British troops sailed from New York for Georgia, followed on 26 December by another 8,000 men under the command of General Clinton.

On 11 February 1780, Clinton's expedition landed on John's Island, near Charleston, and preparations were begun for an attack on that city. General Clinton laid siege to Charleston from 11 April until 12 May with a force of some 14,000 men. The fall of the city on 12 May was, perhaps, the greatest British victory and the worst American disaster of the war. General Lincoln and about 2,500 Continental soldiers were taken prisoner and large amounts of cannon, small arms, and ammunition were appropriated.

On 12 June, General Clinton, convinced that the conquest of the south would be an easy task, sailed for New York with about one-third of his troops, leaving Lord Cornwallis with about 8,345 men to continue their campaign.

The writer OBSERVATOR (*MC* 8/10/79, *PA* 8/11/79) wrote of the advantages of the British conquests in the south. It was, he informed his readers, a means of putting an end to the rebellious colonies obtaining credit in France from the sale of American goods:

> No circumstance of time since the commencement of the American rebellion ever engaged the attention of the nation at large under such favourable expectations as the present moment: favourable, because our military operations on the Continent are principally directed against a valuable southern province, which has hitherto enabled our revolted subjects to obtain a very extensive credit in France from the large remittances annually made therefrom in various articles of merchandise, the produce of that colony, the most saleable and nationally serviceable of any produced in British America; and favourable, because we have the greatest reason to believe, (notwithstanding the accounts announced in some of our public prints to the contrary) from the apparent security on which the expedition was planned and put into execution, that it has already been attended with complete success, and that in consequence thereof North Carolina and Virginia must naturally voluntarily come in or be subdued.

To RESOLUTION (11/12/79), the military success experienced by British arms in the southern colonies was not sufficient and harsher measures were demanded:

> To acknowledge the power of Congress, to naturalize Englishmen, or any born in Great Britain, is to acknowledge not only their independency, but their sovereignty; and if Cunningham and Paul Jones, when taken were not hanged, I wish the present water-gruel Ministry were, who are only ruinous to their friends, and crouching to their oppressors. To give no more quarter to rebels, than Oliver Cromwell did in Ireland, may save blood in the end.... To retaliate as the Hessians and Highlanders did, might prevent their hanging more of their fellow subjects in Philadelphia and Carolina, born under English allegiance, if not natives of Great Britain.

Lord Cornwallis had some outstanding achievements in the summer and early autumn of 1780. Major General Horatio Gates and a force of 3,000 were overwhelmed by Cornwallis and also an army of 2,400 at Camden, South Carolina, on 16 August. On 26 September, Cornwallis and his army occupied Charlotte, North Carolina. For the writers of the *Morning Chronicle*, Lord Cornwallis was an unquestioned hero. At least for the month of October:

A LOYAL AMERICAN (*MC* 10/16/80):

Let the Carolina merchants instantly open a subscription for those heroes who have fought so undauntedly under the immortal Earl Cornwallis, and by whose valour the most important part of America has been retained and brought into the King's peace, which will encourage them to go on in their victorious career, and will inspire an emulation amongst our soldiery, when they experience the bounty of their countrymen in England.

J.B. (*MC* 10/18/80):

The force under Gates, if his Lordship [Cornwallis] had retreated before him, instead of beating him and dispersing them, were the very force somewhere which might have besieged Charles-Town, and perhaps Savannah too; but now they are not to be found any where; the danger is over, and I hope our loyal fellow subjects there and in North Carolina will take care not to let them rally; and as they are likely to get rid of the traitors who correspond with them, and those who barbarously murdered their brave country men, as Englishmen were always called by them, when they wanted help from them ... I hope both those provinces of North and South Carolina will, as well as Georgia, be soon established in their old constitution, and enjoy the liberties and properties under a British Sovereign, they have been cheated and robbed of by Congress men, Committee men and Sequestrator.

"z" (*MC* 10/20/80):

Britain is capable in any one campaign to put an end to the American contest; vigour, and exertion of the force we already have there, is all that is wanted. Why it has not been done, is not my province to enquire; but the success of Lord Cornwallis on the frontiers of the Carolinas, where his opponents were, as seven to two, and commanded by the same general as reduced the Northern army to capitulate, fully justifies the assertion.

Fame for Lord Cornwallis was transitory. In part as a result of the catastrophic defeat of an entire Loyalist force under Major Patrick Ferguson at the battle of Kings Mountain, South Carolina, Cornwallis decided to abandon his invasion of North Carolina.[4]

The Battle of Yorktown

On 4 August 1781, Cornwallis occupied Yorktown and Gloucester Point on the York River, Virginia. This was a defensible position permitting communication by sea with Clinton in New York, and with expected reinforcements it would allow a renewed offensive campaign in Virginia. Unfortunately for the British, Comte de Grasse's French fleet with 28 ships of the line established a naval blockade of the James and York rivers at the end of August and ended Cornwallis's communications with Clinton. The French fleet under the command of Admiral de Grasse outfought the British fleet under Admiral Thomas Graves from the 5th to the 9th of September in a generally indecisive engagement. It did, however, strengthen the blockade and assured the isolation of Cornwallis's army. On 28 September, an allied army of 9,500 Americans and 7,800 French troops moved forward from Williamsburg, and two days later the siege of Yorktown commenced.

Cornwallis hurriedly wrote to Clinton: "This place is in no state of defense. If you cannot relieve me very soon, you must be prepared for the worst." The British had been fortifying Yorktown since August "a work of great time and labour," and the small town was ringed with trenches and redoubts. The settlement of Gloucester on the other bank of the York River had also been strengthened and was occupied by General O'Hara and Lieut. Col. Tarleton's troops. By 8 October the allied trenches and gun positions were ready. Cornwallis had abandoned the outer defense works and retreated into the town. Lafayette's division took over the trenches on 9 October, and heavy, accurate artillery fire was opened on the beleaguered royal troops. On 15 October, Cornwallis, who had been promised reinforcements by Clinton, wrote to his superior: The safety of this place is so precarious that I cannot recommend that the fleet and army should run the great risk in endeavoring to save us." He held out until 17 October, when he sued for an amnesty.

On 17 October Cornwallis opened negotiations for surrender, and two days later he capitulated. The siege ended with some 7,000 British soldiers as prisoners of war. The American War for Independence was over, and Britain had lost her last chance to impose the omnipotence of Parliament on her former colonies of North America.

The postmortems on the surrender at Yorktown were not dissimilar to those on the capitulation at Saratoga. AN AMERICAN REFUGEE (*MC* 12/1/81) advised his readers: "But God forbid, that the loss of these few troops should make the British despond, and give over further attempt against Virginia."

Posing a rhetorical question for his readers, REGULUS (*MC* 12/14/81) asked if they were ready to give up America. He then perceptively advised them that the war in America was now a French war:

> But is the loss of Lord Cornwallis and a few thousand troops, of such magnitude as induce you to give up America? Is the loss of a finger, because it is painful, to justify the amputation of the arm? Can such a misfortune

make Britons despond, and even abandon themselves to despair, at a time when every faculty, every sinew of the state ought to be exerted to recover our possessions, and restore the glory of our country! It is no longer an American war, but a French war in America.

As with the letter writers' reaction to the surrender at Saratoga, the call was to conquer:

PROBUS (*MC* 12/11/81):

The spirit of the nation is too high, its resources too many, not to repair his [Cornwallis's] loss, and revenge his fate . . . the die is cast, we must conquer America, or this country ceases to exist as a powerful commercial kingdom. The Americans are already exhausted in their finances . . . their paper has long since failed them. This is a war of necessity. To a commercial people, the real way of estimating our loss is reckoning the value of the men, or the money that will replace them, and the highest calculation will not exceed three quarters of a million sterling. Thus honour and necessity urge us to pursuit, while our wealth, spirit, and resources, offer the most pleasing hopes of success. This country has often received much greater blows, yet we have hitherto risen superior to them. In such a moment as this, our spirit and firmness will do wonders. The King has set the noble example, we have but to follow it.

REGULUS (*MC* 12/14/81):

The conquest [of America] is still very practicable . . . with only a small additional number of men to replace Lord Cornwallis's lost army. . . . There is not a doubt if you persevere, and adopt a proper method, that we shall subdue our enemies there.

By the year 1778, the scribblers and, it is not improper to assume, their readers were unhappy with the conduct of the war in North America. Their frustration found an appropriate outlet in the letters to the printer. Few escaped their wrath. Generals, admirals, members of the ministry or Opposition, all were subject to the scorn and ridicule of the scribblers.

No members of the military were treated with greater contempt and ridicule than Sir William Howe, commander in chief of the British army, or his brother Lord Viscount Richard Howe, Admiral of the Fleet. LUCIUS (*CM* 12/30/78) was savage in his condemnation of General Howe. The "desertion of Burgoyne," the battles of Brandywine, Germantown, and Red Bank were catalogued as the bungling of the general. Nor would it be prudent for the minister or the king to rush to the protection of so blameworthy an individual:

To Sir W.H.: You issued forth, for the conquest of America, with the fairest hopes, and under the most favourable auspices. You conducted a greater force than the New World had ever seen, nobly provided in every article, and fully adequate to the purpose of its destination. You were attended by a most powerful artillery. You were supported by a numerous fleet, under an experienced commander, of whose steady co-operation, in any purpose, you had the most perfect assurance. Your troops were distinguished for their spirit as any that Europe could produce; and they were to be opposed by a militia, at that time, without arms, ammunition, officers, or discipline. The people were zealous in the cause for which you were to fight.... You were placed in the greatest situation that could animate a human soul. For the fate of the British Empire depended on your conduct.... Permit me, Sir W. to consider how the confidence of your country has been repaid, and its expectation fulfilled. It is, at all times, the duty of a good citizen to scrutinize the conduct of men in public employments. In our present situation, indifference is a crime, and even moderation approaches to a fault.... I cannot attend you through the operations of another year. Honour and humanity recoil at the very mention of them. Your retreat from the service; your desertion of Burgoyne, and the consequent destruction of his gallant army; the loss of two months in the season for action; the attack at Brandy-Wine, decorated with the name of victory;[5] the surprise at Germantown, where the valour of your troops compensated your negligence;[6] the merited defeat and slaughter of the Hessian troops at Red Bank....[7] All these together form the most singular assemblage of t-----y and disgrace, that ever was exhibited in so short a time, or in the conduct of a single man. It defies the power of malice to discolour, or faction to exaggerate. In vain will you trust to the favour of your Sovereign, or retire under the wings of ministerial protection. The Minister himself has much to fear: And a Sovereign of Great Britain, if he wishes to be safe, must abandon his minions to the justice of the people.

The year 1779 brought little comfort for General Howe. His lack of success in America continued to give license to the press. Apprising his readers, CATO (*LC* 2/13/79) wrote:

Such, Sir W. is the career you have run. Delay without prudence, success without advantage, is the history of your campaigns. The loss of America, the ruin of your country's greatness, an indelible disgrace fixed upon the honour of its arms, the lives of many brave men sacrificed to no purpose, a foreign war—a war which may involve us in bankruptcy, and reduce our empire to this little island; these, Sir, form the melancholy catalogue of your achievements.

Nor was Lord Viscount Howe to remain untouched by the fury of the letter writers. TIMILION (*LC* 3/3/81) sought an explanation for two years of inactivity by the king's fleet:

Is not the Public and your own honour as much concerned to know why you did nothing with the King's fleet for the two years of your command, as it is to know in what year it was that you played at Chess with Dr. Franklin? And while you are thus silent upon all the most interesting, and important charges brought against you, must we unavoidably conclude, that you cannot give any satisfactory answer to them; when we see you thus eagerly attempting, whenever you can, to answer even the most trivial ones?

In addition to attacking the Howe brothers individually, the scribblers found them as enticing collectively. FIDUS ACHATES (*MC* 1/12/78) accused them of espousing the cause of the rebels in Parliament and, more importantly, of cooperating to prolong the war as a means of filling their pockets:

> I am a friend to government, love my King, and wish to see the dignity of my country supported with firmness and spirit; but I could never find out why the two Howes were sent out to command our fleets and armies, and to subdue rebels, whose cause they espoused in Parliament. Being brothers, it was said in their favour, that they would more readily co-operate in the means of conquest: but it seems not to have entered into the heads of those who sent them out, that they might co-operate to fill their pockets, and this seems to be what they have done; for the General seems to have lengthened the war, by his delay and unaccountable movements, in order to have the longer time to grow rich; and the Admiral, to let the American privateers and merchantmen escape from their ports, in order to make prizes and recaptures to enrich himself, which could not have been done if these vessels had been prevented from leaving their own ports.

ARISTIDES (2/11/80) addressed his letter of censure to Lord Viscount Howe, but it was a condemnation of the military actions of both brothers:

> On looking back to your correspondence, we find nothing in your conduct there that can do you honour; but much, very much, which we suffered in those parts, to the national disgrace. After the defeat at Long Island, when Washington and his army lay at your mercy, and either of you might have taken them all prisoners; you seem to have been as little disposed to intercept them at sea as the General on land. He gave them three days leisure to prepare for their flight over to New York; and you for six tides kept your fleet out of sight of the Ferry, as if you intended they should not be intercepted in their passage. My Lord, the taking of Washington and his whole army would have effectually disabled the rebels from ever raising another; and would have saved to his Majesty the lives of 100,000 subjects; and to the nation the expense of 50 millions.

After the surrender of an entire army, it was not to be expected that General Burgoyne was to escape the writers' hostility. The disgrace of an army lost was not to be accepted lightly. The passage of time had changed the measure of Burgoyne and his capitulation at Saratoga:

PLAIN SENSE (*PA* 5/26/78):

To Lieutenant-General Burgoyne: However you may be displeased, you cannot be surprised that you are addressed by an unknown Individual. I have felt my full Share of the general Disgrace which has fallen upon the Arms of England, intrusted to your Hands; and I am, therefore, entitled to explain to you, what Measure of Retribution I expect. General Burgoyne, you may be assured that I am touched by Feelings that are not particular; and that

I deliver not my Opinion only, but that of Millions.... Be assured that a real, and not a mock Enquiry; a perfect, and not a partial Discovery, is expected from you. Should the People be disappointed by you; rely on it, that you cannot divert their Rage to an American Commissary; or, at all interest them in a Dispute about the Rent of the Prisons in which your Army is confined; or make them Parties in litigating the Price of Bread, that sustains those Lives which were forfeited to the Courage, and spared by the Mercy of your Enemy:

A CONVENTION OFFICER (*PA* 2/18/79):
Re: The special parole granted to Burgoyne by the Congress;
I will not say that you settled your Line of Conduct with the Congress, and stipulated the Terms upon which you came Home; that was not necessary to obtain their Favour; they had sufficient Obligation to you. You had given them a British Army; you had delayed, and trifled, until they collected a Force to oppose you; sparing their frightened Fugitives who were within a Day's March of your troops, you allowed them Time to recover their spirits, and receive Reinforcements. When you surrendered, your extreme Politeness carried you to an excess of praise towards their Ragamuffins, which even they had too much sense to believe; you freely declared to them that Conquest was impossible; you persuaded them to believe so.

An unsigned letter (3/22/79):
From all of which it appears, that notwithstanding your numerous Errors before your Arrival on the Hudson River, notwithstanding your cutting off your own Supplies in the very commencement of your Campaign, a Thing unheard of, still you had three Opportunities of the fairest and fullest Success.... By such Conduct, Sir, did you defeat an Expedition conceived in Wisdom, and promising a Certainty of Success.

Despite the surrender of an army and a capitulation that ended the authority of Great Britain over the rebellious colonies, Lord Cornwallis remained essentially free from criticism. Only FABRICUS, writing for the *London Chronicle* (12/27/81) and the *Morning Chronicle* (12/28/81), censured his conduct in a reproach based on the failure of Cornwallis to fully appreciate and recognize the value of Loyalist support[8]:

His Lordship knew immediately on his arrival at Portsmouth, from the best authority, that there was a post within his reach, which he might have taken, where he would have been joined by a greater number of loyalists than that of the combined force of France and Congress, if he would accept of them on those terms upon which freemen ought to enter into military service and without which none ever will. I mean if they had been allowed to enlist under officers of their own choice, and to act only for the defense of their own provinces. This measure was earnestly recommended to his attention by his superior in command; who had abundant reason to believe and to know the certainty of success. And yet he paid no regard to this recommendation; but totally neglected a measure which would have saved his army from captivity, his country from disgrace, and in a short time have ended the rebellion.

The success of British arms in the Southern plantations was transitory. The victories on Long Island and in the Carolinas came to nought. Whatever the blunders of the military or of the ministry, the logistics of conducting a war 3,000 miles from a home base in the eighteenth century were insurmountable.

CHAPTER SEVEN

The Perfidious French

The dissension between Britain and her colonies in North America was viewed by the French as an extraordinary opportunity to revenge the defeat of the Seven Years' War.[1] As early as December 1774, Americans in London had hinted to a French diplomat that the colonists might be interested in French aid in the event that their quarrel with Britain ended in military conflict. In September 1775, the French foreign minister sent an envoy to Philadelphia to encourage the Americans and to intimate that they might have the use of French ports. In March 1776, the French asked the Spanish government whether it would join in the project and received an affirmative answer.

By 1783 the French were more than generous to the Americans. Subsidies and loans brought France's cash investment in the United States to more than eight million eighteenth-century dollars. Although the Spaniards were not as committed as the French, they also supported the Americans with cash and munitions.

News of the British victories on Long Island and reports of Burgoyne's easy capture of Ticonderoga made the French reluctant to enter the conflict. By November 1777, however, it became known in Paris that Washington's army had performed creditably at Germantown and that Baron de Kalb, who was serving with Washington, believed the colonists would drive the British into the sea. Then on 4 December came the startling news that Burgoyne had capitulated at Saratoga. The shattering blow dealt to British arms by the northern American army convinced even the most cautious Frenchman that the Americans would not readily submit. The more astute concluded, and not without reason, that since Britain would almost certainly offer concessions leading toward peace, France must move promptly if she moved at all. On 17 December, without waiting to discover whether Spain would join with France, the French foreign minister promised America formal recognition, a step certain to bring his country to a declaration of war from London.

The texts of two treaties between France and the United States were prepared and signed on 6 February despite receipt by the French of a definite refusal from Spain to join in the war. In June 1779, Spain entered the conflict when it became apparent that Britain would make no offer of concessions to ensure her neutrality.[2] (A more complete history of the relationship between the warring countries is provided in Appendix C.)

During the years 1776 through 1779, the interest of the letter writers of the British press was centered primarily on the endeavor of the French and Spanish to assist the rebellious British colonies in North America. Subsequently, they concentrated on the possibility of a direct conflict of the forces of France and Spain with Great Britain.

As early as 1776, there was both fear and apprehension among the British populace that this was an opportune time for France to declare war on Britain or that the perfidious French might well attack without the formality of a declaration. In June, CLEONITUS (*MC* 6/3/76) advised his readers that "France and Spain are hourly expected to open attack." An unsigned (9/20/76) letter in the *Morning Post* reinforced that fear: "We know that whenever they go to war with us, it will be without the formality of a declaration. . . . Never was there an opportunity so complete for the purpose as the present moment when the attack would prove the signal of undoubted success." Again in an unsigned letter (*MP* 11/25/76), the scribbler voiced the uneasiness that "the House of Bourbon means a war with us, which can hardly be doubted."

To those political writers who regarded the poor financial condition of France as a deterrent for a break of relations with Britain, BRUTUS (*MP* 10/19/76) replied:

> There are political writers, who are every day attempting to persuade us that the House of Bourbon will not, or rather cannot, break with Great Britain; from France not being ready for a war, her finances in disorder, great debts not paid, and every department of the state crying out in vain for funds to answer the demands made on them. This argument is a very false one.

Although it was limited in scale, there remained an opinion which declared that France was not about to risk an open conflict with Great Britain. COURAGE SANS PEUR (*PA* 11/1/76) declared, "It is nonsense to expect France to enter the war." LUCIUS (*MC* 8/21/76) suspected it was the king of Spain who had "designs" against Britain, but he thought that France "would rather voluntarily enter into our views."

The comforting words of a COURAGE SANS PEUR and LUCIUS did little to allay the fears that a formidable enemy was poised to invade the home island. The scribblers of the *Morning Post* were enlisted to inform their readers of the arming and the might of the forces of France and Spain. The writer MELA was chosen by that newspaper to alert its readers, and from August through the end of the year MELA's letters sounded warning:

MELA (8/21/76):

In truth, Sir, it must appear to every man of tolerable sagacity that this country stands on the brink of a precipice. France is arming, and with great speed; this is a fact, let the tools of Administration assert what they please; the fleet of Spain is formidable.

MELA (8/27/76):

The power of France is much greater than many of our politicians are willing to allow.

MELA (10/7/76):

By an appearance of friendship to Great Britain, they [France and Spain] bullied our court into a dangerous security; and have been ever since making the most formidable preparations by sea and land that ever were known in the Spanish monarchy, and of late to an equal degree in that of France.

MELA (11/11/76):

[There is] the greatest reason to believe that the House of Bourbon mediates some very great stroke inimical to this country or its allies. The accounts which came last from Spain make the fleet prepared there.... While this is doing in Spain, France is preparing very fast.

MELA (12/16/76):

Your correspondent who signs himself a Brave Briton! writes very consistently with that bullying signature. "The hour of apprehension past, through the persevering vigilance of an able ministry!" I have no doubt but this is the language of administration: But it is the language of folly and deceit; to show nothing more is necessary than to examine the force which the House of Bourbon has now actually ready for the sea and part of which may be for what he knows actually employed against us.

As was not uncommon for the British press in the eighteenth century, the *Morning Post* provided a platform for those writers dissenting with MELA. They argued that Great Britain was at the zenith of its power and that for France to challenge that power would result in certain defeat:

ANTI-MELA (6/26/76):

To weaken both [the colonies and Britain] by a tedious civil war is really their [France and Spain's] interest; and this can only be done by their keeping out of the war and supplying the Americans clandestinely, which it is probable enough they may now do with arms and ammunition. This is playing a sure game. To engage in a war would be engaging in a certain loss.

ANTI-MELA (11/15/76):

I may truly say if we are within a few years to have a war with them [France and Spain], we can never have it at a better opportunity than at present.... We can never look for more forward preparations, or a greater certainty of opposing with success any attempt which France or Spain may make upon us.

"M" (12/20/76):

Let us not therefore be apprehensive of the power of the House of Bourbon—of a family governing countries which have long been upon the
decline—of countries that have not for half a century produced a great
General, Admiral, or Statesman. This kingdom is in the zenith of vigour and
prosperity, abounding with men of the most splendid talents.... Let us not
degrade ourselves then with fears which ought rather to attend the situation
of our rivals.

Despite assurances of the might of the British fleet and its triumphant
power, there remained the fear of an invasion and conquest of the home
isles. Could Britain remain a sovereign state?:

T.H. (*LC* 8/17/76):

A plain honest man would naturally think such manoeuvres of the French
Court should mean something very material seeing that a body of 25,000
as fine troops as any in Europe may be collected together in twenty-four
hours, within twenty-two miles from the English coast, no ships to impede
their passage across the channel, no garrisons to oppose their landings on
any spot.

MELA (*MP* 12/6/76):

If we were at present attacked very moderately in the East and West Indies,
and on the continent of North America,—should we attempt to defend them
we should be open not only to invasion but conquest.

RALEIGH (*PA* 11/19/76):

The ineffectual attempts to raise the falling Stocks—the poor success of the
Press for Sailors—the large demand for the Service—the recent Bankruptcy,
and melancholy Certainty of more—the multitude of our ships that are every
day and everywhere taken by the American Privateers,—all these circumstances combine to show with irresistible conviction, that our danger is imminent and our distress infinite.... That France and Spain may have a
superior Fleet at sea in the Spring to any we can possibly produce, is beyond
a question. With fifty thousand French Troops landed in England, under
that superiority at Sea, let me ask the boldest man living, HOW LONG WE
SHALL EXIST AS A SOVEREIGN STATE?

PACIFICUS (*MC* 9/4/76 and *LC* 9/5/76) reassured his readers on the
prospect of a war with France and Spain, saying that the law of nations
would not permit such an endeavor:

The disaffected Republicans, elated with the late affair at Charles-Town,
but dreading at the same time the success of General Howe in putting a
speedy end to rebellion, flatter themselves that the Court of France and
Spain will seize the glorious opportunity, which, in their opinion, now offers
to impose their own terms on the subjugated English.
The law of nations—received opinions in every civilized country—
common policy—the dread of retaliation—All these combined motives must

militate against the preposterous idea of one state drawing the sword against another, for the sole and express purpose of forming an alliance with subjects in rebellion.

If the French in the island of Martinico, or the Spaniards in Mexico and Peru, were to declare war against their King, would it be advisable, would it be sound policy, to say nothing of justice and honour, for the King of England, in times of perfect peace with his neighbours, immediately to join issue with such rebellious subjects, and for no other reason but because it is mighty convenient to assist Rebels?

Moreover, if the French or Spanish had ever seriously thought of attending to the solicitations of the Congress . . . in order to reduce this country to an abject submission to any terms that might be imposed on her, the French and Spanish Courts would not surely have delayed their hostilities, until we had an army of upwards of forty thousand men in America, and a fleet of ships superior to any maritime force that can be opposed to us.

It was not only the law of nations, but the simple fact that many of the states were friendly to Britain and the rest were not in a position to hurt her that reassured A YEOMAN OF KENT (*MP* 10/9/76): "The public are amused from time to time with paragraphs inserted by authority, that none of the powers of Europe are likely to take advantage of England's being so deeply engaged in this American war; as many of the states are in strict amity and alliance with us, and the rest, however disaffected, are not in a condition to hurt us."

All of the above related to the conflict which had surfaced between the empires of France, Spain, and Great Britain. What were the readers of the newspapers thinking about America, the cradle of the conflict? It was the aid which France had chosen to afford America and the possibility of that assistance resulting in the independence of America which had brought on the threat of war between the great powers. To the scribblers of the *Morning Post*, the independence of America would be the undoing of both France and Spain:

ANTI-MELA (*MP* 9/17/76):

France has been known to move only with its own interest. If North America becomes independent she will infallibly become a great commercial and naval power. . . . They will carry their free trade and bold spirit into all the ports of Spanish America. . . Spain would be undone. . . . Would this be in the interest of France, or the Bourbon family? Yet they are natural consequences of the independency of North America.

ANTI-REBEL (*MP* 10/25/76):

I have no suspicion of a French or Spanish war . . . of what possible advantage would the independency of America be to them. . . . If the Americans were independent of Britain and allowed to build what ships of force they pleased, they would soon possess themselves of all the French and Spanish property.

To many a letter writer in 1776, Great Britain had the option of scaling down her efforts in America or completely eliminating them. The important problem was to deal with the threat of France and Spain:

ANTI-MELA (*MP* 6/25/76):

We should abandon the American war to the frigates, and fall with a heavier weight than ever upon France and Spain.

A.B. (5/3/76):

We shall be fully and deeply committed in the present mad and villainous war with America; in which with all our strength, while we are ignorantly destroying ourselves, France may easily accomplish her purpose and gratify her resentment.

RALEIGH (*PA* 12/3/76):

The only alternative remaining is the ruin of the Empire, or the recall of our Fleet and Army from America. . . . Inaction at New York and despair on the side of Lake Champlain seem to close the prospect of this Campaign. His Majesty has been pleased to tell us that we must look forward to another Campaign. But has he given us any ground to look forward to it with Hope? In this dangerous and almost desperate situation of our affairs we rely upon Ministers who have proved themselves less vigilant and less informed than almost any other men in the Nation. Every man saw the preparations of France and Spain for months before they perceived them. . . . What reasonable hope can we have of meeting them at sea, if they should choose to attack us; and, with Hope lost, what can remain for us but absolute despair and ruin.

There was little change in the principal problems facing the British in 1777. The debate of war or no war continued, as did the fear of invasion and the arming and formidable power of the French and Spanish. And, of course, hostilities continued in America. What was added to the polemic, as perhaps fits a people with great problems, was a pinch of unreality, of fantasy. The *Morning Chronicle* in an unsigned letter (3/19/77) reported that the king of France had ordered all American ships to leave the kingdom.

Writing for the *Morning Post* (7/21/77) in a letter that was copied by the *London Chronicle* (7/24/77), TITUS had a singular scheme to free British troops from America for a war against France and to continue the subjugation of the rebellious colonies:

We have a gallant fleet ready for sea; and if the frigates at present in America were to convoy Sir William Howe's forces from thence to the West Indies, certain it is there is no power there to resist him. . . . As to North America it would be very wise to convoy 50,000 Russians, Prussians, and Germans to that continent; to leave them to themselves unattended by a fleet on condition of conquering for us.

Fantasy or no, the problems for the British remained the same. The question of war became paramount in the polemic of the scribblers. The

Morning Post designated the scribbler MELA to continue as its spokesman and to caution the readers of that newspaper about the growing threat afforded by the French and Spanish to the British Isles.

MELA (*LC* 2/1/77):

As the preparations of France and Spain give so much reason for suspecting that they mean no friendship to this country; so we may, without danger of exaggeration, assert, that they could never wish for a better opportunity to quarrel than the present one, while we are so deeply and dangerously engaged with an American Rebellion.

MELA (*MP* 2/5/77):

The successes which have rendered the campaign in America so brilliant will instead of proving the speedy means of peace and establishment, occasion a general war . . . more expense being certain ruin to Great Britain whether victories or defeats are the consequence. . . . Upon this principle a French Minister must infallibly consider the present crisis as an opportunity too valuable to be missed. North Americans now would be united with themselves.

MELA (*MP* 2/14/77):

If time has matured the ill disposition of the Americans into a revolt, and we find our hands almost full in bringing them to obedience, is it surprising that the House of Bourbon should think it a favourable opportunity to attack us?

MELA (*MP* 7/10/77):

When I see five millions sterling borrowed in one year to support a struggle with our own subjects, I cannot avoid calculating what must be had to carry us through the war not only with those subjects, but with France and Spain at the same time. France and Spain are completely armed and wait for the favourable opportunity to attack us. Let a Spanish armament sail for Ireland—the Brest one for the Thames—the immense force in the West Indies attack our Island there—and a war break out in the heart of our oriental possessions . . . armies, fleets unpaid . . . the country in confusion and the enemy at the gate.

Letter writer NUMA (*MP* 4/2/77) accused the perfidious French ministers of speaking nothing but peace, while their actions spoke of war:

Every day—I might say every hour as the season advances, the designs of the House of Bourbon become more suspicious. Nothing can exceed the friendship which seems to animate their professions—but while the memorials of their ministers and secretaries are thus overflowing with assurances of peace, their motions speak nothing but immediate war.

The scribbler who had been most vigorous in alerting his readers to the arming of the French and Spanish, MELA (*MP* 7/23/77), now recommended an immediate declaration of war:

> That country [France] is now in the possession of the greatest game ever
> played: she is every hour securing to herself the whole trade and advantage
> of British America; and she is carrying on a most successful war against Brit-
> ain without suffering the expense, losses, or danger of a war in return....
> The French were fitting out many privateers to cruise upon the trade of
> England under American colours.... Britain will learn when it is too late
> that she has nothing to trust but an open war, as far preferable to so
> dangerous and insidious a peace.

The ministerial writers refused to accept the possibility of France
or Spain ready and able to attack Britain. Countless reasons were offered
to counteract the theory of an impending assault. NUMA (*MP* 3/10/77 and
LC 3/11/77) suggested that France and Spain would continue to arm, but
would not openly declare war. He believed that France fully appreciated
that a war would scarcely give her anything of importance, and the independence of America would not be to her benefit: "They [France] certainly will arm in proportion as you increase your forces in America, but
they will do nothing more; a war could scarcely give them anything of importance; but if it established the independence of America, it would lay
the foundation of what would take away all that Dr. Franklin can offer
them for their assistance."

COURAGE SANS PEUR (*MC* 1/2/77) was persuaded that "the French navy
is not in a condition to make face against us, neither are their finances in
any order to undertake a war." Suggesting to his readers that all talk of war
was simply a "chimera," ANTI-MELA (*MP* 2/10/77) wrote: "Nothing appears
clearer than the futility of apprehensions which are daily expressed as if that
[war] was an unavoidable event, which in fact is only a chimera in the brains
of some distempered politicians!"

VIGILANS (*MP* 3/12/77) found little reason to fear a combined attack
of the French and Americans: "I am not at all apprehensive of a French
army united with an American one; such allies would be quarrelling among
themselves before half a campaign was over."

NUMA (*MP* 3/27/77) was satisfied that French involvement in Europe
would preclude any acts of war against Britain:

> In such a general squabble and confusion [in Europe] what probability,
> possibility I might say, is there that Great Britain armed and prepared as she
> is should be engaged with the House of Bourbon.... There is every prospect
> of seeing that House so well employed in Europe, as to leave them not even
> the ability of assisting the rebellious Americans.

Once again NUMA (*MP* 5/14/77) assured his readers that there was little
reason to fear a war with France. "If France really means not to break
with us, her policy will be to supply them [Americans] most powerfully
underhand." Undoubtedly this was a practice expected of the perfidious
French.

The fear of invasion now gripped the pens of many a scribbler. TITUS (*MP* 3/5/77) warned his readers of the danger presented by a formidable Spanish navy in addition to the continuing preparations of the French:

> The Spanish navy never was more formidable than at this time. . . . It is also certain that they have 16,000 of the best troops of Spain encamped near Cadiz; which there is from transports and other circumstances every reason to believe intended for Ireland. . . . French preparations go on with a vigour and accelerity. . . . If they should pour into Scotland and England, while Spain attacks Ireland, and with that formidable power they have in the West Indies and the Isle of France, attack us both in the East and West, while so great a part of our force is tied down to North America—how shall we be able to resist it?

Fear of invasion intensified; MELA (*MP* 6/10/77) was distressed at the inadequacy of the British navy when measured against the combined fleets of France and Spain. His chagrin was directed to Lord Sandwich:

> Report says that we have 27 sail, but suspicions are abroad that they are not all manned, which is an object of the highest consequence—yet, Sir, does the fate of the kingdom depend on our fleet. What pretensions do any men in power have to a force equal to resist the forty-three said of line of battle ships [France and Spain]? I must be free to assert that I have heard of none. . . . As to the smaller ones, the enemy has them in great numbers, while the American station has left us quite defenceless as to them; we have in one word none.

Invasion, wrote CRITO, (*LC* 9/11/77 and *PA* 9/13/77), was imminent: "In case of a war with France, whether it may happen this, next, or the Year after, I have good reason to believe we shall find an invasion of this Island will be among the first operations of it."

There were writers, however, who were confident of the power and strength of British arms. The British navy, they assured their readers, was capable of repelling all attacks of the French and Spanish fleets:

An unsigned letter (*MC* 6/7/77):

> To remove any apprehensions which weak and ignorant people may entertain of danger from a French war, I enclose a list of our men of war that are now actually at sea, fully manned. This force now on our coast is sufficient to bid defiance to all the naval force of France and Spain.

COURAGE SANS PEUR (*MC* 8/29/77):

> Nor are they [French navy] in any way capable of making head against the British fleet . . . a force sufficient to make the boasted navy of France cut as contemptible a figure as they did in the last war.

NUMA (3/18/77):

> If advices were now to come of the French, of Spaniards, or both commencing hostilities against us, we should by a sudden exertion, and two or three

days more vigorous press, be able to send forty-five sail of the line to sea; a force much more than sufficient to repel the whole power of the House of Bourbon.

Not only was Britain prepared to resist any military incursions by the French, but NUMA advised his readers in the *Morning Post* and the *London Chronicle* that the poor financial condition of France could hardly support a war.

NUMA (*MP* 7/27/77):

The Gentlemen who imagine we are on the verge of a French war and full of apprehensions at it, do not consider the state of the finances of that monarchy. It is a fact known to all the world that they run in debt considerably every year by anticipations of their revenue in order to support their reduced peace establishments; where then are they to find supplies for a war which according to all appearances would be general. To reduce the power of Great Britain is no part of a pacific administration in France, for it is not at all inconsistent with the welfare of that kingdom.

NUMA (*LC* 6/26/77):

British politicians who are disgusted with administration make it, at present, a fashion to represent the power of France, at this moment, as so great as to threaten the very existence of this empire. I have many reasons for entirely dissenting from that opinion, and for believing on the contrary, that if that kingdom was from the most erroneous policy that ever yet influenced her councils, to attack this country in support of the rebellious Americans, that she would engage in a war far more ruinous to herself than to us. From hence it appears that the French ministry for a war must create new taxes, or seize on new revenues ... the wren pecking at the Eagle.

There were other means to defeat the designs of the French. A reconciliation between Britain and her North American colonies would prove of equal advantage to mother and child:

PASTOR FIDO (*MP* 12/23/77):

If England and America do not soon shake hands together, the determined and hereditary enemies of this nation are meditating a blow which if they are allowed to strike, will effectually ruin Britain and her Colonies.

GUSTAVUS VASA (*MP* 7/24/77):

America has now declared her independency of the mother; it is the duty of every honest man who has the real good of his country at heart to wish a reconciliation that will prove of equal advantage to Britain and her colonies; those who wish otherwise, if any there should be, are enemies to the state and traitors to their King and country. The ratification of the Treaty of Paris was a more desperate wound to the commercial glory of this country than any that had ever before been given; and it was from that moment that America began to think seriously of independency and that France beheld the sunshine of commercial splendour breaking in upon her empire. It was then that the French Administration displayed to all Europe their penetration and superior wisdom in establishing a treaty of peace after an unsuccessful war, that would not only soon repay the nation the many millions they had lost, but they also saw an ample field opening into view that would soon gratify their revenge upon this country without drawing the sword against her.

If all else failed, there was still the hope that France would be so embroiled in the conflicts of Europe that she would have little time to discomfit Britain:

NUMA (*PA* 4/7/77):

English politicians will persuade themselves that the preparations of France and Spain because they are formidable must be designed against them: nothing farther from the truth. . . . The tensions in Eastern Europe would be infinitely more formidable and dangerous to the security and importance of the House of Bourbon than anything within the compass of Great Britain to effect.

Scribbler "x" (*MP* 5/22/77) was convinced, and so counseled his readers, that the "law of nations" would confine the war between Great Britain and her rebellious colonies to just that. The Americans were, in truth, revolting against Europe, and should meet with European chastisement:

I have said it is the duty of every state, because there is a general system of law called the law of nations which each state is as much bound to observe the law of the district wherein he resides; a violation of the law of nations is as much reprehensible in a state as a violation of the particular law of a district is to an individual. . . . Law is the protection of property. . . . It is strange that any European port has ever suffered the Americans either to trade with them or to dispose of prizes there; it is so easily discerned that such permission is not only a breach of the law which ought to subsist among nations, but an opening to piracy, and robbing. The restriction of a nation, and restriction of an individual to due observance of the law is sound policy and truly consistent with liberty . . . for what is liberty without law to protect it? The dispute being only betwixt Great Britain and America, there it should be confined; and as America is revolting against Europe, so should it meet with European chastisement, rather than encouragement.

The year 1778 was hardly under way when news reached London that the French and Americans had on 6 February signed a Treaty of Amity and Commerce as well as a Treaty of Alliance. The press reaction was foreseeable. War was now the centerpiece of the polemic. Letter writers filled the press with notions of Britain triumphant, peace and reconciliation, and condemnation of the ministry. Now that the French had clearly revealed their intentions toward America, it was necessary and proper for Britain to declare war on her traditional enemy without delay.

MENTES (*CM* 9/14/78) wrote of a group of men aligned to no party, men who never would have wished Great Britain to rush into a war with France. Now, however, that the die was cast, they favored a vigorous prosecution of the war:

> There yet remains a set of men among us, bigoted to no party. These men say, that as the Spirit of a Nation evaporates in airy flights, so likewise it must be buried in low submission. It is their opinion, that though baffled, we are not yet totally defeated, even in America. They would not have us give up our claim to the dependence of America, nor withdraw our forces from thence. These were the men who never would have wished Great Britain wantonly to precipitate herself into a war with France; but the die being now cast, they would have her prosecute the war with a vigour becoming itself.

A warning of a revengeful France and Spain came from the pen of ANTI-DECEPTOR (*LC* 7/25/78): "The present opportunity of weakening Great Britain, and revenging themselves, is too tempting to admit of a supposition that they [France and Spain] will not take advantage of it; therefore our ministers are unpardonable if they have not prepared for such an event."

BRITTANNICUS (*PA* 8/1/78) recommended an immediate declaration of war and predicted universal support from the people: "His Majesty immediately declaring war against the perfidious Family of the Bourbons, would re-unite his People; all his good subjects would join and applaud him, and Britain, now abject, would once more become glorious and triumphant."

For T.D. (*MC* 5/7/78), the perfidious French were attacking the dignity of Great Britain, and every true Englishman should strive to punish them:

> History does not furnish an instance of a stronger or more flagrant aggression on the dignity of this realm, than the affront we have received from France; it ought therefore to be the ardent wish of every true Englishman that our utmost endeavour should be exerted to punish this unprovoked insolence, whatever sentiments he may entertain with respect to the merits of our unfortunate contest with America. War should have been declared immediately after the notification of the French Ambassador, and prosecuted with vigour.

Addressed the king to endorse an immediate declaration of war, MILES (*MP* 1/10/78) assured his readers Britain would prevail:

> To the King: The present juncture of affairs is so critical, and the honour of the nation so tremblingly alive, that a war with France to be immediately declared, can alone prevent the imputation of supineness, can alone preserve pure, and unsullied the dignity of the crown. Although it is too true that the savage monster of rebellion has in some degree baffled the British Lion, at last has not totally been overcome, yet we should consider that the fury of the latter has not been half roused, and that the generosity and gentleness

of his noble nature, would wish only to chastise, not entirely destroy. The transparent gleam of victorious moonshine that enlightened America for a moment, shall now be lost in the clouds and darkness of repentance, in the midnight horrors of despair! She will now crouch like a slave at the lightening of Britannia's lance; and tho' France, as a step-mother, should aid the daring parricide, yet shall they find too late, that not all their united power can conquer, or alarm a nation, who have Right for their champion, and Valour and Humanity for their Sovereign.

The bard "w" (*MC* 7/4/78) expressed his belief that war with France was imminent:

> Farewell the scythe, the sickle and the plough,
> Farewell the nymph, but with a lover's vow;
> Farewell to rustic toil and awkward gait,
> 'Tis honour calls, and to defend the state.
> 'Tis British courage fired with martial zeal,
> For Britain's sons will fight for Britain's weal.
> Let France her legions boast, make naval brags,
> Courageous Britons will pull down her flags.

HISTORICUS (*LC* 9/10/78) reminded his readers that the race is not always to the swift, nor the battle to the strong. Contrary to reports in the press, A MEMBER (*PA* 5/2/78) supported the ministry and found no evidence of tardy preparation of the fleet:

> Men ought to consider that the placing of a Nation in a Train of Safety at Home, and in a Condition to act offensively Abroad, is not the Work of a Day; and I will venture to affirm, that not a Moment has been lost, nor any necessary Measure neglected in accomplishing those two great ends.... Preparation being so much advanced, Action must immediately follow. The most formidable Fleet that perhaps ever covered the Ocean will sail next Week. The Skill of the Commander, the Spirit of Officers, the known Bravery of our Sailors, seem to promise certain success. In short, I will venture to foretell, that, in less than two Months, France will sincerely repent her having espoused the Cause of Rebels, against an Empire, as capable as ever to correct her Folly, and to chastise her Insolence.

The writer signing his name A BRITON (*LC* 9/10/78) agreed that "the time is near at hand, perhaps before this shall be announced to my countrymen, of the proud Monsieurs changing their tone and bluster, having received a drubbing from the English fleet."

A shortage of seamen to fully man the British fleet had plagued the military since the beginning of the war in North America, as the colonies were no longer a source of sailors for the British navy. MERCATOR (*MP* 7/7/78) considered the problem solved with the arrival of the West India Fleet:

> The commodities the ships [West India Fleet] bring home, will not be more acceptable to the merchants, and individuals, than the hands will be useful to the State at large. The men of war, who wanted some men to complete their complement, in order to join Admiral Keppel, will now find a sufficient number; so that we shall immediately be able to teach France what it is to rouse the British Lion!

With a powerful navy commanding the seas, the fear of a French invasion subsided. England was ready. A TRUE BRITON (*LC* 7/2/78) scoffed at the idea of an assault from the fleet of the House of Bourbon: "A great deal has been said about the naval armament at Brest, in order to alarm our fellow subjects, as if an invasion of this country required nothing more than a favourable wind for three hours, and could be performed as easily as commanded."

AN ENGLISHMAN (*MP* 8/1/78) was perhaps more eloquent, but the message was the same:

> I will admit that the American war has from a variety of causes been attended with unfortunate effects; I will also admit that the perfidious interposition of France will prolong, and increase the expense of that war; but that the noble, the martial ardour, which ever animates the breasts of Englishmen, is or can be suppressed by these unavoidable difficulties, I hope I shall never admit. Can any man when he is assured that we have a fleet at sea, for the defence of our coast only, consisting of thirty capital ships of the line, exclusive of frigates manned by brave British tars, and commanded by the noblest spirits of the age, with the gallant Keppel at their head; I say, can any man when he is assured of this fact, feel the least anxiety for the safety of this island? But my friends were there not a single soldier in the field, and France should dare to attempt an invasion, he would ill deserve the name of Briton, who did not leave his dearest ties and connections, and fly to the banner of his King and country, to redeem, to vindicate their honour.

By 1778, France had completed her treaties with America; Britain was left in the unfortunate position of conducting an unsuccessful war some 3000 miles from home. Although Spain had not yet declared its intentions, France had recalled her ambassador from Briton and a state of war existed. The people of Britain were anxious, and part of that anxiety showed itself in a press less than sympathetic towards the North ministry. It was believed to be a corrupt and debased ministry that had precipitated a war with the French and put the British Empire on the brink of ruin.

Although some two years had elapsed since America had issued her Declaration of Independence, it was not until 1778 that the scribblers of the British press appreciated the reality of the circumstance. France was now a declared ally of the rebellious colonies. British arms in America had failed to produce the expected victories, and the supremacy of the British fleet was in question. How was Britain to handle American's assertion of independence? The letter writers, undoubtedly representing the dilemma of the British populace, offered a multiplicity of options.

The letters published by the *Public Advertiser, London Chronicle,* and *Morning Post* favored independence for America; the *Caledonian Mercury* suggested reconciliation; and the *Morning Chronicle* seemed to search for a compromise. NOVANGLUS (*MC* 2/28/78) sought an equitable, honourable, and permanent accommodation of all differences in order to return to a natural connection between America and Great Britain:

> It is evident, that a connection or alliance with some reputable maritime power is indispensably necessary to the colonies. An alliance with France, is in every respect as unnatural as their connection with Great Britain is natural. They sucked in prejudices against Frenchmen with their mother's milk. The antipathy has been strengthened by reason and habit. They do violence to their own feelings in holding any kind of commerce with France. Nor is the intercourse much better relished by the French themselves.... I cannot entertain a doubt, but that if a treaty can be but once entered upon, an equitable, honourable, and permanent accommodation of all differences between the two countries will be the result.

A BRITON in the *Caledonian Mercury* (10/19/78) was persuaded that brotherly love would heal the breach between England and America. France and Spain were the common enemies:

> In the present critical conjecture of affairs, not only our own freedom depends upon our conduct, but the freedom, welfare, and preservation of our American colonies. Almost ruined by intestine broils, during an extensive, unnatural war with their parent state, the United Provinces begin to see into the duplicity of our common enemies, the French and Spaniards. The arrogance of the former, in the American service, is become disgusting to men used to civility, and to be treated with brotherly love, as was the case between them and England before the unhappy dispute commenced; and no doubt will gladly heal the breach already made, to the mutual joy of each other as soon as opportunity permits: but on the contrary, if we continue perplexed and irresolute, both parties must suffer...: We boast of public spirit and patriotism, let us show it in our unanimity; let us make choice of some plan or other after our re-union, and pursue it with vigour.... Let the business of the British empire go on to crown the mother and the daughter with immortal glory.

The scribblers of the *London Chronicle, Morning Post,* and *Public Advertiser* hoped that if American independence were granted the former rebellious colonies might be an eager ally in the war against France. ACADEMICUS (*LC* 4/16/78) suggested that Britain and the colonies join in a concerted attack on France:

> We are not in a situation to repel a numerous well disciplined army from France. Therefore, as the Americans are determined to resist to the last drop

of blood, as there is little appearance of success on our part, it appears to me that the present war should be discontinued. This of course would establish the independency of America, which I have endeavoured to show, in the course of this debate, would be a very happy resolution for both countries. Let us, therefore, recall our armies from America, put the West India Islands in a respectable state of defence, and let us fall upon the French with full and united force that we may humble the ambition and arrogance of that perfidious court.

On 21 June 1779, Spain declared war against Great Britain. She made no alliance with America and refused to recognize her independence, but began joint naval operations with France. The entry of Spain into the conflict raised the concern of the British scribblers. In April, before Spain declared her intentions, DION (*MP* 4/22/79) expressed his contempt for the Spanish military:

A war in the present situation of Spain would inevitably be only one effort; they might send their Cadiz fleet for four or five months to join the French, but if it was not attended with all the success they expected, they could not support the exertion. An Army would be sent against Gibraltar, but it would be only to exhaust themselves. At the same time that these disgraces would inevitably attend the measure, their trade would be ruined, and the wealth of America be at once arrested by the British Cruisers and privateers. Thus we have, as we always had, every thing to hope for from a Spanish war, and nothing to fear.

CIVIS (*MP* 7/20/79) expounded the same want of anxiety for the force of Spanish arms because he believed that Spain, already at war, nonetheless trembled at the thought of losing her colonies in the New World. The independence of America would make this loss a fait accompli:

Learn, Sir, from the cautious wording of the Spanish manifesto that haughty Spain fears us, even while she is daring enough to insult us. She has colonies herself; and trembles lest we should spirit them up to a rebellion, which might rob her of the golden possessions of Mexico and Peru. She studiously avoids giving any opinion relative to the war in America, because she must, by a declaration in favour of American independence, virtually free her own colonies for allegiance to and dependence on old Spain.

Open warfare with France and French treaties with America were events that were now firmly placed in history. AMERICA AMICUS was nominated by the *Morning Chronicle* to address the Americans and enlighten them of the treachery of the perfidious French. An alliance between a deceitful Congress and the scheming French could only lead to the destruction of America:

AMERICA AMICUS (*MC* 7/31/79):
It seemed irreconcilable with common sense, that you, the Americans in general, should not desert these incendiary imposters [Adams and others of

the Congress], and embrace the terms which were to be offered for your return to your former happiness. This, I expected, would be the event, in spite of all that seduction and falsehood could urge on your side of the water, by those who were in search of supreme power, or by those in Opposition on this side, who, by their speeches and correspondence, have fastened the prolongation of the war for the same end in this kingdom. In this opinion, however, I was deceived; but when the news, that the Congress had entered into an alliance with the French King, was first known to me, I exulting cried, "Surely this procedure will remove that film which has so long obscured the fight of the Americans; they will now clearly discern the desperation of the Congress, and that they are determined to bring destruction on that country, rather than resign the power which they have usurped; for is it possible to be convinced that the King of France can entertain an idea of making the Americans independent of Great Britain, but for the sake of enslaving them to himself?"

AMERICA AMICUS (*MC* 8/4/79):

You will still continue to be seduced by the Congress, and by the treacherous delusion of the Opposition in this kingdom, to believe that France or Spain can have your independence in view, could be the same thing with concluding, that you intend to ruin your country, and to enslave yourselves. I shall show you with what art both France and Spain have gradually proceeded to make you dependent on themselves whilst they profess to make you independent of all nations.

AMERICA AMICUS (*MC* 8/9/79):

The strongest agitations which possessed the French and Spanish were their fears lest the arms of Great Britain should be enabled to subdue you in a short time; and thereby frustrate all their hopes of reducing you and this kingdom; but when the conduct of General Howe in Long Island, permitted your forces to escape undiminished. . . . Notwithstanding this diminution of your anxiety, there still remained no small dread of reconciliation between you and your parent state, and of consequence of the fatal effects which would thence result, and repay them for their insidious transactions. To remove this terror, the seduction of old Franklin, and the imperial intentions of the Congress prompted the latter to declare the American provinces to be independent of Great Britain, by this event and by that at Saratoga, which raised you from little less than despondence, the French were induced to advance, more openly in your pretended interest, but they nevertheless preserved, as much as possible, the original plan of reducing both you and this nation to all possible impotence.

The scribblers of the British press were unanimous in their condemnation of the perfidious French. Their denunciation was simply a reflection of the convictions of their readers. Fear of invasion, loss of trade, and the eclipse of empire, brought every Englishman to fever pitch. The castigation of the French was perhaps the only subject that resulted in near unanimity among the letter writers.

CHAPTER EIGHT

Despair

Early in 1776, less than one year after the news of Lexington and Concord had reached London, letters to the printer were beginning to reflect a general dissatisfaction with the war in North America that grew into the frustration and despair that extended into the press for the remainder of the war. Those early letters represented a wide-ranging displeasure with the conduct of the war and with the war itself. They reached their zenith in the years 1776 and 1777 and remained significant in 1778, but were gradually replaced by letters portraying the promising circumstance and the golden future of the British in America.

Among other aspects of vexation, the letters gave voice to a general depression. That depression was not confined to one or two of the newspapers, but reached deep into nearly all of them. Nothing but evil could result from the war. It was a despondency so intense that it was better to shun the news from North America than become exposed to the reality. So wrote A BRITON in the *Public Advertiser* (9/20/76):

> An humble by-stander being lately asked what his conjecture might be on the news so anxiously expected from America, in the actual position of things there he gave the following answer: "That he had not for himself any the least curiosity; and thought that any contingency there infinitely beneath the Public Impatience; not that the stake was not of the highest importance to every individual of the Nation that was capable of feeling for its welfare; but because, in the Manner that the Game was a-playing, it was morally and politically impossible for anything satisfactory to result from it, and since, Knowledge was but Sorrow's Spy, it was better not to know." What hope then remains for this distracted Country? Surely little or none. Even to point out the obstacles to retrieval of all this execrable discordance into Harmony, would be but a vain Task, since there is but too much reason for not presuming any likelihood of their removal. On the present face of things then, what remains there for the impotency of good intentions, unseconded by so much as the shadow of hope, but a wish of seeing the sovereign convinced, at length, by his own melancholic experience, resolutely open his eyes on all the cruel detriment to his service and to his Honour, from friends at once

so very false and so very inferior to the trust he has been seduced to repose in them?

For A BYE-STANDER (*PA* 10/21/76: LC 10/22/76) the late action at Long Island was only the beginnings of bad times:

> I find that the late action at Long Island has made a considerable impression upon the Public; the friends of ministry thinking everything gained, the friends of America every thing lost. For my own part, I suppose it only the beginning of sorrow. War is various; man is various. The conqueror at the end of a war has perhaps only won half as many battles that were fought in the course of it; and the very men that gained one battle by their firmness, lost another by their panics. At Bunker Hill, Quebec, and Long Island we have succeeded; at St. John's, Charleston, and in the maintaining possession of Boston we have failed. But because the last action was in our favour, we think we are to succeed in the next. But liberty, Mr. Printer, takes a great deal of killing; and while east and west are the Geographer's distinction, the courage of free men is the same thing on both sides of the Atlantic. The unexperienced cowardice of their militia is now lost in a standing army; yet prejudice assimilating every thing to its preconceptions, and American's bravery is called his bold day, or the bravery of safety and entrenchments; and if our own men are pricked on to action, we say, the devil could not stand the fire, the situation was against us; or allow with composure that an Englishman, like other men, may feel fear. The Americans are daily improving in arms and in hatred; their country is a continued fortress; they are the native engineers in it; action will soon mark out their Generals; and their numbers are easily recruited. I repeat then, we see only the beginning of sorrows—benefits to neither—misery to both. It will have little effect upon me to hear that New York is taken or that the works at King's Bridge are forced: they have laid their account in the possibility of these things and almost expected them. I shall only ask, do the Americans despond? Is more than one province conquered? Or can a single regiment march from one end of the continent to the other? Till General Howe can answer these questions favourable to his country, I say war is before him; a growing war, a war that may be joined in issue, in a year or two, with a foreign war.

Regarding the matter of courage, liberty, and the military expertise of the Americans, PHONCION (*PA* 6/28/75) elaborated on the fears of A BYE STANDER:

> Among sensible men the chief hope of our long remaining the Sovereign of America was founded upon the supposed facility we would have in crushing their first attempts towards rebellion. From the concurrence of a thousand unhappy circumstances we have let slip the golden opportunity. We are no longer to deal with an Alliance ill enough cemented to be broken by the first external shock, or ready to dissolve by the first internal fermentation, with a Government wavering and unstable, with a people too unskilled in the way of employing their resources to be deemed formidable, with soldiers uninured to warfare, or not sufficiently drubbed into heroism to cope with

ours. We must now contend with a Nation which emerging from the first disorders of an altered constitution has assumed a regular and solid form of Government, which become acquainted with the extent of its resources, has established a settled revenue, and levied Troops, who, if we adopt the solid impartial principle that the characters of men depend chiefly on moral circumstances must soon be equal to our own.... As for what may be the final end of this dispute I will not pretend even to hint an opinion. Although there cannot in nature be any such thing as absolute Chance, yet relatively to us there is almost nothing else.

Speaking of the military prospects of British forces in America, MR. GLOVER (*MP* 7/1/76) could only anticipate a grim future:

These [Americans], many hundred thousands in multitude, with enthusiasm in their hearts, with the petition, the bill of rights, and the acts of settlement, silent and obsolete in some places, but vociferous and fresh as newly born among them—these hot with the blood of their progenitors [English] the enthusiastic scourges at one period, and the revolutional expellers of tyranny at another; these, unpractised in frivolous dissipation, and ruinous profusion, standing—armed on the spot, delivered down from their fathers, a property not moveable, nor exposed to total destruction, therefore maintainable, and exciting all the spirit and vigour of defence; these under such circumstances of number, animation, and manners . . . are we to encounter with a handful of men, sent three thousand miles over the ocean to seek such adversaries on their own paternal ground.

Again and again scribblers cautioned their readers that the task of conquering and successfully occupying the rebellious colonies might be beyond the capabilities of the British forces. In the *Morning Post* (4/2/76), BROMFIELD wrote: "For this kingdom to pretend to conquer and hold by the sword a country more than ten times as big as itself, and already abounding with millions of inhabitants and those rapidly increasing, is more ridiculous and absurd than our former wars in Judea, France, Flanders or Germany."

The majority of scribblers were convinced that the loss of America would bring impending misfortune; Britain would be void of a friend and powerful ally. JUVENIS (*MC* 8/23/76) regretted the loss of the affections of her alienated colonies." MELA (*MP* 5/31/75) wrote of the loss of an ally: "No one can with good reason doubt that [when] we have lost the continent of North America, we lose with it the assistance of three millions of people in time of war." Lamenting the loss of countrymen, friends, and allies, AN ENGLISHMAN (*PA* 2/3/76) wrote: "What ought most dearly concern us, we have parted with a people who have for ages past been to us most cordial as countrymen, most affectionate as friends, most faithful allies."

But Britain was a trading nation, and uppermost in the minds and pens of the scribblers was the loss of trade with the colonies. The discontinuation of the exclusive trade with the Americans would precipitate a multitude of related difficulties. The damage to credit, the decrease in revenue, and the injury to the sinking fund were issues attended with great care.

Reminding his readers of the original purpose of the colonies and the value of their trade, THE MERCHANT (*MP* 8/27/76) ridiculed the ministry:

> General Use of the Colonies: There are two great parties at present in England, one for the Americans, and the other against them; and the temporary object of their failure of success envelop too much of every argument concerning the colonization. One says the loss of the American trade will ruin the kingdom; another that we do not feel it as the sinking fund does not suffer; but let both parties consider what is the general use of colonies, and how they operate upon the interest of the nation that plants them. They are a regular demand for the manufactures of a country. Other exportations are subject to many vicissitudes, to duties laid by foreign powers or encouragement given to rivals, but an export to a colony that is treated upon commercial principles is permanent, and depending only on a nation's self. If Britain loses North America, it is no flaw in the colony system; it is a proof only that there are no blunders in politics too great for the Ministers to commit, and ought to be ranked in the same degree of insanity as laws enacted for the professed destruction of agriculture, fisheries, or manufactures. To tell us that our trade has not suffered is an idle imposition. The North American export was known to be immensely great; other demands may have made up for a part of it, and the Americans may yet get the rest thro' other channels, but to tell us that the trade is nothing;—that four millions export is not felt by a nation whose total export to all the world is not fifteen, is a foolish paradox. Look about the country, and see if we have not idle poor enough! The use of exports is to make foreigners support the poor. Why are our poor rates so high as to threaten destruction to the kingdom, if we want no trade at present? But where is the fruitful principle of increase gone, which attended North America? Where is another trade?—Let our Ministers point it out; that has doubled every twenty-five years, with the population of that continent? This is lost to posterity. It is a part and a principal part of the use of colonies, that they increase so rapidly as to create in themselves the nobles of all markets.

The *Morning Post* employed the writings of its unfailing antiministerial scribbler MELA to impress upon its readers the difficulties now facing Britain in the most important matters of revenue, credit, and trade. On 31 May 1776, he wrote:

> The immediate power of this country depends pretty minutely on the public revenue, and the capability of increasing it, which in other words is credit—for as long as the government receives an increasing income, so long as she may borrow upon the credit of it: the monopoly of the American commerce will be lost with the continent, and with the trade most certainly the revenue on that trade must vanish also; this appears to be a position too clear to be denied.

On the first of June, MELA cautioned his readers that not only would the Americans seek other markets but that they would probably find those markets far more advantageous:

> The Americans will gradually go to other markets, and will find those manufactures which they cannot yet establish amongst themselves to be had cheaper of France, Holland, and Germany, than of us; and they will not be long in finding out that it will be fifty times more advantageous to them immediately to export their tobacco, etc., to those markets to which we sell it loaded with duties, five times higher than the prime cost.

All of this would be catastrophic to public credit, according to MELA (*MP* 6/4/76): "In the present situation of Great Britain, the wealth of the kingdom is so dependant on public credit that it is impossible to say what could be the amount of public taxes when that immense convulsion [loss of American trade] happened of a failure of credit from taxes not being productive enough to pay the interest on the public debts." The debt, MELA (*MP* 12/16/76) declared, was so worrisome that prudence had suffered and been cast aside: "This kingdom is so burthened with her debt, that measures which would otherwise be of the highest prudence are of the most fatal tendency. To hear applause therefore of victories gained, is to hear of the people rejoicing at their own ruin!"

Again MELA (7/30/76) cautioned that America was lost and the struggle beyond reconciliation:

> It requires no great political sagacity to foresee that America is lost to this empire; if the war is alone to decide it, and we are unsuccessful, she will become immediately independent; if it is successful, she will be a military government, instead of commercial colonies; and a reconciliation at present would, I fear, be a moon-shine; they will accept no terms from the men who have made the attack upon them.

In an unsigned letter (9/19/76) the *Morning Post* agreed that the "commercial, profitable America" was worse than lost: "You may by persisting conquer it at the expense of 50 or 60 millions—but commercial, profitable America would be as much lost as if the Congress were a States General— nay worse than lost, for you would have America to keep by a standing army, inheriting a dead expense where once you gained nothing but profit."

The writer signing his name ONE OF THE MAJORITY (*PA* 2/8/76) wrote of the dreadful cost of the war:

> At the most moderate computation this rebellion will cost Great Britain Ten Millions of Treasure, and Twenty thousand Lives. Should we value the lives at nothing, the interest of the money must amount to £400,000 per annum.... What is the object of the war? Are we to throw away so much Treasure and so many Lives to gain a Point, which, when gained, is not worth one per cent on our money.

If some of the aforementioned scribblers had the ministry in mind in their condemnation of the war, there were others who were more explicit. All in all, there was a blanket denunciation of the Lord North government. The letter writer AMICUS X.Y. (9/11/76) wrote:

> At the beginning of the American disturbances, the choice of our Ministers announced to us a set of men, superior in wisdom, capacity, and knowledge; but whether so or not, let dispatches, as far as they have appeared, their measures as far as they have operated, determine for them. In the former there has been strange assertions, without proof; discussions, without argument and violent aspersions, without dignity or moderation, but neither candour in the charge, nor judgement in the design, which the result will (I fear) fatally evince to every thinking person, whose life, reputation, or property may fall a sacrifice to the ill concerted cause he may unhappily espouse.

Proclaiming his frustration, AN ENGLISHMAN (*PA* 2/6/76 and 2/14/76) wrote:

> The deplorable State to which the ministry have reduced this Country and America, seems to have been as unprovoked as it was ruinous and unwise.... Our commerce is half ruined; our Colonies wholly lost; our taxes increased, and our Abilities diminished....
>
> The People are supine, the Opposition pusillanimous, the Ministry profligate. Reckless of the fatal consequences which have been so often stated to them, the Ministry pursue with redoubled violence their mad Career to arbitrary Power, in the Face of experience which would have taught any man less desperate that the End was unattainable and the Pursuit ruinous to the whole Empire.

BRUTUS drafted a damnation of ministerial policy in America for the *Public Advertiser* (10/29/76):

> If we consider the present plan of Government, if we contemplate the present measures carried on against America, we can foresee nothing but a series of Destruction, without any national advantage. It has been the determined resolution of the present Ministry to sacrifice the lives of brave men by a war destructive in its commencement, ruinous in its progression, and ineffectual in its consequences. Can it be imagined that Men of acknowledged Bravery will give up their Freedom, in support of which they have no other alternative but self-defence? We are not now to be told that the supplies of Government are derived from the People, or that a vote of Parliament fixes the current service for the year. Let us hope for better men and better measures; let the complaints of the People, let their grievances be redressed. We may abuse our freedom, but if there is a proper spirit among the people we can only lose it with the Constitution.

Although the scribblers in 1776 had explored the question of the impracticability of either conquering or holding America, little was said in justification or expectation of peace. Only MELA (*MP* 11/21/76) wrote of peace, and then simply as a salvation from the present course of ruin:

Without supposing any dreadful losses or unfortunate defeats, what I contend for is that the mere expenses would ruin us by being in fact insupportable. Even success would have the same effect. The enormity of our debt is the breath of ill success; Every nerve is alive to the slightest impression. In such a situation the present prospect is that of ruin: War is destructive; Peace alone can secure us.

The year 1777 brought little variation in the cries of frustration and despair that were voiced in the British press. The letter writers were now stressing the difficulties with which the British were contending in their conquest of the rebellious colonies. And if the colonies were conquered, would not the cost in men and treasure exceed the benefits to be enjoyed by the mother country?

COMMON SENSE (*LC* 9/6/77) examined the strength of the American army and the determination of that army to make each British victory gained too dear. And if final victory was achieved, he argued, the expense of maintaining the necessary military force for the occupation of that country would be ruinous to the victor.

I come now to consider the facility which the Americans are said to be driven from all their posts, even after they have fortified them in the strongest manner, and whether it be so sure a sign as some people represent it, of their speedy submission to the British government. But first, I must observe, that the assertion of their being driven from all their posts with so much facility, is absolutely groundless. They certainly were not driven from Bunker's-hill in that manner. That they were not is but too evident from the sable weeds and melancholy look of many a worthy family in England, which now laments the loss of some of its nearest and dearest relations slain in that short but obstinate engagement. . . . They mean to make the present war a war of posts, where every victory you gain cost you ten times what its value; and not a war of pitched battles on the plain, where your superior discipline, and consequently your superior collective, though not personal bravery must give you an advantage. . . . It is one thing to conquer a country, and another to conquer a people. We may over-run, or, if you will, conquer America; but we can never preserve it unless we can contrive to maintain numerous armies, not only in three or four distinct places, but almost in every province; all the revenue we can ever derive from America [may not] defray the expense of such a military force.

CATO (*MC* 8/21/77) combined his frustration at the unnatural war in America with censure of Lord North:

You must now, my Lord, see the danger this nation was in when you ventured on this unnatural war, which neither the representation, nor the remonstrances of those who were well acquainted with the nature of the country, and the natural disposition of its inhabitants, could dissuade you from. Your hundred thousand men have not been able to hold what they took possession of by surprise, or were in possession of when the matter in

dispute began. Contending for trifles has exhausted our treasure; and opposing mercenary men, to men fighting for the natural liberties of mankind, has
depopulated our kingdom and dyed our harbours with blood: from Bunker's
Hill the stream ran to Boston, while the groans of dying men rend the air,
and agonizing cries of the wounded melt the most hardened heart to pity,
to gain the wretched trifle of two-pence in the pound of imported tea.

In the *Morning Chronicle* (9/4/77), CATO continued to warn Lord
North, and to alert his readers, of the inability of the British military to conquer and to hold the rebel colonies:

> I tell you further, my Lord, you may take Philadelphia, the Americans will
> find their account in it; you must govern it, and so divide your army into
> such small divisions that with chasing the main body of the rebels, they will
> be no more able to cope with them at last by garrisoning every place they
> take, than they were to drive them from their strong posts to the Northward
> of Philadelphia. This is their wish, to protract the war is our ruin they well
> know, and indeed as we have lost their affection, in future, by military form
> alone can we keep them obedient subjects, and the enormous expense to
> support it, exclusive of the great clog on industry, agriculture, etc. such ar-
> bitrary government must produce, a greater sum will be expended than can
> be collected ... so that we have been engaged much to the purpose in shed-
> ding the blood of our brethren, exhausting our own treasure at the time, and
> stretching the credit of the Crown beyond what it ever will be able to pay,
> but must end, to the ruin of thousands, in a general insolvency.

An unsigned letter in the *Morning Post* (8/12/77) expressed keen disappointment at the campaign of 1777:

> If ever the prospect of this country were melancholy to consider, it is at pres-
> ent. Advices from America so late as July 6th, and nothing effective done or
> attempted. Our grand army retreating under the supposition of a feint! Pro-
> crastination is victory to the Americans. Time is everything to them....
> They have nothing to effect but to keep us at the expense of twelve millions
> a year doing nothing, but seeing our trade carried into the ports of France;
> such a situation is triumph to America and wealth to France; but it is
> disgrace, ruin, and defeat to us.

With despair over Britain's position, A BRITON wrote to the *Public
Advertiser* (8/29/76):

> Such too is our own cruel dilemma, that we hardly know what events of our
> operations we have to wish. In the case of overpowering them, of traversing
> the country there from end to end, of keenly pursuing the Wildgoose chase
> ... of wearing them down, in short, what then? The conquest, as it would
> absurdly be called, would bid fair to ruin us. Every victory gained over them
> would still be our Loss, and the maintenance of such a conquest ultimately
> THEIR GAIN. What better could be hoped from a total want of a Plan, as
> well as of Principle; and all this most congenially combined with infinite in-
> solence, infinite MEANNESS.

The year 1777 brought a new dimension to the cries of frustration. The scribblers were now evincing sufficient resolution to accuse the ministry of distributing news from America that was sheer fabrication. Although it was yet early in the contest to hunt for a scapegoat, the ministry was already a prime target and General Howe would soon be too.

JUNIUS JUNIOR (*MC* 9/5/77) accused Lord North of distorting the military news:

> My Lord, the tales you tell in Parliament are vain and delusive. Erroneous in your first principles, you have been deceived into false hopes that hostile power in America was justified by the laws of nature and of nations, and that the object of that Power was worthy of its exertion. You have been deceived in the calculated advantages to be derived from such a supposed conquest, and it is now too late to know and to feel that even when our constitution has been violated in the persecution of unprecedented schemes, and when our arms are employed in an unjust cause, that our profit is — BLOOD AND DEVASTATION!

Traditional traders with America were in desperate straits. Although many of the contractors supplying the military made large fortunes during the war, a connection to government was, in many cases, a prime requisite. Of the forty-six contractors employed by the government between 1775 and 1782, eighteen were members of Parliament and eighteen more has some connection with members of Parliament.[1]

THE MEMORIALIST expressed the chagrin of the traditional trader in the *Public Advertiser* (12/5/77). He charged "the Contractors, both in and out of Parliament, perceived a Policy in the Continuance of the War." A CONTRACTOR (*MP* 4/25/76) detailed the operations of the "new" American traders:

> Since our late unhappy contest with America the trade to that country has entirely shifted hands. The late American Merchants are now left to brood over their outstanding debts while the new ones are all as busy as bees. Mr. Wilkenson never had such a shipping trade to America in all his life as he has had for these twelve months past; Mr. Atkinson's supply of port has been uncommonly large; Mr. Hannau's exportation of sour crout has been the most advantageous trade he ever was engaged in. Mr. Nicoll has been drained of his Beaume de Vie [a medicine advertised in the newspapers] for the use of the army and navy; Mr. Melish's exportation of sheep and hogs has been such as cannot be equalled, etc. These new American Merchants have put the trade on a much better footing than it was. They avoid opening accounts with the people abroad, and have all their demand paid in England.

Slowly there emerged from the turmoil a call for peace. The people were tired of the war. MELA (*LC* 6/7/77) wrote: "I am perfectly convinced, that let Gen. Howe have what success he will, we are not one jot nearer an end of this unhappy quarrel." The writer MODERATOR (*PA*

5/21/77): "Let us remember we are parties whose interest is at stake; and if we go on wrangling to the end we shall, both England and America, be in the case of the two determined suitors, we shall have nothing but the Shell, the Oyster will be swallowed by those who encouraged the brawl." And in the *Public Advertiser* of 10 October 1777, WARNING proposed an alternative which to this point was taboo, to withdraw British troops from America:

> We will not examine whether his Majesty turns pale and is frightened when he receives news from his General and Admirals in America; but this we can honestly assert, that the Nations's Eyes are opened; they are tired of this cruel, unnatural, and ruinous war.... Plunged as we are in a variety of difficulties there is yet time to extricate ourselves from them by the only method which is left us. Withdrawing our Forces, and leaving Americans to themselves. If an Union between the Colonies and Great Britain could be brought about, nothing would be more warmly desired by every lover of this country. But I fear the hatred which our unhappy conduct has rooted in the hearts of the Americans will never be obliterated.

The writer signing his name as BOBO (*MP* 7/31/76) recommended an amnesty:

> An American pine will not easily bend, and an oppressed American is still more inflexible than his timber. These people [Americans] appear to have rather blundered into an impropriety, than entered into a rebellion; and should it even be termed rebellion, it may be said that it lay in their way, and they found it. They have drawn the sword, they know not how, and what they seem to wish is to sheath it with security; I therefore recommend to you to publish an amnesty, without exception or proscription, and you will find the mechanic and husbandman, whose families depend on their labour would immediately from inclination, joyfully return to the enjoyments of that situation they were no longer under the necessity of defending by force of arms; and the officers and leading men once deserted by their soldiers, would be left without protection, and embrace it from necessity. Conciliation was offered, it is true, but there was too much jealousy in the composition to make them palatable; the olive branch was hung out, but it was held at the point of a sword, and the cautious American was afraid to meddle with it lest he cut his fingers; and when every vindictive method failed, when foreign mercenaries have been called in to assist in conquering an injured people without effect, thou then hold forth terms of accommodation by offering to pardon the offence of such as have sinned against us. The Americans have nothing to do but to act defensively, or rather will conquer by INACTION; she will harass your troops without end, and fatigue, NECESSITY, and the ultimate will be sufficient for their destruction, without drawing the sword against them. In return we may burn their towns from Boston to Baltimore, which will certainly distress, but cannot conquer the Americans. Your Lordship may WITH TRUTH declare at the council board, THAT THE HAND WRITING HATH APPEARED UPON THE WALL, AND AMERICA IS DEPARTED FROM US FOR EVER!

By 1778 the absurdity of any attempt to conquer the rebellious colonies and the need for peace and conciliation became the focus of the letters to the printer. The writers held the ministry and the military responsible for the lies and tragedy of the American affair. There was no longer a hope that any offer of conciliation would meet with the blessings of the ministry, but there remained a critical need to disengage from the war in North America, as MEMENTO wrote in the *Public Advertiser* (1/10/78):

> A great Law Lord declared that the question of Original Right or Wrong, Justice of Injustice, was not to be considered; for that the "Justice of our Cause must give way to our Situation." If this assertion was founded in Wisdom then it certainly is now, and ought to be adopted when it tends to stop the effusion of blood and the total ruin of this country.... Without entering into a particular State of the present condition of this Kingdom, which is too woeful for contemplation, it is evident that though it is not yet absolutely ruined, it is certainly on the brink. It may perhaps go on another year before it is totally overwhelmed in Bankruptcy and Disgrace; but the pursuit of the present project for another year will make the public ruin irretrievable.

Reconciliation, however, was not to be had for the asking. CAUTIOUS (*LC* 3/17/78) doubted the likelihood of a cessation of hostilities. First, the British had offered nothing new, and secondly, the Americans would place conditions on an armistice, namely, withdrawal of troops, with which Britain could not comply:

> The plan now adopted for quieting the troubles that prevail in America ... offers nothing to the Americans, but what they insisted on before the commencement of the hostilities....
>
> It is probable that an indispensable preliminary towards the engaging in any negotiation, the Americans will insist on our withdrawing our troops from that quarter of the world; and this, I apprehend as a condition with which we will not comply, and consequently will raise an insuperable obstacle to the formation or conclusion of any kind of treaty.

In support of the American independence, ACADEMICUS (*LC* 10/10/78) reminded his readers of the constitutional petitioning by the Americans and the want of consideration shown to their appeals by the ministry:

> Our conduct all along towards the Americans has not only been marked with severity, but has been in many instances absurd and ridiculous to the last degree. They remonstrated at times, in a constitutional manner, against measures which they considered as unjust and oppressive, but no attention was paid to them, though these were the remonstrances of a virtuous, a loyal, and an affectionate people. To all this however it may be replied, that they now act a very inconsistent part in refusing to embrace the opportunity lately offered to them, of being restored to that happy union which they formerly seemed so desirous of seeing established. This objection indeed is specious, and I will not pretend to say how far the Americans may be acquitted of the

charge of inconsistency or insincerity in this respect; but surely our ministry have no shadow of right to blame the people of America for acting in the same manner as they themselves did in similar circumstances. Often has America thrown herself at the feet of Great Britain without the least hopes of redress. Is it any wonder then that America should, in her turn, lend a deaf ear to the prayers of Great Britain? Would our ministry have given up the cause at this period if they had any prospects of success, or any hopes of the speedy reduction of America. The Americans themselves are sagacious enough to see through the motives of our present conduct. Besides, they have already tasted too much of the sweets of independence to become dependent any more; they are too sensible of the benefits of an unrestrained commerce with the whole world to admit to any restraints upon their trade and navigation; and they are too much elevated with the glorious prospect of a rising empire ever to think of becoming tributary to Great Britain.

Refusing to apologize for a change of opinion regarding the war in North America, CAUTUS (*PA* 9/2/78) now considered the conquest of America as hopeless. More significant was the danger of an invasion of the British Isles and the need to have the army in America returned to defend Great Britain:

> I profess to you, I was once myself a very sincere Advocate in Defence of the War against America, though no Zealot in that or any Party Question: From whence I reap Benefit, that I set some certain Bounds to my political Wishes. I am not ashamed to own that my Opinion of Today differs from my Opinion of Yesterday; just as I put on a Cloth Waistcoat this week, though for a Fortnight before I scarcely endured my Linen one. The Weather is changed, Mr. Printer, and I dress suitably to the Cold or the Heat of the Day. Our political Weather is grown cold too, and my Wishes and Views are cooled in Proportion.... I have long given up the Conquest of America as a hopeless Project; but we are here told, with Coolness and Candour enough [General Howe at his inquest], I must confess, that we are in the most imminent Danger of losing a Force, which I believe no one will doubt may be necessary to the Defence and Safety of our own Island.

Writer D. BURGESS (*PA* 9/15/78) managed to voice his contempt for the British military, his concurrence with a plan to remove the troops from America, the need for those troops to defend Britain, and contempt for the ministry in one short letter:

> Tho' I despair of our finding a General among us good for anything, after the Failure of Howe, Carleton, and Burgoyne; yet since it has been at last found that we have one General that is good for something. I hope the Success of that General will be improved in his own way, by our Army in America speedily retreating hence for ever; as we shall by that Means prevent a further Loss of Men and Money, and preserve the Remains of our Forces for a much nobler Purpose than the distressing the Innocent—the Defence of our own Country. From the Exultation of the Ministry on the Arrival of the Army at New York, a Retreat seems now the utmost they expect.

If D. BURGESS was uncharitable to the ministry, his letter merely reflected the opinions of many of his fellow scribblers, especially those whose works appeared in the *Public Advertiser*. On 16 June 1778, AN OBSCURE BYSTANDER offered a most damning denunciation of the ministry. What made his reproach more condemnatory was the fact that he was the paradigm of all scribblers. He was, in short, the average Britisher, or so this working scribbler wanted his readers to view him:

> I am past the Time of Life to be of any active use to my Country, but I have such a Competency of Fortune as makes me liable to contribute, without being distressed by that Contribution, to the general Support of Government of all Kinds of Taxes; and if the greatest Part of my Fortune could really assist towards the Credit, the Honour, I may almost say the Existence of an English Government, I should not grudge it; but I must own, retired as I live from the World, and unengaged as I am with any Set of Men whatever, I cannot but feel Grief, Mortification, and Humiliation, as an Englishman, for our present fallen State. I have never been conversant enough with the World to be a Politician, and therefore don't pretend to judge of the Expediency of whatever has been undertaken, or of the Propriety or Impropriety with which the Objects have been pursued; but I must feel the consequence in the Events, and be sensible as an Individual concerned, that from a great, flourishing, formidable, envied Empire, of which I was proud of being a Subject, there now remains only a dismembered, withering, insulted, despised State; most unaccountably too has this happened; we have had no Plague to destroy our Fleets and Armies; we have had no Slaughter of great Officers fallen in Battle; yet are we in the Space of three Years mouldered as it were, Moth-eaten, Mite eaten; and are not our Ministers and Officers these Moths and Mites? Should not the small sound Remains of us be preserved if possible, by brushing from them these annihilating Insects; but who amongst us is there with either the Spirit to undertake, or Skill to effect this Salvation: Scarce do Men seem apprehensive of their impending Ruin, so far are they from exerting their Powers to avert it; and in this Period of Profligacy and Impiety, there seems to be but one Text of Scripture in which all agree, "Take no Thought for the Morrow."

The scribblers of the *Public Advertiser* continued to voice their frustration in the same fashion throughout the year:

GRACCHUS (3/6/78):

The Ignorance, the Inability of Administration must visit the Children to the third and fourth Generation, the Landed Gentlemen must pay for your Misconduct, the Merchant reduced to Bankruptcy curses your Inexperience, the Manufacturer feels the Loss of our Trade, while Commerce and all its advantages aggrandise the Enemies of your Country. You must find yourself reduced to this humiliating Circumstance, not to tax the People for acquired Victories, but for Defeats; no triumphant laurels to deck your Fleets and Armies, but they are glad to skulk into the first Port with the small remains of their gallant Troops, to hide their own misfortunes and your Ignominy.

G.N. (3/26/78):

Ministry, in rigid Compliance with the Ignorance or Obstinance of these under whom they act, have at length, and in spite of repeated Remonstrances from the People, conducted the affairs of this Nation into such difficulty and danger, that we can neither proceed with Safety, nor retreat with Honour.

HAMDEN (1/24/78):

That the Colonies are lost to this kingdom there is too much reason to fear. The Contrivers and Promoters of that unnatural and impolitic War, carried on against them with such unremitting rancour for more than three years, now stands aghast, and tremble for the consequences of their temerity.

Not even George III was to escape the anger and disappointment voiced by the writers of the *Public Advertiser*:

G.N. (9/12/78):

What is the Cause? but that Ministry for more than three years past have been carrying on measures in direct opposition to the voice of the people; and which have been unremittingly execrated by all who were not immediate participants of temporary advantages for promoting them, or expectant in future. These men, despicable in themselves and contemptibly impotent, but when armed with the power of the State and Countenance of the S__n [Sovereign], formidable to oppose and counteract the public Inclination, have at last conducted the Nation into such a scene of Distress as cannot be paralleled in the annals of our History.

ANGLICANUS (5/15/78):

We are exhausted of Men and Money, our Commerce rapidly on the Decline, our principal Merchants becoming daily the Victims of it. The K__ has thirteen Children to console him for the Loss of as many fine Provinces. This is a Reign of Mockery; the continual Reviews of his Land Forces taught him to believe his Troops were invincible. He is now amused with the Review of his Fleet. Well will it be for Old England, if that does not prove equally ominous.

If the scribblers of the *Public Advertiser* were insolent in their treatment of the ministry and the king, they showed no sign of repentance when criticizing the military and the falsehoods and inventions that were broadcast by that ministry to the people of Britain.

A.B. (9/2/78):

The last Gazette Extraordinary, according to the usual Policy of the present Government, has concealed everything disagreeable in the Accounts they have received from North America, and published only what they think will be the least alarming to the Public. The General's [Clinton] is a long Military Account of the King's Grand Army having evacuated Philadelphia, and retreated before Part of the American Army to Sandy Hook Island. His Letter has as little of the modern Parade in Descriptions of Military Operations as any with which the Public have of late Years been favoured; and when entirely striped of Martial Phrases, and uninteresting Particulars, amounts to no more, than he had the Honour to inform Lord George Germaine he evacuated the Capital of America, pursuant to the King's Instructions, on the 18th of June, 1778.

CONNOISSEUR (12/9/78):

It is highly pleasing to think that when Posterity shall look into the History of these illustrious Times, and shall read of the glorious Capitulation at Saratoga, so honourable to the British Name; when they shall read of the skilful Retreat of the British Forces from Washington encamped in the Jerseys; when they shall observe in many signal Advantages seized by our Generals after the Battles of Long Island, White Plains, and Brandywine, and the decisive Victory gained off Ushant by our Fleet . . . I am convinced that Posterity will be totally at a Loss to determine, whether the English Nation under the present auspicious and animating Reign have most excelled in Art or in Arms.

There can be little doubt that the *Public Advertiser* treated the ministry, the king, and the military with something less than perfect veneration. It did, however, offer letters of excellent prose to the readers of the press and to posterity, as did the other London newspapers. Few surpassed the splendid letter from G.N. (*PA* 4/4/78) which follows:

In the critical Moment of Suspense, in the awful Pause between Peace and War, if Ministry are not to be moved by the dire Calamities attending the latter, if that Scorpion Scourge has no Miseries in Store for them in common with the Bulk of Mankind; yet, let a Regard to their own Credit, and their Feelings for the Public, have so much Influence with them, as not to lead us into this Vale of Misery, there to leave us wretched and forlorn, without so much as a Prospect of restoring and conducting us, after all our Sufferings, into a State of Security equal to that in which we stood previous to our having engaged in so hazardous, so tremendous an Undertaking. To effect even this, it is necessary we should become victorious; but should that Event be otherwise determined, we must ingloriously desist after a profuse Waste of Blood and Treasure; sit down in Disquietude and lament our Wounds and Losses, reduced to a much worse Condition than that in which we are at present; and withal loaded with Opprobrium, if not placed in a State of dangerous Insecurity. In War, nothing is certain, but the Desolation with which it is constantly, and inevitably attended. The Event depends upon a Multitude of unforeseen Incidents, not to be scrutinized into by human Penetration; and, as the least of these may be decisive of the future Consequences, that Determination must ever remain uncertain and doubtful, and not more capable of being ascertained, but by the final Event, than they are in all Games of Chance and Hazard. . . . Whoever are, or are to be Ministers, let them keep their Eye, if they DARE to look at it, on the Debt of the Nation; let them "bona fide" consult their Conscience and their Reason, whether it be prudent, or even safe, to increase the Tumour of that hydropical disease, the National Debt. A War will certainly increase the Malady, will promote that Event; and it is not in the Sanctity of Names, however great, or good, but in the prudential and wise Choice of Measures, in a Word, by Peace alone, that so fatal a Catastrophe is to be averted. I do not affirm, that there can be no Instance, in which War is not preferable to Peace; particular Cases are entitled to particular Exceptions. We are beset with Evils; their Nature is such, that War adds Force, and Virulence to their Poison; and, therefore, is to be avoided. If there be those who think Peace is disgraceful, let them remember it is the least of these Evils; and as the least, the best.

The message G.N. offered to the British ministry in the eighteenth century remains a compelling mandate to all politicians some two hundred years later.

CHAPTER NINE

Euphoria

By the year 1778, letters reporting the dawning of a golden age for Britain were replacing those of gloom and depression.[1] The writers were now applauding the ministry and the military, and their approbation continued through the years 1779 and 1780. Letters to the printer reported a flourishing trade, and support for the government was at its zenith. Scribblers advised the populace to ignore tidings of doom and destruction. All was well; all that was needed was to restore the spirit of Britons.

The letter writer who signed his name A PATRIOT (*CM* 1/14/78) was optimistic about the British spirit:

> I see the spirit of Britain reviving. Give it encouragement, my countrymen! Show your readiness as individuals to support the Government in this necessary war; necessary, for the support of your trade, and of your being as a commercial, supreme, and independent state! which you have been for so many ages past, and which you have surely a right to be. Remember your all is at stake, and act as men!

A VETERAN (*MC* 1/14/78) was confident that the British lion would react to American military moves: "But they [Americans] no sooner become formidable, than the British Lion begins to roar; a noble spirit animates all orders, it catches from man to man, and proves that the present generation are the true descendants, legitimate offspring, of the ancient British heroes and patriots, for ever recorded in the annals of fame."

The letter writer G.E.W. (*MC* 7/18/78) assured his readers: "There is no doubt of surmounting all the apparent difficulties, if once more we unite, heart and hand, in the common cause, for the mutual benefit of ourselves and threatened country. Rouse ye, my brave Britons, to arms! to conquest! to glory! gird on the sword of valour!"

AN ENGLISHMAN (*MP* 9/25/78) believed the outlook for Britain was promising:

> We see that the clouds, with which our political hemisphere has been so industriously darkened, all instantly disappear; the thunders which have been

described as bursting over our heads, have existed only in imagination, and the lightnings which were to blast this devoted country, prove to be no more than an "ignis fatuus," conjured up by the demon of faction for the infamous purpose of delusion. So far then from having anything to dread from the power of France, we have every reason to presume that her unexampled treachery will be condignly punished, and the neck of rebellion will speedily bend to the feet of justice.

There remained little question that the might of British arms could and would subdue the rebellious colonies. The loss of an army at Saratoga might be construed as a victory. FIDUS VETERANUS (*MC* 8/29/78) found success at Saratoga: "I have beheld with pleasure that the British forces, with their usual intrepidy and ardour, have defeated the Rebels in every action, even in those under Burgoyne, previous to the day in which his army was obliged to surrender to the mandates of famine."

The writers depicted victory; the letters were messages of celebration. All was well. The military situation was healthy and under control, trade was prospering, and America was about to collapse. OPIFEX (*LC* 2/24/78) noted to his readers that British trade had not been unduly affected by the war and stated his confidence in the ministry:

From the debates which have passed on the subject, the whole argument seems confined to the American controversy—whether from the present circumstances, to continue coercive measures, or adopt a more pacific system. That the latter would be most desirable, could the breach be closed by those means of proper terms, there cannot be a doubt. But when the demands of the Americans are impartially considered, and that they contemptuously received overtures already made to them, that nothing short of exemption from parliamentary taxation, or absolute independence will satisfy them, there can be no room for suspense in the breasts of any who wish well to old England, what measures to pursue. To infer inability to reduce them from past losses is concluding very weakly; for it would be absurd indeed to think of succeeding without suffering some partial temporary inconveniences. But amidst all our losses, however magnified, we have this still to comfort us, that we find them much less, do not experience that ruined trade and commerce so confidently foreboded by the Americans and their friends; our trade and commerce appear so far from being in that state of ruin, that excepting some unfortunate individuals, the nation at large scarce feels a decline.... I will dare affirm from the tenor of my remarks that the people will never repose greater confidence in any set of ministers than the present, who have proved themselves the steady and able servants of the Public.

The lack of success of the military was of a temporary nature CIVIS indicated in his letter to the *Morning Post* (7/9/78): "The misfortunes they have daily experienced, not during the last campaign only, but while the troops were in their winter quarters, have given them room to see, that without bringing her whole force into the field, Great Britain with detachments alone is able to break the spirit of rebellion, which like all novelties, had at first a great run."

VETERAN (*MC* 1/30/78) ascribed the lack of success to unusual circumstances that he assured his readers would not recur:

> It is altogether owing to unforeseen contingencies, which, from the nature of things, cannot take place again, that the Rebels have been able to oppose his Majesty's arms hitherto, and that a prosecution of the war, even in the same manner it has been conducted in the two last years, will inevitably return the revolted Colonies to their allegiance, in a few campaigns, and that it may be effected much sooner, and means equally sure.

With General Clinton as the new commander in chief of the army in North America and the earl of Sandwich presiding over the marine department, all was well with the fighting forces of Great Britain. Both CIVIS (*MP* 7/25/78) and A FRIEND TO MERIT AND HIS COUNTRY (*MP* 4/24/78) believed Britain had strength and security with a superior fleet—all of which was the doing of Lord Sandwich:

> CIVIS: In spite of every opposition that a set of base, degenerate Britons raised up against him, [he] has in the ports of Great Britain and Ireland ONLY, raised full sixty thousand for our present naval service. . . . He has fitted out the finest fleet that ever left our ports. . . . He has raised twelve thousand British subjects more, to serve on board the different squadrons. . .
>
> A FRIEND TO MERIT AND HIS COUNTRY: Since you have had the honour of presiding over the marine department of these kingdoms, such attention has been paid to our navy, that the nation in general are under the highest obligation to you for the respectable state it is at the present in; for however clamorous false patriots may be, in deprecating them, I can with truth aver, our shipping were never in a better condition, nor were we ever able to send to sea so formidable a fleet.

Generals Howe and Burgoyne, their successes and defeats, were now of the past. The new victorious commander was General Clinton:

> POLITICUS (*MP* 9/16/78):
>
> The British army under the command of the gallant Clinton, which was to be surrounded, and made captives to the rebel Fabius, if they dared to stir from Philadelphia, marched victorious through the Jerseys, and in despite of the whole rebel force, reached New York in triumph.

> A VETERAN (*MP* 8/26/78):
>
> Re: Clinton's evacuation of Philadelphia: 1. That Sir Henry Clinton carried his grand object of reaching New York, with less loss than ever attended such an operation. 2. That the British army on their march, though obstructed by every difficulty that could be devised by the enemy, and though attacked by the whole united force under the command of Washington, Gates, Lee, Arnold, and their French associate the Marquis de Fayette, repulsed them in every attack; and as the strongest proof of this, carried off every article of

their baggage. From thence it is clear that victory declared decisively in favour of the English troops.

And through the genius of General Clinton, an alteration, a new mode of war promised to subdue the Americans. But it was not a military plan that would reduce the colonies to such a low state that they would be of little or no value to the Crown. Conquer but not eradicate was the policy. So wrote the writer DECIOUS in the *Morning Post* on 1 December 1778:

> The expeditions set on foot by Sir Henry Clinton, are alarming beyond description, as they show at once an alteration in the mode of war and the facility with which it is carried into effect.... This mode of war would cause a temporary distress to the inhabitants, and would soon put it out of their power to maintain their armies; but it would be the means of saving thousands of lives, which must otherwise be lost in a lingering war. Nor would there be any danger of reducing the colonies to so low an ebb, as to be of little or no value to the Crown. There are many intermediate degrees between that abject state, and a condition to oppose a British Army.

OBSERVATOR (*PA* 9/18/78) was less kind to the American rebels:

> But the great day of account is yet to come, and, notwithstanding the seeming fatality under which our arms have operated against them, the means of their subjection is still in our power. When desolation is carried to their dwellings, and poverty stare them in the face; when famine and devastation meet them in their retreat from our justly directed vengeance, and they find they have no asylum to fly to, they will recollect themselves, and comparing their present distracted and ruined condition with their former one, they will estimate the blessedness of that from the misery of this, and finally examining the motives from which they were allured to forfeit it, under the mere imagination of oppression from their present state, they will execrate the wicked promoters of their ruin, and gladly and gratefully acknowledge the supremacy, and admire the condescension of their rightful Sovereign, whom they have been taught wantonly to abuse, and who, after reiterated provocations to his royal dignity and power, has so often graciously invited them to his protection and regard.

Victory was not far off. America remained in a corrupt and divided state. Such was the condition described by the scribblers of the *Morning Post* and *Morning Chronicle*:

A SOLDIER (*MC* 12/12/78):

> It is now beyond doubt, that the next campaign, if carried on with ardour and support, will entirely suppress this unnatural rebellion; nor can a stronger proof be required to ascertain it, than the present deplorable and divided state of the separate Colonies in America: The Floridas firmly attached to Great Britain; the Carolinas and Georgia revolting; Maryland and Pennsylvania praying assistance to stop the tyranny of Congress; Philadelphia despairing; the Jersies depopulated, and New England starving with cold and hunger.

DECIOUS (*MP* 12/5/78):

The Congress assemblies and committees in whose hands the usurped government is placed, are so far from enjoying that confidence of the people that is pretended, that, to keep up their power and influence, they are obliged to have recourse to falsehood, chicane, fines, imprisonment, confiscation, and executions that disgrace human nature. A proper discipline is not yet established in their armies, who for want of a regular subordination are unwieldy and ungovernable. . . . The above is a just representation of the internal state of the rebellious Colonies. They, it is well known, are but the skirt of a vast continent, and are in a manner surrounded by loyal ones. The incursions from Canada keep the frontiers in alarm, and have depopulated a great extent of the back settlements, while the British fleet commands the ocean with a decided superiority, and an active General commands the army in the midst. Such, and so great are the calamities upon the common people, that it is impossible the pressure should be much longer inured. It is too much to be expected from human nature; especially as they may be avoided, by accepting such noble, and liberal offers as are made by government. . . . if vigorous measures are pursued such an event [revolution in the colonies] may yet be as sanguinely expected as it is devoutly to be wished.

Most, if not all, the London newspapers, the *London Chronicle, Morning Chronicle, Morning Post,* and *Public Advertiser,* had, at one time or another, presented a scribbler to reassure their readers of the health of British trade. POLITICUS (2/26/78) framed a letter to the *London Chronicle* seeking to calm the fears of those who looked upon an independent America as a rival for English manufacture. Then two days later he explained his reasoning. The long process of division of labor so necessary for successful manufacture would elude America for centuries:

Some people are apprehensive that if America becomes independent it will soon be able to rival England in manufactures, and consequently commerce. These fears appear to me to be altogether groundless. . . .

It is division of labour that is responsible for producing manufactures not only in greater perfection, but in greater plenty than they could otherwise be produced. If a man must employ several years in learning a trade, it is natural to conclude that some hundreds of years must necessarily elapse before a nation can excel in any particular manufacture. . . . Let us, therefore, no longer alarm ourselves of America's rivalling England in trade and manufactures. If ever that happens, it must be after the expiration of some centuries.

The letter writer J.S. (*MC* 8/27/78) insisted that any decline in trade resulted from the actions of the American privateers during 1776 and 1777:

I can see no cause for the supposition of the decline of commerce, unless a small deficiency in the ordinary produce of the customs should be reckoned such; but this may very easily be accounted for upon other principles. But after all, if any person will still maintain that our trade has suffered interruptions, I will grant that it has. The depredations of the American privateers were a severe scourge during the years 1776 and 1777. The sea is better guarded, and the spirit of the nation roused; the prizes that have been made by America this year are but few in number. British cruisers have been so vigilant and successful this year, that a little longer perseverance must totally annihilate the trade of America.

The scribblers of the *Morning Post* were entirely satisfied with the condition of British trade with America. POLITICUS (9/16/78) informed his readers that "all of our commercial fleets, laden with incredible wealth, are safe in port." And PIZARRO (9/4/78) argued that "America is not worth the expense of contending for; that was she in union tomorrow, more would be required to support her, than would ever be worth to this country."

Giving comfort to his readers, J.S. (*PA* 8/28/78) assured them that the foreign trade of Great Britain was even more prosperous than it was before the war:

It is demonstrable from incontrovertible principles, that the foreign trade of Great Britain now flourishes more than it did before the commencement of the American war, or, in other words, that America, so far from either directly, or circuitously adding to the balance of trade in favour of this nation, rather impeded its commercial prosperity, it would be unnecessary to enlarge further upon this subject, did I not desire to rectify some mistaken opinions that have been industriously propagated, and seem to have been adopted by the ingenious writer, whose sentiments I have hitherto combated, whether through inattention or design, I know not.

Despite the euphoria and a firm belief in final victory, there was a call, modest at best, for peace and recognition of the independence of America. The writer PEACE! PEACE! (*PA* 1/19/78) proposed an invitation for amity and union, an opportunity for America to be a valued trading partner and sturdy ally.

Some four months later the *Public Advertiser* published another letter calling for peace and American independence. ULYSSES (*PA* 4/1/78) wrote in favor of independence with certain provisos, maintaining that people of the same culture could surely live in harmony:

Let us immediately acknowledge the Colonies independent, if we can get Terms, and make with them some Treaty of Commerce; it matters not much at present what this Treaty is: Future Times will undoubtedly mend it. Similar Customs and Manners, similar Government and Religion, the same Origin and the same Language, the same Bravery, Spirit, and Freedom, will some Time reconcile us to each other.

The letters of euphoria in 1779 continued to beseech Britons to emulate the "illustrious heroes of antiquity," insisted that the "genius of Britain" would rise superior to every danger, and argued that "the invincible spirit alone saved them from ruin." Now, however, there was a difference. For those who wished to believe that there was an alteration in the fortunes of the British military, there was a glimmer of hope.

Sir Henry Clinton had replaced Howe as commander in chief of British forces in North America. A new strategy was introduced. Philadelphia was to be evacuated and New York retained as the center for the military. The southern provinces were chosen as the arena for a fresh British offensive. The new stratagem resulted in the most successful military operation of the war. Savannah, Georgia, fell to the royal troops on 26 December 1778, and shortly thereafter Augusta capitulated. There followed other victories for the British forces. Little wonder that the scribblers of the London press celebrated.

DECIOUS (*MP* 3/6/79) rejoiced that Great Britain had regained a province rich in raw materials. And there was good reason to look forward to other victories:

> The successes of his Majesty's arms under Lieutenant Colonel Campbell are far from being inconsiderable. One stripe is already torn from the American flag, and a whole province, abounding with tar, lumber, rice and indigo, restored to the empire. The twelve rebellious colonies, are but the margin, or border of the vast continent of America, and are, in a manner, surrounded by loyal ones. The directing of the force against one, or perhaps both ends of this line of provinces, bids fair to reduce them all successively; especially if it be established as an invariable rule of conduct to complete the conquest as the army advances.

As well as a celebration for the victories in the southern provinces, there was a certainty that the British military was now about to seek the aid of loyal subjects in those provinces. The writer J.R. (*MC* 8/9/79) articulated for the Loyalists:

> It was the prevailing opinion amongst those best acquainted with Provincial politics that Charleston must certainly fall into our hands, but that the murmurs of all classes of the people who would be friends to the British Government, were they properly encouraged and supported, were very great, on account of their long continued inattention to the security of the Southern Colonies, which, had our force been properly recruited therein, must long since have been regained.

DECIOUS (*MP* 3/4/79) wrote of the support already evidenced by the new commander in chief, and General Campbell for the Loyalists in the southern provinces, a succor which had been notably missing in the past:

> It has commonly been the policy of Generals who had a country to conquer, to avail themselves of some factions of party within such country. But instead of availing himself of a friendly party to assist in suppressing rebellion, one would almost think that a certain General meant to avail himself of the rebels to extirpate every friend to Great Britain in America. Happily for this

country a different line of conduct is adopted by the present Commander in Chief, the good effect of which appears already. A test has been established in Georgia, and while loyalists are protected, rebels are proscribed. The immediate consequence was, to use Colonel Campbell's own words "the inhabitants, from all parts of the Province flocked, with their arms, to the standard, and have cordially embraced the terms which have been offered."

The writer signing his name A PLAIN MAN (*MC* 6/11/79) was elated at the favorable outlook for British pursuits which reached beyond the victories in the southern provinces. The number of native American troops serving British interests and the American seamen sailing on British privateers were proof of divisions within America: "America is not united against England. The numbers and the courage of the native American troops, now in the British pay, is a proof that comes home of itself to the point. The hundred and sixty privateers fitted out in New York, and manned principally with American sailors, ... have ruined the rebel American trade."

The year 1779 brought little change in the perception of the scribblers as to the stability of the rebellious colonies. They believed America's foreign trade was ruined and her currency was near collapse. Washington was experiencing inordinate difficulties in raising an army. Plainly, the rebellious colonists were a destitute people. So babbled the scribblers of many a London daily:

AN AMERICAN (*MC* 4/12/79):
A proper exertion will produce the Crisis in the American fever which various symptoms indicate to be at hand; the wants of the people, destitute of internal resources, and ruined in their foreign commerce; the depreciation of their currency now reduced to twelve or fourteen to one; their inability to raise an army or to support one if raised, the appearance of an approaching famine: all these circumstances, with a thousand others, are working a grand and desirable revolution.

MENTOR (*MP* 4/23/79):
Under this state of real facts the public will judge how far it is probable that Washington will be at the head of 30,000 men in the ensuing campaign, or even on third of the number. But let us suppose, that he should succeed in procuring half the number, they must be undisciplined, scarcely acquainted with the manual exercise, never before in action, and incapable of keeping order, in case they are pressed by one third of their number of British regulars. They will be half starved, half naked, undisciplined banditti, like their predecessors, who never stood the British bayonet for the space of ten minutes, and who had they ever been pursued in any one instance, must have been totally routed, and destroyed, and an end put to the rebellion.

A FRIEND TO OLD ENGLAND (*PA* 1/2/79):
We nurtured and supported the children of America more than our own, and when they were able to go alone, they requited us with ingratitude. The

Americans therefore have been, or might have been, the happiest people on the face of the earth, under our Laws and Government, had they even submitted to a small share of taxation, instead of resisting, to obtain ideal Independence, with real Slavery; for if facts speak anything, they are slaves to Congress, and they have only this country to depend upon to make them free, and stop the rapid progress of their present declining state.... Her commerce is gone ... she has no navy; nor by privateering, because her ships are either taken or destroyed.

With all the protestations of "all's well" in Britain, there remained pockets of disbelief. The *Morning Post*, a staunch supporter of the ministry, now spoke openly of the colonies as lost to Britain. The loss, the letter writers were quick to assure their readers, would in no way materially affect Britain or its people.

CLIO (*MP* 6/2/79):

The public prints have of late swarmed so with the most melancholy predictions of the declension and ruin of this kingdom, from the revolt of America, that a moderate man would suppose there must be at least some truth in it.... There is every thing within these islands necessary for a great and powerful people, and therefore it is folly to suppose that we are almost to suffer annihilation should we have lost the American provinces.

EUMENES (*MP* 8/21/79):

Your paper, I am sorry to see, too often filled like others, with essays and paragraphs, the tendency of which is to spread a desponding spirit through the kingdom: but I do not think there is the least reason, real or ostensible, for such ideas. I am well persuaded that the power of Great Britain, founded upon solid and undeniable resources, is fully equal to her present situation; and though the family of hungry Oppositionists are ever ready to represent us as undone, because we have lost thirteen provinces, for my part, I believe there never was a dominion of such extent upon earth as the American colonies, that yielded so little to any country as they did to us, of which the great and striking proof is, our doing so well without, as with them. Our customs prove that our trade has lost nothing by losing America; and the full and ample employment of our manufactures speak the same thing.

The call for the people of Britain to rouse themselves and show the spirit of their ancestors had not diminished in 1779. Nor had scribblers failed the ministry in support of its exertions. Unanimity and utmost exertion were to be the watchwords:

ALFRED (*LC* 8/24/79):

At the present important crisis, it is the duty of every friend to his country, to endeavour, by the utmost exertion, to rouse the people to a just sense of their own consequence and to remind them of those illustrious heroes of antiquity, who have ever stood forth in the hour of danger to defend their country against the attacks of its enemies. Where unanimity prevails, there is little doubt of success, and we have only to convince the general disturbers of our tranquillity, that we have both the ability and spirit to resent an insult. English glory was never yet tarnished.

POLITICUS (*MP* 7/28/79):

Experience, however, has taught us that there is a spirit in Britons which rises superior to difficulties; and when properly exerted, never fails to crown their endeavour with success: this spirit will undoubtedly manifest itself on the present occasion, and be attended with its usual happy effects.

OBSERVATOR (*PA* 8/24/79):

When verbal and written declarations [of the Ministry] shall be realized into substance, then will the confidence and affections of the people be secured; then will the whole nation be rivetted in a firm and faithful union, and the hateful name of party will become extinguished; the stern virtue of our ancestors will awake, and every Englishman will be animated with a noble emulation for the welfare of his country; the flood gates of opulence will be let loose, and the British youths will ardently rush forward to the field of glory, draw the sword and throw away the scabbard.... Britannia will once more reign triumphant o'er the foaming seas.

The *London Chronicle* and the *Morning Post* advised their readers that even if all endeavor to end the war successfully failed, the security of Britain would remain intact because it would not suit the purpose of the nations of Europe to upset the balance of harmony.

HISTORICUS (*LC* 9/23/79):

The great care of Europe is to maintain a kind of equality so as to secure the common repose. A general system must be preserved for that purpose: and however our politicians may talk or write of the subjection of Great Britain, that is an event that never will be permitted to happen; it is not consistent with the real interest of Europe, and that real interest must and will be preserved.... But Spain, France, and America, leagued against England, if our valour and the native spirit of our people are not adequate without foreign assistance to the preservation of our kingdom, will soon feel the weight of other belligerent powers. It is a duty as natural for them to concur for the common safety, as it is for the fellow citizen of an empire to unite against the invaders of their liberty.

HISTORICUS (*MP* 9/20/79):

Supposing that every syllable uttered by the patriotic fabulists was truth, and that England was as defenceless as these enemies to its happiness wish it to be, there exists a certainty that the belligerent powers of Europe would instantly step in to stop any increase of power to the ambitious House of Bourbon. For it is a maxim laid down, and from which each power will never depart, that a balance must be preserved for the tranquillity of the whole....

By 1780 the scribblers displayed less interest in the war in America. Knowledge was truly sorrow's spy. As all letters concerning America diminished by the eighties, so did the letters of euphoria. The *Morning Post* continued to emphasize the successes of British arms, while many of the other London morning dailies put their faith of victory in the chaos and desolation prevailing in the rebellious colonies. VERAX in the *Morning Post* (7/4/80) proclaimed the success of the military:

> And while we make progress with our arms forward, we leave no enemies behind us, strong enough to show themselves. What we are doing seems to be a solid and effectual reduction of the rebellious part of the Colonies, and a restoration of the well-affected to the peace, amity, and friendship of the Mother Country; and bids fair to be followed by a general Restoration of that whole Continent to its constitutional and natural dependency on Great Britain, which is the only safe state it ever can enjoy.

The *London Chronicle, Morning Chronicle,* and *Public Advertiser* saw most promising possibilities in the utter collapse of the rebellious colonies in North America. The writer signing as A BRITISH FREEHOLDER (*LC* 1/27/80) informed his readers that "the American contest beards the most promising aspect. Congress seems convulsed, and their cause nearly expiring."

The *Morning Chronicle* (2/12/80) presented a writer called A ROYAL VOLUNTEER whose two years of service in America with the royal army gave him impeccable qualifications. He argued that the transgressions of the colonies would enable British arms to crush the rebellion:

> I am just arrived from America, where I have been for near two years, constantly with the Royal Army.... I shall frequently furnish you with such facts as I imagine will be acceptable, and doubt not your readily publishing them. In the meantime I beg you will insert the following truths: The present defection from the republican cause daily increases: in order to quiet a commotion which had broke forth among a party of their troops a few weeks before I left New York, the pay was increased to 65 paper dollars each man each month: However, many of them were determined to serve no longer, and several have come over to his Majesty's service.... It is a truth not to be doubted, that we have it at present in our power to crush the rebellion, and bring those unhappy wretches to a sense of their duty. The number of desponding mortals that are now starving, on account of the continuance of this destructive war, may fully convince us, that by acting in a proper manner they will be easily subdued.

In an unsigned letter (1/13/80), the *London Chronicle* expressed its euphoria in a different manner. Union with America was not to be grounded on military conquest or any internal failure of the rebellious colonies. Rather success would lie in the unique benefits that Britain could furnish to the security and trade of America:

> Were the Americans left to their unrestrained choice, Britain is the country, and the only one, with which they should desire an union. Her constitution insures real substantial liberty to every subject—all are under the protection

of equal laws—none are exposed to the caprice of arbitrary will—the property and person, the civil and religious liberties of every man are perfectly secure. Britain is the only state whose maritime power can effectually protect America from foreign insult or invasion—she is the only state whose immense trade can employ and give vent to the various commodities of this western hemisphere to advantage—and she is the only state who can fully and on advantageous terms supply America with the several manufactures of linen, woollen, metals, etc. that she requires. No other state can furnish these of equal quality, in the same quantity, and at the same price. Let me add, that the ties of blood, religion, language, laws, and manners, strongly impel each to a coalition, which cannot be said of any other state with respect to America, but Britain. Providence, nature and reason, therefore point out and demand this union—and that union, I firmly believe and trust in God, will take place.

The spirit of the British revived, and the lion commenced to roar. But the war with the rebellious colonies and their allies was too much for British arms. The successful military action in the southern colonies was of short duration, and the promise of assistance from the Loyalists never fully developed. The surrender of Burgoyne at Saratoga, the subsequent entry of the French into the conflict, and the capitulation of Cornwallis at Yorktown was more than the British establishment could withstand.

CHAPTER TEN

American Brethren
and Fellow Subjects

Americans considered themselves to be Englishmen, and Englishmen regarded Americans as Englishmen. Thus it was to be expected that scribblers of all political persuasions would be inclined to employ such expressions as "fellow subjects" and "brethren." The application of those terms by both the ministerial writers and their antagonists in the Opposition indicates that all factions in Britain considered the war with the colonies in North America to be "unnatural."

To those writers intent on the subjugation of the rebellious colonies, the American brethren were the "rebellious brethren in America," "deluded brethren," and "bastard brethren." Antiministerial scribblers were less inventive. Americans were simply "brethren" or "fellow Christians and fellow subjects." Readers, in turn, were reminded that "Britons on both sides of the Atlantic are Brethren."

The number of pro- or anti–American letters indicates the changing opinions of the British reading public as the war progressed.[1] In 1775 and 1776, letters expressing sympathy for the colonies in America were equal to those supporting the ministry and damning the rebellion. Two years later those convictions had altered. In 1778 and 1779, most writers voiced unhappiness with their American brethren.

In 1775 many scribblers viewed English liberty as firmly entwined with America freedom. RALEIGH (*LC* 6/10/75), writing a few days after the news of Lexington and Concord reached London, forecast the success of the rebellious colonies coupled with the rekindling of British liberty: "The seat of empire seems already dedicated for the western world. Happy Britons, if they shall owe the revival of their liberty to the success of their American brethren."

The antiministerial scribblers were anxious about British liberty and saw a connection with the freedom of the colonies in North America, as ONE OF THE PUBLIC (*PA* 6/1/75) apprised his readers: "The Americans have been, as a Part of the British Empire, in Possession of every right which the Constitution gives ever since they were a People there settled. . . . Be not deceived, my Countrymen, nor suppose the present Struggle is to vindicate the Sovereignty of Britain; it is to establish Despotism in the Crown and enslave America."

Again, on 19 June, ONE OF THE PUBLIC informed his readers of the continuing threat to liberty both in Britain and in the colonies:

> Ye, my Countrymen, are deceived by appearances, and wickedly instigated by the enemies of Liberty, think the Americans are in open arms against this Country; ye execrate them as rebels whom ye should reverence for their virtuous fortitude; they are fighting for us, and on them depend the Liberties of this Country. . . . There is a general conspiracy against freedom. . . . In America it is endeavoured to be established by a Tory Administration by Force of Arms.

Americans were a "free people" as well as a "free-born people." Thus did ONE OF THE PUBLIC (*PA* 6/8/75) challenge the reigning concept of the supremacy of Parliament: "If Parliament can take what it pleases, when it pleases, and how it pleases, what is left to the People so miserably robbed, so cruelly plundered. . . . It is to preserve their Liberty with their property that Americans have resisted the executions of the late Acts of Parliament, because a submission to them must destroy them as a free people."

A COMMISSIONER OF SUPPLY (*CM* 10/9/75) warned his readers to beware of haste in entering into the present war. Again the concept of the supremacy of Parliament was challenged:

> I trust that none of you will testify your approbation of the present war, till you have carefully perused the charters of all the different Provinces, and until you are clear in your own minds, that not withstanding what is contained in these charters, upon the faith of which our brethren settled in America, the British Parliament may assume the power of establishing their taxation. Many of you have sat upon Juries and have not grudged long and painful attention, where the life of only one man was at stake; and will you, without due examination give your voice where the lives of thousands are at stake?

The writer A FRIEND TO LIBERTY (*MC* 8/12/75) suggested to his readers a connection between an administration seeking to subvert the English constitution and the slaughter of American fellow subjects: "When an administration dead to every sense of honour and shame, secretly undermine our constitution at home, and openly attack the liberties, and wantonly spill the blood of our American fellow subjects, opposition from every part of the kingdom become laudable and absolutely necessary."

Although the war had barely begun, there were scribblers who voiced disapprobation. The letter writer CANDIDUS (*MC* 10/6/75) was dismayed that there were Britishers so totally divested of every principle of humanity as to express approval of the subjugation of the Americans:

How greatly it is to be deplored that there can be found men, subjects of the
British empire, so totally divested of every principle of humanity, and of the
sympathy for the miseries of their fellow creatures, which has hitherto been
the distinguished characteristic of Britons ... by advising the most ample
supplies ... and by every other method to rivet the fetters which have been
so long forging for their American brethren.

The writer signing his name as simply "w" (*PA* 9/18/75) censured the
Public Advertiser for harboring ministerial writers and condemned scribbler
"u" for "wishing to send regiment after regiment to America to slay fellow
subjects."

The ministerial writers in 1775 displayed a temperate stance towards
the rebellious colonies. It was early in the war, and there remained the expectation of a timely and advantageous peace. How could the rebellious
rabble in America contend with British arms? The battle of Bunker Hill had
resulted in grievous losses to the royal forces, but they had succeeded in
securing their objective. Did not the *London Gazette* assure its readers of
the great victory in Massachusetts Bay?

There was an exception to the moderation of the ministerial scribblers.
In a letter addressed to Lord North, QUIDNUNC (*PA* 7/4/75), coupled a
vitriolic attack on the council of the city of London with one on our
American Brethren: "I have been endeavouring to find out some popular
Object for a Tax, whose evident Utility may reconcile it to the Mayor,
Alderman, and Common Council of London, and remove any Degree of
Odium that is likely to attend an Imposition for the humane Purpose of cut-
ting the Throats of our American Brethren in cold Blood."

There was concern among the scribblers for the plight of those
Americans remaining loyal to the king. ANTI FACTION (*MC* 11/10/75 and *LC*
11/11/75) believed that the oppressors in America, working under the ploy
of liberty and freedom, had in fact persecuted a vast number of fellow subjects. He briefed his readers:

The people of England can never be made to believe that administration
have any hostile designs against the constitutional liberties of America; on
the other hand, they are firmly persuaded that the coercive measures now
pursuing, so far from being inimical to freedom, are indispensably necessary
to support the freest constitution the world ever produced, and to rescue a
vast number of our fellow subjects in America from the despotism not to be
exceeded in the annals of mankind.

The *Public Advertiser* (11/7/75) offered its readers a letter from the
scribbler APPIUS entitled "An Address to the People of Great Britain from
the oppressed Loyalists of America." APPIUS urged the maintenance of
parliamentary authority throughout the empire and speaking in the quise
of the Loyalists, he stated: "In the midst of all our distresses, nothing
had given us severer anguish than that our Oppressors have craftily

imposed themselves on many of our fellow subjects in the Mother Country, as maintainers of freedom and the rights of humanity."

OPIFEX (*LC* 10/7/75) shared with APPIUS as well as all ministerial writers the necessity of maintaining parliamentary omnipotence. He assaulted both the Middlesex freeholders and his American brethren for lack of respect for Parliament: "The public may see by the instructions given to the Representatives of Middlesex that their Constituents have quite laid aside common decency and respect towards Parliament and that they are not willing to be outdone by their American brethren in phrases of contempt; "our inveterate enemies in the present Parliament."

To EGO (*CM* 10/16/75), his American brethren had been duped and all those not voicing approbation of the conduct of the war remained enemies to America: "I must declare it the indispensable duty of every loyal subject to hold every person who may endeavour to persuade the people against ADDRESSING HIS MAJESTY upon the present emergent state of affairs to be not only an abettor of the faction at home, but a real ENEMY TO AMERICA. It is beyond a doubt that the generality of our American brethren have been duped."

Should Britain require assistance in quelling the rebellion in North America, it was readily available from Europe according to THE ATLANTIC LINE (*MP* 11/1/75): "All our European neighbours are not only pacifically inclined toward us in the present crises of the state, but have also made us ... friendly tenders of assistance against our rebellious brethren in America."

Such terms as "Fellow citizens," "fellow subjects," and "brethren in America" were employed by the ministerial scribblers in 1776 to identify those colonists who remained loyal to the crown. These writers asserted that supporters of Congress, those "pretended advocates for Freedom," were guilty of "unheard-of-cruelties to the Loyalists."

APPIUS (*PA* 9/17/76) wrote of the ways in which the American rebels were repressing the Loyalists:

> I confess I was once an Advocate for the Americans; their claim to be exempted from Parliamentary Taxation, seemed to me to be founded in Justice; and I thought that it was equitable at least to give them a security against an oppressive exercise of it. But some of their late proceedings have convinced me, that their opposition is not dictated by true Patriotism, but by a spirit of tyranny and despotism. I shall not insist on their having destroyed the liberty of the Press, and preventing any thing from being published amongst them which controverts the measures of Congress; I shall not mention their having obliged peaceable citizens, at the peril of the loss of their Lives and fortunes, to subscribe associations, however contrary to their principles and opinions.... We there find these pretended Advocates for Freedom audaciously depriving their fellow citizens of the common privilege of

investigation and speech, precluding them of the benefit of a Trial by Jury, subjecting them to punishment of ex post facto laws.

CORIOLANUS (*PA* 11/12/76) cited the case of James Rivington, a printer of New York, to brief his readers on the perfidy of the rebellious colonists, who had cut off Rivington's ears and slit his nose:

> He is now driven from America, without business, and deprived of the means of maintaining a family, consisting of twelve persons, who he left behind in New York.... [He is] proscribed and proclaimed an enemy to America. Let every Englishman who may read this plain narrative, learn to value, as he ought, the blessings of equal Liberty and Law, which he enjoys in this Country: Let him not suppress his generous indignation at the perfidy of Traitors, who, while they [were] declaiming on the sacred nature of Property, were destroying the property of their fellow subjects; while they were clamouring against Tyranny, were abolishing the Freedom of the Press, whose religion is selfishness, inhumanity, and hypocracy; whose Liberty is the Power of persecuting others.

Notifying his readers that it was an honorable course for Britain to conquer America to give freedom to the Loyalists, PACIFICUS (*MC* 8/5/76) wrote:

> In England treason assumes the name of Liberty, and Rebellion called Natural Right. Unheard of insolence and absurdity! I rejoice, however, that a spirit of unanimity is obvious among us. The views of Congress to establish independency by the sword are now so manifest that no unprejudiced man can entertain a doubt about them. The supporting measures thus glaringly opposite to the interest of Great Britain and of America, may suit the purposes of needy patriots, of men in the pay of France or Spain, and of disaffected republicans. But I have too good an opinion of my countrymen to suppose there can be many of them thus lost to every principle of virtue. Unfortunately for the patriots, the resources of this great commercial country are so great that the loss of the Colony trade is scarcely felt in the different manufacturing towns throughout the kingdom; but, exclusive of all commercial regard and of the many millions the Colonies have cost this kingdom, it is surely becoming the honour of Britons to conquer, that they may give freedom to their brethren in America. And it is worthy of a government like that of Britain to overlook every expense when the object is nothing less than to relieve some thousands of good subjects on the other side of the Atlantic from the cruelty of the severest despotism that was ever exercised in any part of the world against men, whose only crime is their allegiance and attachment to the religion, the laws, and the constitution of Britain.

DETECTOR AMERICANUS (*LC* 9/7/76) addressed a very pertinent query "To the Opposition, or Friends of the American Rebels in Britain":

> With whom are we to be reconciled? When the leading party in America leave off to destroy our property, withhold our debts, oppress our fellow

subjects and oppose the laws ... In America, they are straining every nerve, pressing every argument, every topic, nay contradictions, into their party, to prove the immorality, profligacy, imprudence, futility, littleness, and the absurdity of a reconciliation with Britain. Have you not seen that famous essay of that insidious old fox F____, called Common Sense, written professedly to guard America against the snares of reconciliation.[2]

To those scribblers who in 1776 challenged the ministry and the purpose of the war in North America, the continuation of the conflict could only end in the ruin of the British Empire. ARTABANUS (*MP* 9/12/76) counseled his readers about the immense debt and the loss of trade resulting from the confrontation:

> The present alarming state of this empire must rouse every man who pretends to have at heart his country's welfare; and when he beholds in one view that nation sinking under an immense debt, her revenues wasting, trade decreasing, all affection of the colonies lost, the duty of civil power exchanged into a military one, a brave army fighting unwillingly against their fellow subjects and the kingdom moulding away for want of men of experience, abilities, and virtue.

ARMINIUS (*MC* 11/30/76) agreed with ARTABANUS. Troubled by the burdensome taxes and the loss of beneficial commerce, he addressed his report "To the People of England":

> Can it appear in the least advantageous to you to have daily more and more burthensome taxes heaped upon you, together with the loss of a beneficial commerce, to no other purpose than that of pleasing the whims of Administration, who any one of common sense must perceive are pursuing the most unconstitutional and arbitrary purposes, which you suffer with unaccountable insensibility and are made the instruments of the displeasure against your brethren the Americans.

Forecasting a confederacy of America and Britain resulting in a mutually beneficial commercial empire, MICROMEGAS (*CM* 7/29/76) wrote, suggesting the Howes, as commissioners for conciliation, address the Americans as follows:

> Countrymen and brethren, ye are all Britons alike; your first right is freedom; no deduction is to made there from; no partiality or notorious inequality can be allowed among freemen; Americans and Irish are not to be treated as Britons one way, and as foreigners another; both justice and policy forbid it. The line was happily drawn between you, therefore return to your former state. The infancy of America is ceased; 'tis not a mother and a daughter; Britons on both sides of the Atlantic are brethren; let each be the supporter and each the supported, till millions constitute the greatest commercial empire the World ever knew.

As in 1775, writers associated the liberty of the British with that of the Americans. OLD CASTLE (*MP* 5/23/76) suggested to his readers:

Mutuality of interest between the governors and governed is so necessary for the preservation of political liberty that it is impossible to destroy the one and retain the other; this is the great security of British freedom, and what renders our constitution so justly the admiration of those who have experienced the fatal effects arising from different principles; it is the avowed purpose of destroying this, that has so much alarmed the Americans; surely with reason, and has involved Great Britain in a war which must end ingloriously whether she is successful or not. I am conscious that every considerate man will concur to put an end to this unjust war; it is a duty we owe our country, ourselves, and our fellow subjects. The discontent with which it has been carried on is a proof that it is contrary to the inclinations of the people. Had Administration good motives for prosecuting it they would not hesitate to offer such terms as would secure the rights of British subjects to the oppressed Americans, and which, if refused, they would be sincerely supported by the inhabitants of this country. When they did not, when they insisted upon unconditional submission, it is not difficult matter to guess their intentions.

In addition to their disapproval of additional taxes and loss of liberty, the scribblers were incensed by the cruelty of the British forces. The writer signing as A LOVER OF PUBLIC LIBERTY (*LC* 2/20/76) questioned the need for such behavior:

Supposing the Americans [are] so bad that we think it lawful to wage war against them in such a cruel way as has been banished from all the civilized parts of Europe for near a century past, to forget they are men, fellow Christians, and FELLOW SUBJECTS, and to fire upon and set fire to the habitations of helpless and innocent infancy, decrepid old age, dying sickness, and tender women, and to drive them from their habitations into fields and woods, amidst the rigour of winter.

The writers of the British press were less enchanted with their "brethren" and "fellow subjects" in 1777 than they were in 1775 and 1776. The mission of the ministerial writers was to disparage the Opposition, expose them to ridicule and contempt, and hold them responsible for the war in North America. The tone of their letters became more strident, as when COURAGE SANS PEUR (*MC* 6/8/77) vented his anger on the minority:

To the Minority: ... after you have lighted the torch of rebellion, let loose all the horrors of civil discord, broken the allegiance you owe your King, forfeited the esteem of your country, when Victory sat smiling on our brows, your deluded brethren, ready to fall a sacrifice to their rash ambition, we are to be lulled asleep by an ignominious patched up peace; and olive branch, forsooth, offered by the first empire of the world, to a rascally Banditti in the Colonies, at the same time in actual rebellion against lawful Sovereign; for no other reasons than because a few individuals of the same mould as themselves are displeased at seeing the flourishing condition of their country, which rests on the basis of as solid and firm a foundation as theirs would be rotten and mouldering.

HISTORICUS (*MC* 7/24/77) briefed his readers on the culpability of the Dissenters: "The Dissenters in England, in conjunction with their brethren in iniquity, the English patriots, and their bastard brethren in America have had a large share in promoting the recent troubles in America."

By end of 1777, the news of the surrender of Burgoyne at Saratoga had reached London. STEDFAST (*PA* 12/13/77) responded by declaring every man a conspirator who would propose withdrawing troops from America:

> I will not offer such injury to the native spirit and established bravery of my loyal Countrymen, as to entertain a single idea that an event which has befallen a few of your fellow subjects in one part of America, when such signal successes have attended them in others, can induce them to believe that a defeat of so little moment can be a cause of national concern; and although they will sincerely lament the loss of such brave men, who have died in the defence of their Country's Rights and Dignity, against the most ungrateful of all Rebels, yet I am persuaded that no other sentiment than resolutions of pursuing those Rebels to the utmost State of Humiliation, and of the branding every man with a stigma of conspirator against his King and Country, who shall insidiously dare to propose the withdrawing our Troops from America, on any terms by those of submitting to their lawful Sovereign.

The writer simply signed J.A. (*PA* 11/14/77), an antiministerial scribbler for the *Public Advertiser*, responded to the disaster at Saratoga in a manner unlike that of STEDFAST: "None but Barbarians could read Mr. Burgoyne's Account without being grieved; nor can any honest Heart help being affected at the Carnage on both sides. Are they not our Brethren?"

By 1778 it was apparent that the war in North America was not responding to the expectations of the British military or the British populace. Burgoyne had surrendered his army at Saratoga, and the spectre of France entering the war on behalf of the colonies was rapidly becoming a reality. The lenity of the administration as well as the "affected Patriotism of the Opposition" provided grist to the mill for the scribblers.

Taking little comfort from the performance of the ministry or the Opposition, MEMNON (*PA* 5/7/78) wrote:

> Opposition say that our present Misfortunes arose from the arbitrary Principles of Administration; I affirm, that they have proceeded from the affected Patriotism of Opposition. The present set of Patriots opposed the passing [of] the Stamp Act; they also repealed it, when it had actually carried itself into Execution; and, thus, sowed those Seeds of Resistance which have since produced such a plentiful Harvest of Rebellion. When the Rebellion broke out, they supported it upon Principles of Liberty, instead of repressing it upon those of Expediency. A Clamour was raised, and Rebels were called by the endearing Name of Brethren. A foolish Populace gave Credit to the Assertions of designing Men. They thought their own Freedom involved in the

Contest; and thus the Hands of Government, being weakened at home, they were found incapable of making any spirited Exertions abroad. Instead of combating this unfortunate Turn of public Sentiment, Administration yielded to the Current. Conciliation was the Word; and, to obtain it, they spirited the Nation by Concessions, whilst they encouraged the Insolence of the Insurgents. Men in general became tired of a War that was destined to terminate in Disgrace. When the Insurrection became really serious, the Nation perceived that they had been deceived. They despised Administration for Pusillanimity; they detested Opposition as the Authors of their Misfortunes. Whichever Side should prevail, they were doomed to be ruled either by one Set of Men, whose Want of Spirit had raised Contempt, or by another, who had humbled their Country by laying her defenceless, disgraced and degraded at the Feet of a despicable and insolent Enemy.

CIVIS (MP 8/21/78) censured the ministry for its sufferance of the rebellious colonies and proposed additional troops for America, a suspension of habeas corpus, and punishment for those supporting the rebellion:

If our Ministers are not aware of the fatal tendency of their lenity, let then them look back at the beginning of the American war; let them consider then what a happy event a bold stroke at first might have produced. Severity abroad, and justice at home, would have broken the spirit of rebellion in its first stage, and preserved the colonies for the mother country. When the voice of opposition, strengthened by the seeming timidity of Administration, raised itself in the senate, reprobated the measures of government, extolled the conduct of the noble chiefs in America, and encouraged them to persevere in their rebellion, that was the time to show the resolution, and bold determination. Thirty thousand men should have been sent directly against the rebels; the habeas corpus should have been instantly suspended during the rebellion, and every man who had dared to speak a word in favour of treason, should have been immediately confined, and punished as severely as the laws can punish an abetter, and encourager of rebellion. This bold conduct, this resolute proceeding would have intimidated the whole of the Republican Party; and their pious brethren in America would have soon understood, that they were not to expect any assistance from their confederates in Britain; treason would have dropped its ears; rebellion would have expired without a shot from a cannon. Let ministers weigh well these considerations; let them see their errors before it is too late; let them rouse from their lethargy, and let the world know, that they are ministers, and that there are laws in this kingdom which none shall be permitted to violate with impunity.

For those scribblers seeking a reconciliation with the colonies, the Carlisle Peace Commission of 1778 was a hoax perpetrated by the ministry. Thus did G.N. (PA 4/14/78) counsel his readers:

Were the Ministry in Earnest; did they seriously propose any Thing by this Commission; had they any the least Favourable Expectation from it by

Appearances, do they imagine that the Americans, in their Situation, would treat, whilst a hostile Army was still on their Coast—whilst an inimical Ministry, the Cause of all their Suffering, were still in Place—and with the Commissioners, the mere Creatures of that Ministry? Every Circumstance loudly proclaims this to be a ludicrous Commission; it will prove such in the Conclusion. And if the People of England will suffer themselves to be so easily deluded, I can assure them the strong Intellects, and the clear and discerning Judgement of our Brethren in America will not subject them to the Influence of so bungling a Craft.

From the onset of the conflict in North America, there were writers who voiced dismay and revulsion at the bloodshed resulting from the war with their brethren. The letter writer signing as RACHEL (*PA* 12/4/78) continued the practice as she was "weeping for HER children: "Bishops, Clergy, are you Christians? And will you countenance such cruel Fratricide? For the Americans are your Brethren: Revolters, Rebels, call them what you will, they are still your Brethren. May the Blood that shall be shed lie on your Hands, if you do not fall on your Knees to the Throne, and deprecate such Savage Barbarities."

By 1779, France was openly an ally of the rebellious colonies. The ministerial scribblers could no longer write of the peaceful intentions of Britain's traditional enemy. The writer WAR! WAR! (*PA* 10/6/79) revealed to his readers a change of attitude, an alteration of belief which was not uncommon among the British populace:

> I am aware, Sir, how often the Voice of timid Eloquence has preached up PEACE! PEACE! within the Senatorial Walls. Let it be remembered, Peace, was at that Moment most ardently to be wished for, engaged as we were in a cruel, unjust, and unnatural War with our Fellow Subjects in America. Engaged as we are in a just War with the United House of Bourbon, it becomes the Duty of every Briton to cry aloud for War.

An ABHORER OF ALL PARTY SPIRIT (*MP* 3/12/79) informed his readers that the Americans had prevented all hopes of reconciliation by their treaty with France:

> The usurpation in America play an exceeding high game; a freedom from the claims of British subjects, and the government of such a continent are no trifling matters. To gain their end (and the misery is, our conduct gives them the highest chance of gaining, without risk of loss) they have pursued the most desperate course, by committing every violence, and giving every insult, that so there might be abundance of obstacles to reconciliation; and now they have fixed the matter, by a league with France. Away then with treaty, my fellow subjects, for assuredly none can avail us; spirited exertions only can end the present contest, so as to make America more useful to Great Britain than to any other power. If our Navy can compel France to keep her armies at home, there is no doubt but our force, wisely conducted, can, in one year, lay the Congress power (the source of all our suffering) in the dust.

We are now to fight only for an union of force with America; this re-union it would seem can be of no other service, but to render Britain the more safe. I would be glad to see any advantage pointed out which Great Britain would have beyond any other nation, from such a treaty as the Commissioners appeared ready to make with Congress? And if there is such advantage, how it, or the so much talked of union of force could be secured, should the following article be given up. To agree that no military force shall be kept in the different states of North America, without the consent of the General Congress or particular assemblies.

MARCUS (*CM* 2/3/79) told his readers that if the colonies did become independent, they would not offer Britain favorable trade arrangements:

Flatter not yourselves either, that once being the same people, and still possessing the same laws, and the same religion, will give you a preference in the American market: For as a spirit of revenge has often separated brethren in opposition to their real interests, so will disappointed ambition on the one hand, and a remembrance of past injuries on the other, prevent any friendship from being renewed between Britain and the colonies should they become independent. They have already shown what they can do in defence of rebellion. Should you remain much longer inactive, perhaps revenge may prompt them to confine you to your original island, with hardly one ship of the line to protect what trade the pity of surrounding states leaves you to enjoy. Let me hope, then, that all excuses from fear, of philosophy, or mistaken views of commerce will be thrown aside: That you are resolved to conquer, or fall with glory. If there be any amongst you who still hesitate about their conduct, let them remember, that there are such things as laws of high treason, and our country never stood more in need of their being put in execution.

If Englishmen dwelling in Britain required justification for denying the colonists English liberties, CIVIS (*LC* 4/27/79) supplied the necessary rationale:

It would be superfluous to employ words to establish the supremacy of a parent state over its colonies, since the principle is admitted by all parties; who only differ in what is to constitute that supreme authority.... If Englishmen with their descendants in the American colonies were admitted to enjoy equal political privileges with their brethren in the mother country, the supremacy of this state over those remote dependencies would be reduced to a mere "brutum fulmen," a phrase destitute of all meaning. The bill of rights, our recent confirmation of English liberties, was indeed framed after the settlement of our American plantations.... The framers of this famous statute were better grounded in their political constitution than to think of stretching it over the ocean to America.... British liberties are thus found to be absolutely local; they neither are, nor can be, American liberties. The British government has according [sic] constantly exercised legislative authority over the colonies ... subordination to the laws of the sovereign state being expressly reserved in such grants [charters], in return for support and protection.... Englishmen leaving their country—they are free Englishmen ... destitute of all political privileges whatever; they land politically naked on the American shore, and are to accept the constitution of the colony they make choice of for their settlement.

The voice of those scribblers supporting the American cause grew feeble in 1779. Few could accept or justify encouragement for the rebellious colonies now that a firm alliance between them and the French had been concluded. BRITANNIA (*MC* 12/25/79) could only beseech Parliament to seek peace with the Americans in order to defeat the evil designs of the treacherous French:

O think, think my dear Parliament! what is said you have done, and what you are now adoing, before it is too late; that is before matters are brought to their last extremity. Be not, I pray you, like the sturdy unbending oak, which is split by the rending tempest into a thousand pieces, but like the pliant weeping willow, that, humbly reclining its head, safely rides throughout the storm. In a word, be not weary in well doing, but courteously send again, and again, by your siren negotiators, the olive branch of peace to your American brethren. They cannot, they will not, any longer resist your repeated, pressing importunities, and endearing condescension. They must be insane if they do, but it is far otherwise with them. Believe me, they still love the British nation, in their hearts, a thousand times better than the treacherous French or haughty Spaniard.... Go then, gentle negotiators, once more, across the vast Atlantic ocean, in the spirit of much meekness, great condescension, and all conquering love, and give those high and mighty lords, the Congress Chieftains, and all the dear returning prodigals, the sweet kiss of reconciliation, parted once, but never, never to be parted more. So shall the proud House of Bourbon be defeated in its deep laid plots against free born Britons, and Americans, in order to maintain their grand object, universal monarchy.

To G.N. (*PA* 1/26/79), English liberty continued to be interwoven with American liberty. To forfeit the latter would destroy the former:

The spirit of Liberty, as we all know, and must acknowledge when we speak conscientiously, has been kindled in America; and War, which was to have quenched, has tended only to give Ardour, and to spread the holy Flame. Nearly extinguished in Europe, Asia, and Africa, by the Folly and iniquity of Mankind, and then fled across the Atlantic to recover its Strength, and, if possible, to revive in the new World. Should it be unsuccessful there, there is not a Spot, perhaps on the whole Globe, wherein it is received and cherished in its virgin purity. The Contest therefore on America may justly be considered as the last efforts of Liberty; and the Question is, shall it be persecuted, and expelled from the Earth, and leave us for ever to seek a Refuge in its native Heaven, whence it originally descended to bless Mankind? ... Every Man must perceive, that if America should be enslaved, Britain cannot for any Length of Time after that Event retain and preserve those small Remains of her ancient Liberty she now enjoys. The present War is a War without Hope. For as the avowed Intention of the War is to subdue America, so it is necessary, or rather an inevitable Consequence, that, when subdued, she must be enslaved; since nothing, after what has passed, will be able to restrain, and keep her in Subjection, but Fortifications and a Military Power; and whoever is subjected to these, is in a complete State of Slavery. This Slavery established in America, will soon after be inevitably extended to Britain, and pervade it by the Means before alleged; which Event will most assuredly take Place in the Reign of the first misguided Prince, and iniquitous Ministry, which shall happen next after that Calamity befalls America. Thus our indisputable Rights, and Liberties, will be made solely to rest on this uncertain Basis, the Wisdom of some future Prince, and the Integrity of his Ministers.... If Ministry therefore will not adopt such Measures as shall effectually put an End to this destructive War, it is high Time the People should. It is not Reason, nor is it consonant to Civil Government, nor is it in the Nature of Despotism which is not Civil Government, that a whole Nation should be undone in Compliance with the forward Humour of one Man, or of any Set of Men whatever. And, therefore, if we entertain any Regard for our Liberties; if we value our Property; if we have any Consideration for our own Lives, and those of our Fellow Subjects which are to be sacrificed in this Hopeless War, wherein nothing beneficial can be obtained, and all enjoyment may be lost; it is incumbent upon us to be indefatigable in our Endeavour to stop the Progress of this ruinous War, lest we be overwhelmed with that Destruction which inevitably attends the Continuance, and will be infallibly hurled on our Heads in its rapid Career, while we are blindly and desperately promoting and encouraging the Prosecution of it.

Although the ministerial scribblers in 1780 celebrated the British victories in the Carolinas and Georgia, the foundation of their exhilaration rested with the defeat of the French. The writer A READER (*LC* 1/8/80) objected to the manner in which the Patriots perceived the victories in the southern plantation. Were not those victories frustrating the planned operations of the French in North America?:

I cannot conceive what sort of patriots those can be who take pains to lessen our joy for the late affair at Savannah.... The whole set of operations planned against our North America by the French, and our old deluded, now enslaved, and cheated fellow subjects, overthrown at once, and a cause for dissention and inextinguishable discord among our enemies ... are surely matters more worthy of our exaltation.

Peace with America was a means to assure the success of British arms against both France and Spain, according to LAURENTIANUS (*CM* 4/24/80):

What I propose is that a Petition should be drawn up to the House of Commons, in decent and respectful terms, humbly setting forth, "That some of the petitioners were originally for the American war, and some against it; and therefore praying the Honourable House to take the matter under their consideration, so that we may have peace with our brethren, and be enabled to contend, as we have formerly done, against foreign nations."

To some writers, the success of British arms in the southern colonies of North America should be regarded less as a means of subjugation than as a way to achieve a lasting reunion with the Americans. This was the message PEACE AND UNION (*PA* 6/21/80) suggested to his readers:

> The Capture of Charles-Town is an Event of such a Magnitude, as to raise the Expectation in every Lover of his Country of a happy and lasting reunion with our Brethren of North America. The Consequence of this Country, in the Eyes of all Europe, depends on our maintaining the Colonies; not by subjugation, which I ever believed to be impracticable, nor by holding out to the Americans Terms of unconditional Submission; and Expressions formed by Pride and Presumption, and supported by Tyranny and Cruelty.

HUMANITUS (*MC* 1/1/80) could only shudder with pity at the reported cruelties of the British forces in America: "Great are the calamities of war in general, but much greater in that country, which is unhappily the seat of it. Nature shudders, and humanity drops the tear of pity at the enormities said to have been committed by our army in America, which every man of honour and feeling for his fellow subjects, must look upon with the utmost horror and detestation."

PORTEUS (*MP* 10/14//80) suggested a simple and realistic solution, but one that in 1780 was still anathema to the British populace: "Withdraw your troops from America, and treat with them as brethren and freemen. It has ever been my opinion, and I will repeat it till this House reverberates with the sound. Withdraw your troops from America—disband them— save the country the expense of supporting them. America is lost, and no military power can restore it."

The year 1781 brought a search for a scapegoat. ARISTIDES (*LC* 2/22/81) accused General Howe of granting the American brethren a calamitous reprieve at the battle of White Plains. Lord North and his ministry were held responsible by AN ECONOMIST (*MC* 6/7/81) for the failure of his administration to aid our "suffering brethren [loyalist], who are now left totally destitute by that very government in support of which they lost all their property, and reduced themselves and their families to misery and ruin."

Accusing all British generals, with the exception of Lord Cornwallis, of human depravity, PLAIN TRUTH (*MC* 12/25/81) wrote: "These men, not content with having wantonly wasted the treasures of this nation, and sacrificed many thousands of their loyal fellow subjects to their rapine, would now prevail on you to abandon to your enemies the most valuable part of your foreign dominions and with it more than a million and a half of your faithful fellow subjects."

For A LOVER OF TRUTH (*LC-WC* 7/17/81), it was a profligate ministry that attempted to destroy or enslave the Americans: "The welfare and the liberties of England depend upon the ministry being defeated in their attempts to destroy or enslave our brethren in America; and that therefore every true friend of England must lament every victory that is obtained by men who are only fighting for the destruction of those liberties, which is the duty of every Englishman to defend."

The scribblers on both the ministerial and Opposition sides referred to those persons who had emigrated from Britain to America as brethren, fellow subjects, and Englishmen. The terms were the same but adjectives joined to them were devoid of similarity.

Those colonists who disputed the supremacy of Parliament and the sovereignty of the Crown were described by the ministerial correspondents as "rebellious brethren," "deluded brethren," or "bastard brethren." Americans who maintained their allegiance to the mother country were "suffering brethren" and "loyal fellow subjects." To those scribblers favoring the Administration, the rebellious colonists were intent on depriving their fellow citizens [loyalists] of the privilege of speech and the benefit of trial by jury. The properties of those who remained loyal to Britain were being destroyed, and it was the obligation of the mother country "to rescue a vast number of our fellow subjects from a despotism not to be exceeded in the annals of mankind."

Opposition writers avoided criticism of the Loyalists in America and stressed the plight of those colonists who supported the Congress. They were the "oppressed Americans," "American fellow subjects," and "fellow Christians and fellow subjects." For the Opposition scribblers, those colonists who supported separation from Britain were the "oppressed Americans" and the "enslaved Americans." And it was to preserve their property that they had resisted the executions of the acts of Parliament.

For the scribblers, it was truly a civil war between "brethren." Each professed fidelity to liberty and freedom and each accused his adversaries of suppressing those rights. Each accused the other of wantonly spilling blood and of unheard of cruelties. Each portrayed his antagonist as wicked and the perpetrator of heinous crimes. Each acted as men did from time immemorial in an effort to justify the inhuman atrocities of war.

Epilogue

It is fitting to honor the British press and to the public they served during the American War for Independence. The printers deserve our praise for providing a platform for the diverse views of their readers even as they were harassed by a misguided ministry. And tribute must be bestowed on the populace for thwarting efforts of the government to muzzle the voice of an independent press.

A press that was essentially free served the people of Britain during the years 1775-1781. Despite the unbridled criticism of Parliament, the ministry, and George III, the administration was loath to exercise its ability to prosecute printers for seditious libel. It is beyond doubt that as the law stood the newspapers wrote treason, but the ministry had discovered that they spoke the voice of the people and to put them down would require an army. And so the printers, supported by their readers, questioned, challenged, and denigrated attempts of the ministry to constrain their freedom.

CRITO (*MP* 10/3/75) raised the alarm of the danger of a despotic government insidiously eroding the basic rights of Englishmen:

> Death of the English Constitution: The Court, when it arrives at that plenitude of importance will not be so foolish as to be guilty of cruelties and outrages in their naked form. Everything will still be done according to law, and those acts upon the vigour of which the freedom of the subject depends, will one after another be virtually repealed by explanation and amendments. Oppression in every instance will take the form of law; and the people will see their Houses of Lords and Commons meeting as regularly as now, and inclosures, turnpikes, and such business transacted with great formality; but the liberty of the press will be gone, habeas corpus evaded, and the trial by jury poisoned, the power of the Attorney-General will be dreadful, and the standing forces of the nation much increased. When these symptoms appear, let it be concluded, that ancient forms are but so many farces, and had much better not exist than exist only as cloaks of despotism.

Three years later G.N. (*PA* 5/21/78) sounded a similar alarm. The structure of government would continue unaltered, but that design would act only as a mask for despotism.

> The Influence of the Crown on a corrupted Parliament may entirely destroy our Liberty while the Forms remain; in Speculation every Thing may continue the same, but in Fact there will be a total Change. For the Parliament being thus at the Devotion of the Crown, the Crown as an absolute despotic Power through the Medium of Parliament, complying only with the mere Forms of Liberty as a Mask to conceal under that Disguise the Reality of the Despotism. And I am justified in Conclusions far more extensive than any I have drawn, or mean to draw, from the clear and express Words of Lord Bolingbroke, whose Authority stands thus in his fifth Letter On the Study of History. "For sure (says he) there cannot be a greater Absurdity to affirm, that the People have a Remedy in Resistance, when their Prince attempts to enslave them; but that they have none, when their Representatives sell themselves and them."

Again G.N. (PA 11/4/78) wrote of the spurious facade of liberty which the ministry permitted the populace:

> The People would do well to determine whether they have any Rights and Liberties, or whether they have none. And if they have, they ought to come to a Resolution to maintain and defend, or at once to relinquish them. If they mean to do the latter, then they may as well remain where they are, in the Hands of Ministry, where Legislature has obsequiously lodged them, as elsewhere; but if they mean to claim and defend them, they ought certainly to be removed from the dangerous Touch of such rapacious Guardians. At present, we hardly know with Certainty whether we may account ourselves a free People or not; we seem rather to possess a middle Compound Character between the two; a mostly Composition of both, determinable at the Will of the Ministry, as we do not seem inclinable to determine for ourselves. All we have to bias with Certainty is, that we are permitted to be clamorous in Commendation of what in reality we do not possess; to carry high the mere Ensigns of Liberty, and occasionally to exult in the Sound, while we are crouching under the Badge of Slavery, which by certain, but almost imperceptible Advances, Ministry have been casting on our Shoulders, and mean, unless we reject it with Spirit, I know not; for some Time past a careless indifference, a stupid Insensibility seems to have been so predominant as to render us incapable of being affected either by Glory, or by Dishonour. The Advantages arising to Ministry from so abject a Disposition, they will not fail to improve; and at a convenient Season, when it is least apprehended, will slip on the Chains, and indissolubly rivet the Fetters of Slavery upon us—Fetters more durable than Adamant.

JUNIUS JUNIOR (*MC* 9/23/77) suggested to his readers that the minister was their servant, a most singular concept in eighteenth century Britain. Perhaps, he continued, all virtue did not reside with the king and ministers:

We should have some stronger reasons in a free state for supporting a Minister than that simple one that the King has thought proper to appoint him. There is something too courtly in this; it draws away the attention of the Minister from his country, whose servant in fact he is; whatever the road to power, that is the road that will be trod. If the opinion of the country be of no use, as a means of power and consideration, the qualities which usually procure that opinion will no longer be cultivated; and whether it will be right in a state so popular as ours to leave ambition to popular motives, or to trust all to pure virtue in the minds of the King and Ministers, must be submitted to the sense and judgement of the people.

JUNIUS JUNIOR (*MC* 10/1/77) further apprised his readers that Parliament was no longer responsible to, nor the protector of, the people:

The popular election of magistrates, and popular disposition of rewards and honours, is one of the first advantages of a free state; without it, or something equal to it, we can not, perhaps, long enjoy the substance of freedom. The frame of our commonwealth did not admit to such an actual election; but it provided as well, and better, for all the effects of it, than by the method of suffrage in any democratic state whatever. It had always, until of late, been held one of the first duties of Parliament to refuse to support government until power was in the hands of men acceptable to the people, or while factions prevailed at Court, in which the nation had no confidence. Thus all the good effects of popular election were supposed to be secured to us, without the mischiefs attending on particular intrigue. This was the most noble and refined part of our constitution. The people, by their representatives and grandees, were entrusted with the power of making laws: the King with the control of his negative; the King had the deliberative power of choosing to office; the people had a negative in a parliamentary refusal to support. Formerly this power of control was what kept ministers in awe of Parliament, and Parliament in reverence to the people. If the use of this control on the system and persons of administration is gone, everything is lost, Parliament and all.

In the "Whimsical Reflections of Sam Saunter" (*MP* 7/4/78), the scribbler strongly recommended the necessity of party to protect the people against the veiled invasions of their liberty. To speak of faction in an approving manner was most unusual in the British press of that era:

Since British freedom so much surpasses the boasted liberty of the ancients, can we be too watchful in guarding, and transmitting it entire to posterity. Mankind will never betray their liberties in a collective body; and if ever slavery should attempt to rear her baneful head in Britain, it will be by those imperceptible gradations, which will escape the observations of the multitude, and which none but the most penetrating can decry. It is this that makes party so valuable, and so necessary to the preservation of our liberties; for, as government can never gain over all the men of wit and genius to their side, there will always be a Minority sufficient to check these inroads of tyranny, which are so natural to individuals in power, to obtain the smiles of their prince, and secure their own aggrandizement.

To J.A. (*PA* 10/27/78), the peril to the freedom of the press, that bulwark of British liberty, was immediate and palpable. A Parliament displeased with the press was seeking to reimpose restraints on the publishing of their undertakings. This writer ended his letter with a warning to the people and to Parliament. To the populace he offered cautions of the devious ways of despotism; to the administration he gave notice of the danger that would result from the just anger of an wrathful people:

> In the present Reign, the Modes assumed have been to buy what they were afraid to destroy; and by Severities on Printers, for occasionally printing what they have ignorantly thought harmless; and when called upon, have given up the Authors, have endeavoured to deter such from conveying such Instructions so necessary to a free People to know, and which every tyrant dreads they should. Hence we may evidently see three Things which all Kings and Ministers dread: First, All Information to the People: Secondly, All Freedom of Discussion in the People: And, Thirdly, Any Press which may convey Information, or the free Discussion of others, to the Community at large. This Discussion occasioned the heavy Complaints in the last Sessions of Parliament; and some then lamented that no Act of Parliament existed to punish Printers for publishing their Transactions. But as Despotism acts by Sap, so step by step it moves unseen or unregarded, until by multiplied Exertions it oversets the Bulwarks of Liberty, or the Superstructure is destroyed by the united Efforts of a justly incensed People.

This same writer, J.A. (*PA* 10/27/78), further informed his readers that the Ministry was considering the appointment of a licenser. For those uneasy with a free press, the concept of a guardian of virtue and order, a licenser, had a universal and timeless appeal. For those devoted to the freedom of the press, a licenser was a censor, one who would be empowered to muzzle the press with prepublication restraints, a concept which at this time was alien to British principles. Again a warning was sounded about the threat to liberty that would result from a supine populace:

> Establishing a Licenser is to restrain Genius, not the Press; — and to inhibit all Freedom of Sentiment; nay it is subjecting every Work of Genius to the venal or confirmed Prejudices of one Man, and establishing him as an infallible Judge of every controverted Point, either learned, religious, or civil. And this is the Reason why all Administrations have uniformly followed the Practice of Restraint. This originates from Fear, and Fear is the Consequence of Violence. The Liberty of the Press is so essential to a free State, that it may be called the Touchstone of Freedom, as none such exists in arbitrary Monarchies, or tyrannical Aristocratical Republics. Whenever the Press is restrained, Liberty will soon feel the Pressure, as by Means of a free Communication, in the daily prints, the People will be early warned. But such, at present, is the spine Sluggishness of most, that nothing but extreme

‎‎‎‎

Danger, attended with approaching Ruin, will stimulate; as the Care of Posterity is lost in personal Sensuality, all generous Exertions in Favour of the People will be unattempted, and this Nation be (deservedly) stigmatized for the base Degeneracy.

If the British people were guilty of "Sluggishness," and they were not, the press was not to be submissive to a hostile ministry. In a letter that taunted Lord North and the government, Henry Woodfall, printer of the *Public Advertiser*, restated (2/17/78) the very phrase, employed the very word, *Murdered*, that had resulted in the conviction of four fellow printers and John Horne in the matter of the Constitutional Society advertisement in June 1775 (see Chapter Two). The writer PHILO-ARISTEDES delivered Woodfall's challenge to Lord North: "You ought to know that America will not treat with you for a Reconciliation, except her INDEPENDENCY be first acknowledged: You ought to know that she hath a Right to that IN-DEPENDENCY, and that every American slain for defending it is murdered: Murdered, my Lord, I say, notwithstanding I have the punishment of Mr. Horne, and the Doctrines of the Court of King's Bench before my Eyes."

The warnings issued by the letter writers of two hundred years ago remain as compelling in contemporary society. Administrations of all political tenets find a free press restraining to their pursuits. To deliberate behind closed doors, out of the glare of public scrutiny, is a common goal for most members of government. Leaks of government intelligence to the press, and then to the inspection of the public, are considered violations of responsibility by a licentious press. That is, unless the seepage is managed by a member of the administration.

Licensers, or censors, are no less the favorites of contemporary governments than they were some two hundred years in the past. Often proposed as protectors of the morality and virtue of the people, they are no more than a mask to conceal a further erosion of basic rights.

The active participation of a vigilant populace continues to be essential to preserve the freedom of the press. Such involvement is as necessary in our contemporary society as it was in the eighteenth century. All of which is not to approve of a unbridled press, but to stress the need for caution in attempting restraints. Alexis de Tocqueville's opinion on freedom of the press remains as relevant today as it was two centuries ago:

> I admit that I do not feel towards freedom of the press that complete and instantaneous love which one accords to things by their nature supremely good. I love it more from considering the evils it prevents than on account of the good it does.[1]

APPENDIX A

Henry Woodfall's
Account at Newgate[1]

MR. WOODFALL'S FEES

	£	s.	d.
To the Sergeant-at-Arms, Caption Fees	3	6	8
Seventeen days in custody	17	0	0
Bringing to the bar	0	6	8
Housekeeper	0	5	0
Messenger 17 days at 6s. 8d. per day	5	13	4
Serving the Speaker's order and warrant	0	13	4
Doorkeepers	0	5	0
The Speaker's secretary	1	0	0
The clerk and clerk's assistant	1	4	0
	29	14	0

MR. WOODFALL'S BILL

February 14.	3 Bottles of Port	0	7	6
"	2 ditto Sherry	0	4	0
"	Beer	0	1	4
"	5 Suppers, beefsteaks	0	7	6
" 15.	3 Breakfasts	0	3	0
"	2 Fowls, bacon, greens, leg of pork	1	1	0
"	6 Bottles of Port	0	15	0
"	2 Ditto Sherry	0	6	0
"	Biscakes	0	0	3
"	7 Suppers, duck, mince pies, and cold beef	0	14	0
"	7 Teas and coffee	0	7	0
"	Beer	0	3	0
" 16.	2 Breakfasts	0	2	0
"	3 Bottles of Sherry	0	6	0
"	10 Ditto Port	1	5	0
"	6 Dinners, leg of lamb, 2 ducks, sallat, &c.	0	18	0
"	Supper, beef, and mutton, steaks, sallat &c.	0	10	6
"	Biscakes	0	0	3

			£	s.	d.
February 16.		Beer	0	3	0
"	17.	2 Breakfasts	0	2	0
"		5 Dinners, salt-fish, sauce, and loin of mutton	0	15	0
"		2 Bottles of Sherry	0	4	0
"		2 Ditto Port	0	5	0
"		Suppers	0	2	6
"		Beer	0	1	6
"	18.	2 Breakfasts	0	2	0
"		7 Dinners, sirloin of beef, sallat, &c.	0	18	0
"		Sherry, 1 bottle	0	2	0
"		Port, 7 ditto	0	17	6
"		Brandy	0	0	6
"		Biscakes	0	0	3
"		4 Teas	0	3	4
"		Suppers, beef, sallat, &c.	0	5	0
"		Beer	0	3	0
"	19.	4 Breakfasts	0	4	0
"		7 Dinners, mutton, 2 chickens, and sallat	1	1	0
"		Sherry, 2 bottles	0	4	0
"		Port, 4 ditto	0	10	0
"		Biscakes	0	0	3
"		6 Teas and coffee	0	6	0
"		Suppers, veal collops, sallat, &c.	0	5	0
"		Beer	0	2	0
"	20.	4 Breakfasts	0	4	0
"		6 Dinners, veal, bacon, and greens	0	12	6
"		Sherry, 2 bottles	0	4	0
"		Port, 2 ditto	0	5	0
"		12 Teas	0	10	0
"		6 Suppers, cold duck, beef, and sallat	0	7	6
"		Beer	0	2	6
"		Lipsalve	0	0	3
"	21.	3 Breakfasts	0	3	0
"		4 Dinners, stewed beef, &c.	0	8	0
"		2 Bottles of Sherry	0	4	0
"		4 Ditto, Port	0	10	0
"		4 Suppers, mutton chops, cold beef, &c.	0	5	0
"		Beer	0	2	6
"	22.	2 Breakfasts	0	2	0
"		7 Dinners, leg of pork and potatoes	0	12	6
"		Port, 3 bottles	0	7	6
"		Sherry, 1 ditto	0	2	0
"		4 Teas	0	3	4
"		6 Suppers	0	3	0
"		Beer	0	3	0
"		Oranges and sugar	0	0	6
"	23.	3 Breakfasts	0	3	0
"		7 Dinners, fish, sauce, leg of mutton, &c.	1	1	0

			£	s.	d.
February 23.		Sherry, 1 bottle	0	2	0
"		Port, 3 ditto	0	7	6
"		2 Teas	0	1	8
"		6 Suppers	0	6	0
"		Beer and tobacco	0	4	10
"	24.	3 Breakfasts	0	3	0
"		7 Dinners, veal cutlets, &c.	0	17	6
"		Sherry, 2 bottles	0	4	0
"		Port, 2 ditto	0	5	0
"		5 Teas	0	4	2
"		7 Suppers, beef and mutton steaks	0	7	6
"		Beer	0	3	0
"	25.	3 Breakfasts	0	3	0
"		3 Dinners, mutton, &c.	0	7	6
"		Port, 4 bottles	0	10	0
"		Sherry, 2 ditto	0	4	0
"		4 Teas	0	3	4
"		6 Suppers, fowls and mutton chops	0	10	6
"		Beer	0	3	0
"	26.	3 Breakfasts	0	3	0
"		8 Dinners, stewed beef and fowl	1	0	0
"		Sherry, 2 bottles	0	4	0
"		Brandy	0	2	0
"		7 Teas	0	5	10
"		6 Suppers, fowls and chops	0	10	6
"		Beer	0	4	0
"	27.	3 Breakfasts	0	3	0
"		6 Dinners, beef and tart	0	18	0
"		Sherry, 3 bottles	0	6	0
"		Port, 4 ditto	0	10	0
"		6 Teas	0	5	0
"		3 Suppers	0	3	0
"		Beer and tobacco	0	3	10
"	28.	3 Breakfasts	0	3	0
"		5 Dinners, mutton and sauce	0	10	6
"		Port, 3 bottles	0	7	6
"		Sherry, 2 ditto	0	4	0
"		Beer	0	3	0
"		4 Suppers, cold beef, &c.	0	5	0
March	1.	3 Breakfasts	0	3	0
"		5 Dinners, veal and broccoli	0	12	6
"		4 Teas	0	3	4
"		Port, 1 bottle	0	2	6
"		4 Suppers, mutton chops and sallat	0	5	0
"		Beer	0	3	6
"	2.	3 Breakfasts	0	3	0
"		5 Dinners, mutton, &c.	0	10	0

		£	s.	d.
March 2.	Sherry, 1 bottle	0	2	0
"	Beer	0	1	6
		35	9	3
	Deduct for fowl, overcharged	0	5	0
		35	4	3
	Use of room and linen	1	11	6
	Servants	1	1	0
		37	16	9
	Fees	29	14	0
	The barber and messenger	2	11	6
		70	2	3
	Messenger, &c.	1	17	9
	Received, March 7, 1774, the above contents in full	72	0	0
	(Signed) JOHN BELLAMY.			

MR. WOODFALL TO THOS. BARRAT Dr.

		£	s.	d.
For seven times shaving		0	3	6
To seven times shaving		0	3	6
		0	7	0
	Servants	0	2	6
		0	9	6
Gave Wood, messenger		2	2	0

Olive Branch Petition

To the King's Most Excellent Majesty

Most gracious Sovereign,

We your Majesty's faithful subjects of the colonies of New Hampshire, Massachusetts bay, Rhode Island, and Providence plantations, Connecticut, & New York, New Jersey, Pennsylvania, the counties of New Castle, Kent & Sussex on Delaware, & Maryland, Virginia; North Carolina and South Carolina in behalf of ourselves and the inhabitants of those colonies, who have deputed us to represent them in general Congress, entreat your Majesty's gracious attention to this our humble petition.

The union between our Mother Country and these colonies, and the energy of mild and just government, produced benefits so remarkably important and afforded such an assurance of their permanency and increase, that the wonder and envy of other nations were excited, while they beheld Great Britain rising to a power the most extraordinary the world had ever known.

Her rivals observing, that there was no probability of this happy connection being broken by civil dissensions, and apprehending its future effects if left any longer undisturbed, resolved to prevent her receiving such continual and formidable accessions of wealth and strength, by checking the growth of those settlements from which they were to be derived.

In the prosecution of this attempt, events so unfavourable to the design took place, that every friend to the interests of Great Britain and these colonies entertained pleasing and reasonable expectations of seeing an additional force and extension immediately given to the operations of the union hitherto experienced, by an enlargement of the dominions of the crown, and the removal of ancient and warlike enemies to a greater distance.

At the conclusion therefore of the late war, the most glorious and advantageous that ever had been carried on by British arms, your loyal colonists having contributed to its success, by such repeated and strenuous exertions, as frequently procured them the distinguished approbation of your Majesty, of the late king, and of parliament, doubted not but that they should be permitted with the rest of the Empire, to share in the blessings of peace and the emoluments of victory and conquest.

While these recent and honourable acknowledgements of their merits remained on record in the journals and acts of that august legislature the parliament, undefaced by the imputation or even the suspicion of any offence, they were alarmed by a new system of statutes and regulations adopted for the administration of the colonies, that filled their minds with the most painful fears & jealousies; and to their inexpressible astonishment, perceived the dangers of a foreign quarrel quickly succeeded by domestic dangers, in their judgement of a more dreadful kind.

Nor were their anxieties alleviated by any tendency in this system to promote the welfare of their Mother country, for tho' its effects were more immediately felt by them, yet its influence appeared to be injurious to the commerce and prosperity of Great Britain.

We shall decline the ungrateful task of describing the irksome variety of artifices practised by many of your Majesty's ministers, the delusive pretences, fruitless terrors, and unavailing severities, that have from time to time been dealt out by them in their attempts to execute this impolitic plan, or of tracing thro' a series of years past the progress of the unhappy differences between Great Britain and these colonies, that have flowed from this fatal source.

Your Majesty's ministers persevering in their measures and proceeding to open hostilities for enforcing them, have compelled us to arm in our own defence, and have engaged us in a controversy so peculiarly abhorrent to the affections of your still faithful colonists, that when we consider whom we must oppose in this contest, and if it continues what may be the consequences, our own particular misfortunes are accounted by us, only as part of our distress.

Knowing, to what violent resentments and incurable animosities, civil discords are apt to exasperate and inflame the contending parties, we think ourselves required by indispensable obligations to Almighty God, to your Majesty, to our fellow subjects and to ourselves, immediately to use all the means in our power not incompatible with our safety, for stopping the further effusion of blood, and for averting the impending calamities that threaten the British empire. Thus called upon to address your Majesty on affairs of such moment to America, and probably to all your dominions, we are earnestly desirous of performing this office with the utmost deference for your Majesty; and we therefore pray, that your royal magnanimity and benevolence may make the most favourable construction of our expressions on so uncommon an occasion. Could we represent in their full force the sentiments that agitate the minds of us your dutiful subjects, we are persuaded, your Majesty would ascribe any seeming deviation from reverence in our language, and even in our conduct, not to any reprehensible intention, but to the impossibility of reconciling the usual appearances of respect with a just attention to our own preservation against those artful and cruel enemies, who abuse your royal confidence and authority for the purpose of effecting our destruction.

Attached to your Majesty's person, family and government with all the devotion that principle and affection can inspire, connected with Great Britain by the strongest ties that can unite societies, and deploring every event that tends in any degree to weaken them, we solemnly assure your Majesty, that we not only most ardently desire the former harmony between her and these colonies may be restored, but that a concord may be established between them upon so firm a basis, as to perpetuate its blessings uninterrupted by any future dissensions to succeeding generations in both countries, and to transmit your Majesty's name to posterity adorned with that signal and lasting glory that has attended the memory of those illustrious personages, whose virtues and abilities have extricated states from dangerous convulsions, and by securing happiness to others have erected the most noble and durable monuments to their own fame.

We beg leave further to assure your Majesty that notwithstanding the sufferings of your loyal colonists during the course of the present controversy, our breasts retain too tender a regard for the kingdom from which we derive our origin to request such a reconciliation, as might in any manner be inconsistent with her dignity or her welfare. These, related as we are to her, honour and duty, as well as inclination induce us to support and advance; and the apprehensions that now oppress our hearts with unspeakable grief, being once removed, your Majesty will find your faithful subjects on this continent ready and willing at all times as they ever have been with their lives and fortunes to assent and maintain the rights and interests of your Majesty of our Mother Country.

We therefore beseech your Majesty that your royal authority and influence may be graciously interposed to procure us relief from our afflicting fears and jealousies occasioned by the system before mentioned and to settle peace thro' every part of your dominions, with all the humility submitting to your Majesty's wise consideration, whether it may not be expedient for facilitating those important purposes that your Majesty be pleased to direct some mode by which the united applications of your faithful colonists to the throne in pursuance of their common councils may be improved into a happy and permanent reconciliation; and in the meantime measures be taken for preventing the further destruction of the lives of your Majesty's subjects; and that such statutes as more immediately distress any of your Majesty's colonies be repealed. For by such arrangements as your Majesty's wisdom can form for collecting the united sense of your American people, we are convinced, your Majesty would receive such satisfactory proofs of the disposition of the colonies towards their sovereign and the parent state, that the wished for opportunity would be restored to them of evincing the sincerity of their professions by every testimony of devotion becoming the most dutiful subjects and the most affectionate colonists.

That your Majesty may enjoy a long and prosperous reign, and that your descendants may govern your dominions with honour to themselves and happiness to their subjects is our sincere and fervent prayer.

John Hancock

Colony of New Hampshire
  John Langdon
Massachusetts Bay
  Thomas Cushing
  Saml. Adams
  John Adams
  Rob Treat Paine
Rhode Island & Providence Plantation
  Step. Hopkins
  Sam Ward
Connecticut
  Stephn. Dyer
  Roger Sherman
  Silas Deane
New York
  Phil Livingston

New Jersey
  Wil. Livingston
  John D. Hart
  Richd. Smith
Pennsylvania
  B. Franklin
  Geo. Ross
  James Wilson
  Edwd. Biddle
  John Dickinson
Newcastle Kent & Sussex on Delaware
  Ceasar Rodney
  Thomas Mc. Kean
  Geo. Read
Maryland
  Mat. Slighman

Jas. Duane
John Alsop
John Jay
Frans. Lewis
Wm. Floyd
Lewis Morris
Robt. A. Livingston Jnr.
North Carolina
Will Hooper
Joseph Hewes

Thos. Johnson Jnr.
Wm. Paca
Samuel Chase
Thos. Stone
Virginia
P. Henry Jr.
Richard Henry Lee
Edmund Pendleton
Benj. Harrison
Th. Jefferson
South Carolina
Thos. Lynch
Christ. Gadsden
J. Rutledge

Continental Congress—8 July 1775.

British, French, Spanish, and American Relations 1774–1779

When the news came to France that Britain and the thirteen colonies had come to blows, the Comte de Vergennes was the foreign minister. Although he was quite new in the ministry, having been appointed by Louis XVI after his accession to the throne in the proceeding year, Vergennes was an experienced diplomat. His policies varied little from those of Choiseul, but he was more cautious. Devoted to duty, gifted with a subtle intellect, unscrupulous when the needs of France seemed to require duplicity, Vergennes hovered on the fringe of greatness. He had feared that the crisis in Anglo-American relations might drive the North ministry from power and bring to the British helm the earl of Chatham, who might be able to satisfy the Americans and again lead the united forces of the British Empire against France and Spain. Hence Vergennes decided to be most circumspect.

As early as December 1774, Americans in London had hinted to a French diplomat that the colonists might be interested in French aid in the event that their quarrel with Britain ended in military conflict. Vergennes prudently avoided committing himself. But reports of Bunker Hill and of the American determination to fight led Vergennes to believe that the opportunity so long hoped for by Choiseul had perhaps arrived. In September 1775, he sent to Philadelphia a special agent, Achdard Bonvouloir, to encourage the colonists and to intimate that they would be permitted free use of French ports. Almost simultaneously Vergennes entered into close association with Baron de Beaumarchais, a trusted French agent who was eager to offer help to the colonists for the benefit of France. Whether Beaumarchais influenced Vergennes or Vergennes used Beaumarchais to execute a decision he had already reached is not known. In any case the two men worked hand in hand after the autumn of 1775. In December, undoubtedly with the approval of the minister, Beaumarchais wrote a letter to Louis XVI urging the young monarch to undertake to supply secretly munitions and even cash to the Americans. When the king hesitated to strike clandestinely at a nation with which France was at peace, Beaumarchais emphasized that the chance to injure Britain seriously at little expense must not be ignored because of scruples laudable in private life but out of place in statecraft. In March 1776, Vergennes asked the Spanish government whether it would join in the project. Marquis Grimaldi responded affirmatively and with a frank expression of hope that their aid might lead to the mutual exhaustion of both Britain and America.

Assured of cooperation from Spain, the French foreign minister formally laid the scheme before his colleagues. Its secret execution should be accompanied, he urged, by assurances of friendship to Britain. There should be no commitments to the Americans which would give Britain an excuse to declare war with France. Vergennes admitted, however, that his proposals might bring such a declaration, and he thought France and Spain should therefore be constantly prepared for battle. Vergennes's plan contemplated the establishment of an American republic or many American republics. Like Choiseul, he believed that American independence would cripple Britain commercially while at the same time assisting French trade. In support of his scheme Vergennes argued that the Americans, republican and weak, would not move against the French colonies in the West Indies. On the other hand, he contended, perhaps without faith in his assertion, that there was a real danger of an Anglo-American reconciliation and of an Anglo-American attack upon the French islands.

So it was that France and Spain saw the situation capable of being exploited to their own advantage and determined to offer concealed assistance to the Americans before an agent of the Constitutional Congress even reached French soil. Using as capital two million livres, Beaumarchais sent off the supplies to America, which arrived at the end of 1776 and hastened, if they did not assure, American independence. Later French subsidies and loans brought France's cash investment in the United States by 1783 to more than eight million eighteenth-century dollars. Spain also supported the Americans with cash and munitions.

Vergennes, and apparently the French government, reached a tentative decision to declare war upon Britain, provided that Spain also entered the conflict. Leaders at Madrid were eager to fight but demanded as the price of action Minorca and Portugal. Although Vergennes was willing in August 1776 even to sanction an attack on Portugal in order to obtain the support of the Spanish army and fleet, he drew back when news came to Paris of the rout of the American army on Long Island. Clinging to the policy of secret aid, he decided that no further steps should be taken until it was certain that the Americans would continue to fight in force and for some time. In accordance with that decision, Vergennes cautiously watched events until July 1777, when he officially proposed the formation of a Franco-Spanish-American alliance, defensive and offensive, which would wage war until all the parties to it were willing to make peace. Louis XVI gave his approval, but Spain refused her consent. Charles III had now dropped plans for the conquest of Portugal; he had also acquired a new foreign minister, Count Floridablanca, who was more cautious than Grimaldi. Like his predecessor, he was opposed to American independence. He disliked republics and feared that the American one would serve as a dangerous example in both the Old World and the New. He also foresaw that an independent American nation might eventually prove to be a greater threat to the Spanish Empire beyond the Atlantic than Britain had been. Floridablanca and Charles III therefore suggested Franco-Spanish mediation between Britain and the Americans, the result to be, they hoped, an uneasy truce between the contestants, one which would leave both weak,—to the advantage of Spain and France. Once more Vergennes retraced his steps. He found further reason for prudence in the reports of Burgoyne's easy capture of Ticonderoga.

During 1777, Vergennes and France were moving toward the fateful plunge, with or without Spain. Surreptitiously, yet without great attempts at concealment, munitions and military supplies of all sorts left French ports for America, partly through the machinery set up by Beaumarchais, partly through the activities of French merchants eager to trade with the America. American vessels frequented French harbors, and American privateers brought their prizes to them. In fact, the American commissioners actually fitted out three warships in those ports. French officers, including the Marquis de Lafayette, crossed the ocean in numbers to join the Americans—often on leave of absence from the forces of France. The British government, which was well informed of these goings-on by Viscount Stormont, its ambassador at Versailles, and by a very efficient espionage service, protested on several occasions, but not vigorously enough to bring all these activities to an end. Britain wished to avoid precipitating hostilities.

Although sympathy for the Americans in 1777 permeated all classes in France and even official circles, there is little evidence that French policy was much altered, although Vergennes and those who wished to intervene openly in the Anglo-American conflict were doubtless encouraged so to act. As long as the news from America continued to tell of British advances and American setbacks, France would not move openly for fear that the patriot cause was collapsing. To many in France, the capture of Philadelphia by Howe seemed to mark the beginning of the end. By 24 November 1777, however, it was known in Paris that Washington's army had performed creditably at Germantown and that Baron de Kalb, who was serving with Washington, believed the patriots would drive the British into the sea. Then on 4 December came the startling tidings that Burgoyne had capitulated at Saratoga. The shattering blow dealt to British arms by the northern American army convinced even the most cautious Frenchmen that the patriots would not readily submit; the more acute concluded, and not without reason, that since Britain would almost certainly offer the patriots concessions leading toward peace, France must move promptly if she moved at all. On 17 December, without even waiting to discover whether Spain would join with France, the French foreign minister promised the United States formal recognition, a step certain to bring his country a declaration of war from London. In return, he asked a pledge from the American commissioners that the United States as an ally would not make a separate peace, a pledge they gave.

On 7 January 1778, the French ministry and Louis XVI gave Vergennes their support. Accordingly, the texts of two treaties between France and the United States were prepared, and they were finally signed on 6 February, despite receipt by Vergennes of a definite refusal from Spain to join in the war and despite renewed efforts by Wentworth and others to persuade Franklin and Deane to make peace with Britain. The two treaties with France contained numerous provisions. By the terms of a Treaty of Amity and Commerce, France officially recognized the United States of America, and the two nations agreed to encourage trade with each other. The Treaty of Alliance carried far reaching pledges. If France and Britain fell to blows before American independence was achieved, France and the United States were to be loyal allies and were not to lay down their arms until that independence was formally or tacitly assured. Neither was to make a separate truce or peace without the consent of the other. France renounced forever all pretensions to the North American mainland east of the Mississippi and agreed to keep hands off the Bermudas, leaving the United States free to seize those territories. France was permitted to possess the British islands in the West Indies. Mutual guarantees were included. France guaranteed the independence and territories of the United States as they should be at the close of the war with Britain; the United States guaranteed the existing possessions of France in the New World, together with such other territory as she might acquire as the result of participation in the war.

In June 1779, Spain entered the conflict. When it became apparent that Britain would make no concessions to Spain, Floridablanca, after exacting a heavy price from Vergennes for Spanish military assistance, consented to the secret Franco-Spanish Convention of Aranjuez in April 1779. Simultaneously Spain sent an ultimatum to the Court of St. James offering mediation between Britain and the Americans on terms which George III and Lord North were certain to reject and which they did in fact reject. Thereupon, in accordance with the agreement of Aranjuez, Spain declared war. France was compelled to pledge that she would make no separate peace and that she would fight until Gibraltar was restored to Spain. In addition, France pledged all possible aid to Spain to wrest from Britain Minorca, Mobile, and other areas and privileges. Spain promised support to her ally's efforts to acquire territorial and commercial advantages in Newfoundland, Senegal, the East Indies, and elsewhere. It should be emphasized that Spain did not become the ally of the United States. Spain did not even engage to recognize the new country, and she offered such recognition only at the close of the war.[1]

Notes

Introduction

1. T. N. Foulis, *Memorials of His Time—Henry A. Cockburn 1779–1854* (London: 1909), p. 80.

2. Letters relating to the American question:

'75	'76	'77	'78	'79	'80	'81
613*	502	352	448	262	137#	222

*613 letters were printed from June through December.

#93 issues of the *Morning Chronicle* for the period January through June are no longer extant.

3. The *Gazetteer*, 11 August 1783, printed the following statistics of the number of copies of newspapers printed in the "whole kingdom": 12,680,000 (1775), 13,240,659 (1778), 14,397,600 (1781), 15,272,519 (1782).

4. Ian Christie, *Myth and Reality in the Late Eighteenth Century British Politics and Other Papers* (London: 1970), p. 323.

5. Junius was the most celebrated of the scribblers of the 1760s and 1777s. His letters, originally printed in the *Public Advertiser*, were plagiarized by a significant section of the British press. His early letters were critical of the ministry but generous toward George III, that is, until his Letter 35 of 19 December 1769: "It is the misfortune of your life, and originally the cause of reproach and distress which has attended your government, that you should never have been acquainted with the language of the truth, until you heard it in the complaints of your people. It is now, however, too late to correct the error of your education."

Henry Woodfall of the *Public Advertiser*, John Almon of the *London Magazine*, John Miller of the *London Evening Post*, Robinson of the *Independent Chronicle*, Say of the *Gazetteer*, and Baldwin of the *St. James Chronicle* were prosecuted for printing this Junius letter.

6. Christie, *Myth and Reality*, p. 32.

7. Newspaper publishers did not consider the Stamp Tax to be a persistent and unrelenting evil. Many proprietors favored the tax as a means of discouraging competition. In 1789 when Parliament outlawed the group purchase of newspapers and placed a penalty of £5 on anyone convicted of belonging to such a club, an increase in the Stamp Tax was not an element in the original legislation. Rather, it was included as part of an arrangement by which the publishers agreed to accept another increase in the Stamp Tax in exchange for the government prohibiting the

letting of newspapers. Rather than deploring the action as another means of restricting the dissemination of the news, *The Times*, 27 June 1789, declared that newspapers lent out to read were afterwards returned as unsold, "an imposition which had grown to a prodigious evil. . . . This practice is not only a material hurt to the revenue, but likewise great injury to the proprietors."

8. Piers Mackesy, *The War for America 1775–1783* (London: 1964), pp. 65–73.

Chapter One: Historical Background

1. The happenings described in this chapter were extracted in the main from *People and Events of the American Revolution*, ed. Trevor N. Dupuy and Gay M. Hammerman (Dunn Loring, Va.: T. N. Dupuy, 1974).

Chapter Two: The British Press

1. F. Knight Hunt, *The Fourth Estate: A History of Newspapers, and of the Liberty of the Press* (London: 1950), pp. 187–89.

2. F. S. Siebert, *Freedom of the Press in England* (Urbana, Ill.: 1952), pp. 309–12.

3. Milton R. Konwitz, *Fundamental Liberties of a Free People: Speech, Press, Assembly* (Ithaca, N.Y.: 1957), pp. 202–3.

4. Henry Sampson Woodfall (1739–1805) succeeded his father as printer of the *Public Advertiser* when he was nineteen, although his name did not appear on the masthead until 1760. He published some of the finest prose in his newspaper and gained extensive recognition with his publication of the Junius letters. In November 1793, he disposed of his interest in the *Public Advertiser*.

William Woodfall (1746–1803), younger brother of Henry Sampson, was the printer of the *London Packet* from 1772 to 1774 and of the *Morning Chronicle* from 1774 to 1789.

5. The unjust prosecution and unmerciful sentence of which William Woodfall writes was a prosecution for libel based on the publication of a SOUTH BRITON letter on 16 February 1774 which the House of Commons charged on 2 March 1774 was cause "to alienate upon the Affection of his Majesty's subjects from His Majesty and His Royal Family." For this publication, both Henry Woodfall, printer of the *Public Advertiser*, and William Woodfall were adjudged by the Court of the King's Bench to be guilty and "each to pay a fine of two hundred merks [about £200] and to suffer three months imprisonment and until the said fine be paid."

6. By the 1780s every London newspaper received a subsidy from one political faction or another. There was still a good deal of talk about liberty of the press, but the term had been redefined to mean a newspaper's freedom to decide which faction's money it would accept.

7. D. A. Baugh, *Aristocratic Government and Society in Eighteenth-Century England* (New York: 1975), pp. 2–3.

8. Zachariah Chafee, Jr., *Free Speech in the United States* (Mass.: 1942), p. 449.

9. Marcus Lee Hanson, *The Atlantic Migration 1607–1860* (Cambridge, Mass.: 1945), p. 17.

10. Chafee, Jr., *Free Speech*, p. 497.

11. Sir C. G. Robertson, *England Under the Hanoverians* (London: 1911), p. 169.

12. Laurence Hanson, *Government and the Press 1695–1763* (London: 1936), p. 2.

13. Anthony Smith, "The Long Road to Objectivity and Back Again: The Kinds of Truth We Get in Journalism," *Newspaper History—From the 17th Century to the Present Day*, ed. George Boyce, James Curran, and Pauline Wingate (London: 1978), p. 161.

14. Chafee, Jr., *Free Speech*, p. 500.

15. Siebert, *Freedom of the Press*, p. 5.

16. Henry Sampson Woodfall, printer of the *Public Advertiser*, was charged in 1774 with seditious libel for publishing a letter from John Horne entitled "Strike but Hear." Discharged by the House of Commons on 2 March 1774, Mr. Woodfall settled his account with Newgate prison on March 7.

Appendix A contains a copy of that reckoning which will give the reader some insight into the worth of £100 at the end of the eighteenth century.

17. Alexander Andrews, *The History of British Journalism* (London: 1859), p. 231.

18. Sir William Blackstone, *Commentaries on the Laws of England* (London: 1769), 4:151.

19. Hanson, *Government and the Press*, p. 492.

20. The paragraph is quoted from the *St. James Chronicle*, January 18–20, 1781. The *London Courier* is no longer extant, but the variation in the text would be minimal.

21. *Gentleman's Magazine* 51 (July 1781): 340.

22. Siebert, *Freedom of the Press*, p. 127.

Chapter Three: Addresses and Petitions to the Crown

1. "Addresses" usually supported the actions of the Crown; "petitions" were generally critical of those endeavors.

2. Addresses and petitions to the crown:

'75	'76	'77	'78	'79	'80	'81
70	5	0	0	0	0	0

3. *Morning Post*, 7 August 1775.

4. *Morning Post*, 15 November 1775.

5. Edmund Burke, British statesman, parliamentary orator, and political thinker, played a prominent part in all major political issues from 1764 to his death in 1797.

In 1774 he was elected a member of Parliament for Bristol, then the second city of the kingdom and an open constituency requiring a genuine election contest. For the rest of his parliamentary career, he was a member for Malton, a pocket borough of Lord Rockingham.

6. As late as the autumn of 1775, the legislatures of North Carolina, Pennsylvania, New Jersey, New York, and Maryland went on record against independence. S. E. Morrison, H. S. Commager, and W. E. Leuchtenburg, *The Growth of the American Republic* (New York: 1980), pp. 169–70.

Chapter Four: A Ministry Under Siege

1. William Edward Hartpole Lecky, *A History of England in the Eighteenth Century* (London: 1882), 3:126–27.

2. Letters critical of the North ministry:

'75	'76	'77	'78	'79	'80	'81
56	37	41	45	36	9	19

3. On 12 June 1775, General Gage proclaimed martial law in the province of Massachusetts Bay. He declared all those in arms to be rebels and traitors and offered pardon to all who returned to allegiance to the Crown, except for Samuel Adams and John Hancock, who would be tried for treason.

4. On 30 March 1775, royal assent was given to the New England Restraint Act. New England colonies were forbidden to trade with any country but Britain and the British West Indies after 1 July and were restricted from the North Atlantic fisheries after 20 July. Later the act was applied to New Jersey, Pennsylvania, Maryland, Virginia, and South Carolina.

5. Not all traders suffered from the loss of commerce. Many of the contractors made large fortunes during the war, and of the forty-six contractors employed between 1775 and 1782, eighteen were M.P.'s and eighteen more had some connection with M.P.'s. Peter D. G. Thomas, *Lord North* (London: 1976), p. 98.

Chapter Five. Peace or the Sword

1. Letters on the subject of war or peace:

'75	'76	'77	'78	'79	'80	'81
49	39	33	111	27	19	23

The marked increase in letters for the year 1778 was a consequence of the expanding interest in the Conciliatory Commission of that year and the reality of the French involvement in the war.

2. Dr. Franklin replied: "If continuing the Claim pleases you, continue it as long as you please provided you never attempt to execute it. We shall consider it in the same light with the Claim of the Spanish Monarch to the Title of King of Jerusalem." Alan S. Brown, *The Impossible Dream*, ed. Lawrence S. Kaplan (Kent, Ohio: Kent State University Press, 1977), p. 17.

3. New England colonies were forbidden to trade with any country but Britain and the British West Indies after July 2 and were restricted from the North Atlantic fisheries after July 20. Later the act was applied to New Jersey, Pennsylvania, Maryland, Virginia, and South Carolina.

4. K. G. Davies, ed., *Documents of the American Revolution 1770–1783*, Colonial Office Series (London: Irish University Press, 1976).

5. William Eden, George Johnston, and the earl of Carlisle were named as commissioners on 12 April 1778. On 6 June, the commissioners arrived in Philadelphia and offered the colonies autonomy under the British crown. On 16 June the commission was advised by Congress that the only acceptable terms were the withdrawal of British forces and the recognition of United States independence.

The Carlisle Commission left New York and sailed for Britain on 27 November. Their attempt at peace had failed.

6. The Declaratory Act was passed by Parliament on the same day it repealed the Stamp Act. It declared the British legislature possessed complete authority over the colonies in all cases whatsoever.

7. Benjamin Franklin, John Adams, and Edward Rutledge were directed by Congress on 6 September to meet with Lord Howe. On 11 September the parties met in a friendly but futile conference.

8. In a naval engagement on 27 July 1778, which became known as the battle of Ushant, British and French fleets under the British admiral Augustus Keppel and the French admiral Count d'Orvilliers clashed indecisively off the coast of France.

Chapter Six: The Sword Unsheathed

1. The numbers of letters written concerning each campaign are as follows: Lexington and Concord, 13; Bunker Hill, 8; Boston, 9; Long Island, 13; Saratoga, 32; the South, 11; Yorktown, 14.

2. Piers Mackesy, *The War for America 1775–1783* (London: 1964), p. 42.

3. Comte d'Estaing, Admiral of the French fleet, arrived with his fleet of 12 ships of the line at Delaware Bay on 8 July 1778. They represented the first French active participation in the alliance.

4. Cornwallis's withdrawal from the Carolinas was not without military achievements. On 1 February 1781, his forces defeated the Americans at the battle of Catawba River, North Carolina. On 15 March of that year, Cornwallis with about 2,000 men attacked and defeated a superior force of 4,000 at the battle of Guilford Courthouse, North Carolina. Unfortunately for the British forces, their losses were extremely heavy—93 dead and 439 wounded.

5. Washington was out maneuvered and defeated by the forces of General Howe on 11 September 1777.

6. Mainly because of fog and a complicated plan, Washington was repulsed on 4 October 1777 in a fierce assault on Howe's encampment. The Americans had 1,100 casualties, the British lost 534. The battle was a psychological American success, however, with Washington's boldness in defeat surprising both friend and foe.

7. The British attack by Hessian troops on Fort Mercer (Red Bank), New Jersey, on 22 October 1777 was the first move in Howe's campaign to open the Delaware River, up to Philadelphia, to the British fleet. The 400-man garrison of the Delaware River fort repelled the attack.

8. An entire Loyalist force under Major Patrick Ferguson was killed, wounded, or captured in the battle of Kings Mountain, South Carolina, on 7 October 1780. This disaster was an important factor in Cornwallis's decision to abandon his invasion of North Carolina.

Chapter Seven: The Perfidious French

1. Letters about the French alliance with America:

'75	'76	'77	'78	'79	'80	'81
15	44	63	70	24	7	8

As the intentions of the French became apparent, the letters increased in volume.

Chapter Eight: Despair

1. Peter D. G. Thomas, *Lord North* (London: 1976), p. 98.

Chapter Nine: Euphoria

1. Letters of despair and euphoria:

	'75	'76	'77	'78	'79	'80	'81
Despair	14	47	48	45	23	13	11
Euphoria	7	37	22	55	58	26	15

Letters of Despair changed to those of Euphoria in 1778. All in the spirit of "Play the Game."

Chapter Ten: American Brethren and Fellow Subjects

1. Pro-American and anti–American letters:

	'75	'76	'77	'78	'79	'80	'81
Pro-American	9	7	2	4	3	4	3
Anti-American	9	7	4	7	8	3	3

The pro–American Letters became less frequent as the efforts of the Conciliatory Commission were rejected by the colonists and the French entry into the war became a certainty.

2. *Common Sense* was first published in Philadelphia in January 1776. A British immigrant, Tom Paine sought to further the cause of independence in America, which was still a matter of some dispute. He advocated a confederation of American colonies for the mutual development of their resources and urged Americans to become independent of a Britain that was incapable of protecting them and had exploited them for its own economic interests. He advised his readers that reconciliation was impossible at that point. The "insidious old fox F___" was Benjamin Franklin. Many of the scribblers ascribed *Common Sense* to his pen.

Epilogue

1. Alexis de Tocqueville, *Democracy in America*, ed. J. P. Mayer (New York: 1969), p. 180.

Appendix A

1. John Wade Junius, vol. 1, Appendix (London: 1871).

Appendix C

1. John Richard Alden, *The American Revolution* (New York: 1954): pp. 180–90.

Index

A.B. 83, 128, 154
A.Z. 61
Abhorer of All Party Spirit 177
Academicus 137, 150
Addresses: dissenting 45–47, 47–51;
  Loyal 42–45, 47–50
Advertisers, Age of 28
Alfred 164
America Amicus 138, 139
An American 163
American collapse 163–64
An American Refugee 117
American Revenue Act 14
Americanus 90
Amicus 108
Amicus X.Y. 145
Amor Patriae 88, 93
Angelicus 153
Anglicanus 111
Anti American 66
Anti-Deceptor 134
Anti Faction 63
Anti-Faction 170
Anti-Forestiero 67
Anti-Mela 66, 89, 125–26, 127, 128
Anti-Rebel 127
Appius 170, 171
Aristides 120, 181
Aristidus 74
Arminius 68
Arminus 65, 173
Artabanus 173
The Atlantic Line 171
Auger 100
Augusta 114, 162
Aurelius 82

Baldwin, Henry 34, 35
Battle of Long Island 64, 102, 107–9

Beckford's Ghost 62
Beverly 42, 51–52
Bill of Rights (British) 31, 32
Blackstone 36
Bobo 149
Boston: 102, 106, 107; Massacre 17–18;
  Port Bill 19; siege of 105–7
A Bostonian 11, 60
Bristol 44, 47, 48
Britain, at zenith of power 125–26
Britannia 179
Britannicus 70, 134
A British Freeholder 166
British Legion 113
British military: logistics 11, 67; success
  78, 156–60, 162–63, 166–67; supplies
  11; troop withdrawal suggested 22;
  troops in Boston 16
A Briton 64, 78, 92, 112, 135, 137,
  140, 147
Bromfield 142
Brutus 61, 69, 124, 145
Brutus, J. 60
Bunker Hill 42, 102, 104–5
Burgess, D. 151
Burgoyne, General Jim 11, 40, 71, 93,
  110–14, 118, 120, 121, 175
Burke, Edmond: appointed N.Y. agent
  18, 46, 47, 48
Bute, Earl 53
By-Blow 82
Bye-Stander 141

Caledonian Mercury 7, 48, 49, 103, 107,
  137
Cammillus 61
Campbell, Lt. Col. Archibald 114, 162,
  163
Candidus 169

207

Carlisle Commission of 1778 80, 81, 85, 95, 98, 100, 176
Castle William 106
Cato 84, 119, 146, 147
Cautious 150, 151
Charandes 61
Charleston 115
Charlotte 116
Cicero 75, 89
Cincinnatus 57, 84
Circulation (newspaper) 10
A Citizen 48
Civis 138, 157, 176, 178
Cleonitus 61, 124
Clericus 55
Clinton, General Henry 12, 98, 104, 107, 115, 117, 162
Clio 164
Clytus 82
Coersive or Intolerable Acts 19
Colonial Currency Act 14
Colonial Protest of Sugar and Currency Acts 14
Commentaries on the Law of England 36
A Commissioner of Supply 169
Committee of Correspondence at Boston 18
Common Sense 112, 146
Conciliation 80–89, 97–98, 150; anti 89–92, 97–98
Conciliatory Resolution of Parliament 23
Conciliatory Resolution of 1775, Lord North's 80, 84, 99
Concord 24, 25–26, 42, 65, 81, 102–4, 105
Congress 85, 86
Connecticut 81
Connoisseur 154
Constant Reader 98
Constitutional Society 34, 36, 37, 187
Continental Association 22
Continental Congress 20, 21, 22, 23
A Contractor 148
A Convention Officer 121
Coriolanus 172
Cornwallis, Lord 7, 26, 115–18, 121, 181
A Country Gentleman 69, 70
Courage Sans Peur 89, 124, 130, 131, 174
Crito 50, 60, 61, 63, 83, 86, 87, 131, 183
Curious Dentatus 63

Daily Advertiser 28
Decious 72, 79, 160, 162
Declaration of Independence 85
Declaratory Act 15
Democrates 78
Demosthenes 112
Detection and Truth 30
Detector Americanus 90, 172
Detester of His Enemies 83
A Detester of Tyrants 82
Dion 114, 138
Dorchester Heights 106

E 66
An Economist 181
Edinburgh 49
Ego 171
An Enemy to Imposition 103
An Englishman 67, 105, 136, 142, 145, 156
Entellus 82
Essex Gazette 25, 103
Eumenes 164

F 96
Fabricus 121
Faction 61
Fidus Achates 120
Fidus and Probus 75
Fidus Veternus 98, 111, 157
Figg, R. 63
Fox's Libel Act 41
France 73, 93, 98, 123–24, 180; fear of war with 126–39
Freeholder 51
A Friend of Great Britain 94, 96
A Friend to Legal Liberty 71
A Friend to Liberty 169
A Friend to Old England 163
A Friend to Truth 97

G.E.W. 156
G.N. 9, 77, 95, 153, 154, 176, 179, 184
Gage, General 11, 83
Gaspée incident 18
Gates, Major General Horation 116
Gazetteer 34, 41
Gentleman's Magazine 41
George III 34, 40, 51, 153
Germain, Lord George 12, 40, 87, 107
Glover, Mr. 142
Golden Hill, Battle of 17

GRACCHUS 152
Gratus 72
Graves, General 109

H 94
Hamden 153
Hera Litus 60
Hessians 99, 108
Historicus 135, 165, 175
Homo 29
Honestus 78
Horne, John 35, 36–37, 187
Hospice 65
House of Burgess, dissolution 20
House of Commons, closing of
  Gallery 32–34
Howe, Lord Richard 81, 118, 119, 120
Howe, Lord Viscount 119, 120, 162
Howe, General Lord William 77, 81,
  104, 106, 107, 108, 109, 118, 148, 181
Howe Commission of 1776 80, 81, 85,
  86, 89, 173
Humanitus 181
Humanus 108

Impartial 9, 90
Impartialist 72
An Imperialist 87, 91
Independent 50
An Indignant Englishman 91, 98
Independence, consequences of 94–96,
  127
Invasion, fear of 125, 126
Investigator 72

J.A. 11, 68, 113, 175, 186
J.B. 116
J.R. 162
J.S. 160, 161
Jones, John Paul 71
Julius 77
Junius Junior 67, 68, 148, 184, 185
Junius 49, 65
Juvenis 142

Keppel, Admiral 77

Lane, George 67
Laurentianus 180

Lecky, William 59
Lexington 24, 25–26, 42, 65, 81,
  102–4, 105
Libel 34–37, 40, 41
Liberty (British) 168–69, 174, 183–86
Livery of London 54, 55
Log Book 40
London Advertiser 28
London Chronicle 8, 35, 44, 45, 46, 47,
  48, 49, 50, 51, 93, 99, 104, 111, 121,
  137, 147, 160, 166
London Courant 7, 40, 41
London Evening Post 34, 35
London Evening Post Extraordinary 25
London Gazette 32, 36, 43, 44, 46, 68,
  103, 107, 170
London Packet 35
Long Island, Battle of 64, 102, 107–9
Lord Campbell's Act 41
Lord Mayor of London 53, 54
A Lover of Public Library 174
A Lover of Spirit and Consistency
  in a Prime Minister 73
Lover of Truth 181
A Loyal American 116
Loyal Subject 49
A Loyalist 108
Loyalists 90, 98, 99, 106, 114, 121, 170,
  171–72; resolutions rejected 21
Lucius 109, 118, 124

M 126
Maccrowdey, Rorey 89
Machiavel 107
The Majority 144
Manchester 43
Mansfield, Lord Chief Justice 36, 87
Manufacturer 49
Marcellus 64
Marcus 178
Massachusetts: Government Act 19;
  Provisional Convention 16
Mela 11, 63, 67, 125, 126, 129, 142,
  143, 144, 145, 148
A Member 135
Memmus 108, 109
The Memorialist 148
Mennon 175
Mentes 134
Mentor 97, 163
Mercator 135
A Merchant 111
The Merchant 143

Meres 34
Messala 55
Metaphor 87
Micromegas 86, 173
Middlesex Journal 41
Miles 134
Miller, J. 35
Ministry: approbation 62–63, 70–71,
    75–76, 78–79; disapprobation 60–62,
    63–65, 67–68, 72–73, 99–100, 113,
    145, 151–54
A Moderate Man 64, 76
Moderator 148
Molasses Act 13
Montezuma 57
Mornay, H. 82
Morning Chronicle 7, 27, 28, 30, 35,
    37, 43, 46, 47, 48, 57, 104, 111, 121,
    128, 129, 138, 160, 165, 166
Morning Herald 41
Morning Post 7, 28, 32, 49, 51, 52, 66,
    89, 99, 124, 128, 129, 137, 142, 143,
    144, 147, 157, 160, 161, 165, 166

Neutralis 88
New England Restraint Act 23, 80
New York: Assembly 23; "Committee
    of 51" 19, 20; resumes importation 17
No Creole 88
Non-Importation: opposition to 23;
    reaffirmed 17; resumed 16
Noon Gazette 41
North, Lord 17, 40, 59, 61, 65, 67–69,
    73–75, 88, 146, 147, 148, 170
A North American 70, 71, 97
The North Briton 53
Novanglus 75, 137
Numa 90, 105, 129, 130, 131, 132, 133

Obadiah 82
An Obscure By-Stander 9
Observator 71, 75, 78, 99, 104, 110,
    115, 165
An Observer 64
Oddo 109
Old Castle 173
An Old Correspondent 64
Old England 86
Old Man 100
An Old Officer 107
An Old Soldier 105
Old Truepenny 63

Olive Branch Petition 56–58, 193–96
One of Many 114
One of the Public 60, 168, 169
Opifex 55, 157, 171

P 32
Pacificus 31, 84, 85, 91, 126, 172
Parliament: exclusion of visitors at
    32–34; omnipotence 84, 169, 171
Pastor Fido 132
A Patriot 156
Peace and Union 181
Peace! Peace! 91, 92, 93, 161
Penn, Richard 83
Petitions of Livery of London 54–55
Phalaris 37
Philalethes 30
Philo-Patrie 85
Philopoemen 9, 74
Phoncion 141
Pitt, William 22
Plagiarism 10
A Plain Man 163
Plain Sense 120
Plain Truth 181
Policrites 100
Political Looking Glass 55
Politicus 160, 161, 165
Poplicila 113
Porteus 181
Press: and British opinions 29; libel
    34–37; liberty of 31, 32, 36–37; pro-
    hibition of publishing debates 33;
    taxation of 27
Probus 66
Proclamation of 1763 14
Public Advertiser 166, 170, 175, 187
Public Advertiser 7, 25, 28, 31, 32, 34,
    35, 40, 45, 58, 61, 69, 83, 84, 91,
    95, 104, 106, 137, 140, 145, 148, 149,
    150, 152, 153, 160
Public Ledger 34

Q 106
Quartering Act 14, 20
Quebec Act 20
Querist 96
Quidnunc 170

R. Figg 63
Rachel 177

Raleigh 126, 128, 168
Randall, H. 35
A Reader 180
Real Patriot 33
Reconciliation 80–90
Regulus 117, 118
Resolution 115
Response 63
Restraining Bills 60
Retz 75
Revolutionary Settlement of 1688 31
Revolutionary Whig 63
Rhode Island 81
Rivington, James 172
Royal Subject 48
A Royal Volunteer 166
A Royalist 98

St. James Chronicle 34, 35
Sandwich, Lord 40
Saratoga 11, 40, 71, 93, 110–14, 118, 120–21, 175
Savannah 114, 162
Say 34
Scapegoat, search for 109
Scotus 9
Scribe, Timothy 8
Seditious libel prosecutions 27, 30, 32, 37–40
Seven Year's War (conclusion) 13
Simplex 49
Solomon Doubtful 111
Southern campaign 114–16
Spain 73, 123–24, 180; fear of war with 126–39
Stamp Act of 1712 14, 15, 28
Staples, John 104
Stedfast 175
Suffolk resolves 21
Sugar Act 14
Sydney 32

T.D. 134
T.H. 126
Tages 73
Taxation of press 27
Tea Act 18, 70
Tea importation 19
Tea ships 18
Tell, William 105
Timilion 119

Titus 61, 131
Tocqueville, Alexis de 187
Townshend Acts: Massachusetts resolves 16; repeal 17; Virginia resolves against 17
Trade 66, 88, 160–61, 173
Traders 45, 46, 49
transatlantic communications 12
Trans-Atlanticus 107
True Blue 51
A True Briton 136
Tully 33

U 170
Ulysses 161
Unbiased Patriot 83
Unsigned 32, 49, 50, 52, 57, 101, 103, 106, 108, 121, 124, 128, 144, 147, 166
Ushant, Battle of 71

Vasa, Gustavus 74, 132
Veritas 50
Vero 51
Vespucius 52, 83
Veteran 158
A Veteran 111, 156, 158
A Veteran of Seen Service 66
Vigilans 90, 130
Vindex 50
Virginia Association 17
Virginia Stamp Act resolves 15
Voltaire 32

W 135, 170
W.J. 58
War! War! 177
Warminster 48
Warning 92
Washington, General George 107, 163
Whimsical Reflections of Sam Saunter 185
Whitehall Morning Post 41
Wilkes, John 35, 53, 54, 55
A Wiltshire Freeholder 47
Wing, Wang, Wong 31
Woodfall, Henry Simpson 29, 34, 35, 37, 187, 189
Woodfall, William 29, 30, 35, 37
Writs of Assistance in Boston 13

X 133   Yorktown 7, 26, 27, 116–
                                               18

Y.Z. 101
A Yeoman of Kent 127   **Z** 66, 116